Working Words

Working Words

The Process of Creative Writing

Wendy Bishop
Florida State University

Mayfield Publishing Company
Mountain View, California
London • Toronto

Library of Congress Cataloging-in-Publication Data
Bishop, Wendy.
    Working words : the process of creative writing / Wendy Bishop.
      p.   cm.
    Includes bibliographical references and index.
    ISBN 1-55934-076-2
      1. English language—Rhetoric—Study and teaching.   2. Creative
    writing—Study and teaching.   I. Title.
    PE1404.B58   1991
    808'.042—dc20   91-32342
                                                                              CIP

Manufactured in the United States of America

10 9 8 7 6 5 4 3 2 1

Mayfield Publishing Company
1240 Villa Street
Mountain View, California 94041

Sponsoring editor, Janet M. Beatty; managing editor, Linda Toy; produc-
tion editors, Sondra Glider and Lynn Rabin Bauer; manuscript editor,
Carol Dondrea; text and cover designer, Christy Butterfield; illustrator,
Robin Mouat. Cover photo: © 1991 Gianni Vecchiato.

The text was set in 10/12 Meridien by T:H Typecast and printed on 50#
Finch Opaque by Maple-Vail Book Manufacturing Group.

Portions of Chapters 2, 3, 4, and 5 have appeared in somewhat different
form in Wendy Bishop's *Released into Language: Options for Teaching Creative
Writing.* Copyright 1990 by the National Council of Teachers of English.
Reprinted with permission.

Page 162, copyright © 1991 by Michael Dorris and Louise Erdrich.
Published by arrangement with the authors.

For Marvin, Morgan, and Tait, again.

For my writing community, teachers and students, as always.

Preface

"It's not easy," novelist Joseph Heller says about writing, "But it's exciting, it's stimulating. If it were easy I wouldn't want to do it."

Like writing, teaching writing isn't easy. Novice writers are full of great and varied expectations. Some want to learn immediately about the traditional forms of writing, but others are mainly interested in exploring their personal experiences. Many will find satisfaction in sharing their writing, for the first time ever, with a public audience of peers and teacher, and still others are eager for an immediate introduction to the world of small press publishing. I wrote this textbook to support all kinds of student writers.

In *Working Words*, I've intentionally devoted a great deal of space to illustrations of process, using students' work. Process illustrations are used sparsely in other creative writing textbooks, so their inclusion here signals a distinctly different approach. For some students —particularly for those devoting themselves to creative writing for the first time—illustrations of process will provide a missing clue to composing. Students want to know what *actually* goes on when a writer writes.

In my experience, students best learn to write by trying to write themselves. But they also gain an enlarged understanding when they combine writing practice with an analysis of their composing processes—when they write about writing. And students are very receptive to process analysis if they are provided with nonthreatening examples: other students' brainstorming, invention exercises, exploratory writing, revision drafts, peer responses, and meditations on writing. Seeing what others have done, they are encouraged to make solid attempts themselves.

Approach

Working Words accommodates a new version of the creative writing classroom, derived from graduate workshops but transforming graduate methods to meet the needs of undergraduate writers. Graduate creative writing classes have influenced us all: promising writers share and critique drafts under the guidance of a seasoned writer/teacher. Still, the primary goal of those classes remains to support and encourage the most proficient writers in our universities. Undergraduate students, I've found, do not thrive on this model of instruction—at least not enough of them do. I designed *Working Words* to help novice writers *begin* their education in creative writing.

To the traditional teaching model, I add in-class writing, large- and small-group critiques, and writing about writing. I encourage genre experiments—students exploring poetry and fiction and non-fiction and drama—because students can't identify their own writing strengths, weaknesses, or preferred genres until they have written, seriously, for an extended period of time.

When they work with words, students gain insight into the interrelatedness of reading and writing processes, they understand literature more thoroughly by writing with literary aims in mind, and, of course, they produce writing of worth, for themselves and for their growing readership—friends and family, teacher and school, journals and editorial boards.

Organization

Becoming a creative writer is an act of personal commitment. In *Working Words* I try to help you strengthen the knowledge and commitment of your students by illustrating the process of creative writing.

Briefly, I have divided this book into three parts.

Part I, Thinking about Writers and Writing, allows students who have rarely reflected on their writing pasts and their feelings about writing to do so. Both Chapters 1 and 2 help students to articulate their knowledge and to examine their beliefs. Chapter 2 also offers a brief overview of what writing researchers and practicing writers can tell us about composing.

Part II, The Process of Creative Writing, focuses on the complex and recursive aspects of creating a successful text. Chapters 3 and-5 offer a variety of invention activities to get students started on a drafting sequence. Once they have a text, students are encouraged to participate in self-analysis in journals (Chapter 4) and in shared analysis through conferences and small- and large-group response sessions (Chapters 4 and 6). Later drafts are discussed in light of revision exercises (Chapter 7), while the final chapter in this section discusses evaluation (Chapter 8), examining the final products of students' invention, drafting, and revision cycles.

Part III, The Results of Writing, presents a discussion of the forms of writing. Chapter 9 examines poetry, fiction, and drama, offering examples from student writers. Chapter 10 provides a sampler of other popular forms: sketches, prose poems, science fiction, children's fiction, and nonfiction—the journalist's column and family stories.

While *Working Words* is intended for classroom use, it is also designed to meet the needs of creative writing students who want to explore issues alone. Extensive reading suggestions at the end of each chapter offer direction to those who are ready to forge ahead in an area you don't have time to cover in class.

All chapters in *Working Words* offer starting points for class discussions. Most chapters provide extensive exercises that encourage students to create together and alone, in class and at home. *Working Words* ends with two appendixes, listing professional writing associations and resources for creative writers and providing questions for writing-response sessions.

Additionally, an instructor's manual for *Working Words* offers a more extended discussion of the teaching philosophy that informs this book. The instructor's manual suggests various ways of using this text, offering suggestions for course requirements, plans for both quarter and semester courses, and an introduction to eight types of writing assignments that focus on writing as a process.

Working Words will help your students develop productive writing attitudes and habits, including the habit of thinking extensively about the process of creative writing. I believe that creative writing can be taught, and that every writer's work can be enhanced through an effective course—through your course, using *Working Words.*

Acknowledgments

Working Words came into existence with the generous help of Donna Decker, Patricia Foster, Mary Jane Ryals, and Heather Sellers, teachers of writing at Florida State University for many semesters. They allowed me to tape some of their classes and conferences and shared their students' work with me. Their students, as well, deserve great thanks for opening up their personal writing lives to readers of this text.

Other writing teachers, from around the country, from my past and present, deserve thanks for participating in a continuing dialog about creative writing; these include Will Baker, Brad Comann, Alys Culhane, Kate Haake, Carolyn Kremers, Trecie Melnick, Hans Ostrom, Rod Moore, Ken Waldman, and others whom I have, no doubt, failed to name here. Members of the writing workshops I teach have always been patient with my incessant collecting, as I saved journals, writing exercises, and samples of their creative work. I have tried to ensure that I have permission from all these writers to share their work-in-progress; I would be glad to hear from the few I have lost touch with over the years.

The National Council of Teachers of English first supported my work with creative writing pedagogy, and I appreciate the efforts of all the editors and officials of that organization and their generous permission to reuse portions of *Released into Language: Options for Teaching Creative Writing* to illustrate this text.

My reviewers helped enormously. I appreciated the care with which each reader responded. Thanks to Beverly Connor, University of Puget Sound; Elizabeth Davis, University of California at Davis; Marvin Diogenes; Douglas Lawder, Michigan State University; Bill Meissner, Saint Cloud State University; Lawrence Pike, Macomb Community College; and Constance Warloe, American River College.

I feel very lucky to have met Jan Beatty. She is an editor who believes in projects and makes them come true; I'm indebted to her and to the editing and production staff at Mayfield Publishing.

The English Department at Florida State University has provided me with strong support for pursuing cross-disciplinary writing interests; thanks to all my writing colleagues here.

Contents

PART II

The Process of Creative Writing

PART III
The Results of Writing

*Language is a city to the building of which
every human being brought a stone.*

—*Ralph Waldo Emerson*

A well-known writer got collared by a university student who asked, "Do you think I could be a writer?"

"Well," the writer said, "I don't know. . . . Do you like sentences?"

The writer could see the student's amazement.

"Sentences? Do I like sentences? I am twenty years old, do I like sentences?"

—*Annie Dillard* The Writing Life

Introduction

Some writers wait until their muse inspires them. Some plan ahead for days or weeks what they will say. Then, like myself, there are people who write all the time, hoping that, eventually, something decent will be produced.

I write deliberately. I don't mean that I write "on purpose." Rather, I write for a purpose. I want every word to count. I don't always get what I want the first time around, but I continue to correct and revise until my writing says exactly what I want it to say. . . . I never really know where my writing is taking me, and that is why it is exciting when I finally finish a piece. I've learned to let my writing go.

—JEAN

Taking this class on Fiction and Poetry has reshaped my ways of thinking in so many ways. It has helped me to grow and to understand more. I now read a poem and rather than just reading what is on the surface, I dive deeper into it and try to understand what the poet was thinking, why he wrote it this way, and why he chose to write in this particular form. Being able to ask all of these questions has given me an appreciation of poetry and fiction that I was never able to have before because I didn't really understand them, though I thought that I did. The greatest piano player in the world still took lessons because he felt that there was always something new that he could learn or that some new technique was being used. This same idea applies to writing. There is always more that you can learn and there are always some different techniques that you haven't tried.

—LILY

This book is for those moments when you are not writing, can't write, or need to step back from your writing in order to gain a slight distance and come to understand more clearly what it is you do as a writer. At the same time, my goal is to get you writing again, with more understanding, pleasure, and power than you had before you opened this book. Although I address my thoughts to "academic" creative writers, students of writing enrolled in workshop or craft classes, I hope the discussions, ideas, and writing suggestions will be useful to those in composition classes and to those who compose outside a formal classroom—writers who live in rural areas, students of writing who are studying independently or by telecommunication, nonacademic writers who enjoy reading Writing about Writing, members of informal writing groups, and so on.

Whether working alone or together, writers are complicated, active individuals, and this book helps you, as a student of creative writing, explore their many worlds. It is my contention that, although *doing* your writing is essential, understanding what it means to be a writer—by cultivating a writer's activities, discipline, and productive lifestyle—also contributes greatly to your writing growth.

Throughout this book, I weave together the voices, opinions, and writings of many student writers. Naturally, these voices, opinions, and writings are in progress; none of these writers shared their work as final products about which you might write weighty critical papers. You might interact with their work, though, by writing your own creative piece or imitation or journal entry, considering why a portion of their writing is successful or unsuccessful. Or you might be encouraged to draft an informal position paper in which you challenge another student writer's claims, because thinking and thinking again about writing is a powerful self-learning technique.

You'll find, then, that I have included writings that I care about and that made me think more deeply about writers and writing. For "models" of more polished or professional writing, you and your teacher will want to turn to the many anthologies, literary magazines, and additional textbooks that I list in each chapter. As you commit more seriously to writing, you'll collect some of these books and dip into them yourself.

Working Words offers a broad and general discussion concerning the process of creative writing; it will act as a prompt, a handbook, a guide, a prod, a first place, a way in to the world of the professional. But not everyone needs to become an acknowledged professional in order to find satisfaction through creative writing. Learning from her own first semester in a writing course, Robyn suggests that you

> Look at your writing as a permanent part of yourself. Do the best you can and be proud of it. Leave it open for constructive criticism and change the parts that don't "work" for you. Then say, "this is my finished work, it's good and I'm proud of it."

Through creative writing, I hope that you will become proud of your writing, that you will learn to consider written texts with more confidence, that you will develop techniques that allow you to write more fluently and come closer to attaining your own writing goals—whether they are modest (to write an effective dialog between two believable characters) or ambitious (to write a Pulitzer award winning novel).

Not every writer needs to gather the same information from this text. Although it is written in a certain order and information is placed in numbered chapters, you should plan to roam freely from section to section. To help you, I often suggest that you see other parts of the text. Make this book work for you by ignoring anything that doesn't address your needs.

Another habit of this book needs to be mentioned. Often, I provide commentary on material, either by writing notes to you, by adding more student voices, or by listing questions that you can respond to in journal entries and small-group or class discussions. I invite you to make this book host to your thinking. Write in it. Highlight what you like. Argue with what seems wrong-headed. Share your experiences, and you'll be more prepared to share them again later with fellow writers.

As you begin a writing workshop, consider Rod's advice:

> In a creative writing class the student can't just come to class, try to absorb a lecture and go on about something afterwards. Along with assigned writings, beginning students should take it upon themselves to write on their own—just for the practice and the improvement. The more one writes the easier it becomes. . . . Write a few drafts before you reach your final outcome. Write your ideas and thoughts, then the first draft.
>
> Let this draft sit for a while and then read it. Don't just "read" it, edit it. Go through and see what works and what doesn't. Make your revisions and set it down for a few days to do again. . . . Do the assignment when assigned, not the day before it is due. If you do, it will be easier and more beneficial. What kind of editing or rewriting can a person do at 3:00 A.M.?

Rod's observations should remind you to give yourself time in your endeavors. Your writing is for you as well as for those you are about to meet in class.

Chapter 1

Thinking About Writers and Writing

Every morning you climb several flights of stairs, enter your study, open the French doors, and slide your desk and chair out into the middle of the air. The desk and chair float thirty feet from the ground, between the crowns of maple trees. The furniture is in place; you go back for your thermos of coffee. Then, wincing, you step out again through the French doors and sit down on the chair and look over the desktop. You can see clear to the river from here in winter. You pour yourself a cup of coffee.

Birds fly under your chair. In spring, when the leaves open in the maples' crowns, your view stops in the treetops just beyond the desk; yellow warblers hiss and whisper on the high twigs, and catch flies. Get to work. Your work is to keep cranking the flywheel that turns the gears that spin the belts in the engine of belief that keeps you and your desk in midair.

—ANNIE DILLARD

You are a writer every time you write. I also know you become a better writer by studying writers' lives in the fullest sense, learning about their interests and beliefs, work habits and rituals, writing processes and techniques. You'll also want to read poems, stories, novels, and essays in order to extend your knowledge of form and craft.

In this chapter, I ask you to spend time exploring the beliefs that writers have about themselves and that you may have about writers and about what you must do in order to turn yourself into a better writer. At the same time, you should feel free to use later chapters of this book as you draft and share your first classroom work.

As you begin, it is worth remembering that our cultures shape our writing beliefs and writing expectations. We all grew up in different home towns, conforming to particular political, religious, and family customs. We may have African American, Mexican American, Asian American, Native American, or Anglo American lineages, and we may identify most with particular gender, ethnic, income, or regional groups. Some of us have recently arrived in the United States and are still translating between two very different ways of thinking and speaking. In any given writing workshop, class members' beliefs and attitudes will not be identical. Equally, our early literacy experiences are bound to be varied. Some of us heard wonderful storytellers as children while others of us read classic children's books. Some of us took to reading and writing at an early age, and others of us took our time. Individual members in our class, then, will value different writers' subjects, styles, and voices.

As a writer, you are yourself composed of your beliefs, and no two writers will view the world in exactly the same way; you have to find your way. That's a good thing, actually. Annie Dillard's metaphorical description shows that considering yourself a writer is a matter of writing, is a matter of learning craft, but is, at the same time, a matter of developing these important measures of self-knowledge and self-trust.

Exploring Your Own Beliefs

To clarify your own beliefs about writing, read the following statements.[1] You may feel that these statements are true or false, that they apply to you greatly or not at all. Circle any of the statements that surprise you. Use a highlighter to mark any statements you want to argue with or that contradict your experience. Finally, put a star next to any statements about which your beliefs are particularly strong.

- Writing is for communication.
- Writing is permanent, speech ephemeral.
- Writing is speech plus handwriting, spelling, and punctuation.
- A writer is a special kind of person.
- Most great writers work alone.
- You really can't teach "creative" writing.
- Writing is learned from instruction.
- Writing is learned by writing.
- Creative writing is the hardest type of writing.
- You must have something to say in order to write.

- Writing should be easy.

- Writing should be right the first time.

- Writing can be done to order.

- If you have to revise, your idea probably wasn't very good.

- Writing is a sedentary activity.

- Writing is a silent activity.

- Writing is a solitary activity.

- Writing is a tidy activity.

- Writing should be the same for everyone.

Any of these circled, highlighted, or starred sentences are worth looking at more carefully. Do this by first writing down one of your "starred," strong belief statements. Then list your reasons for feeling so strongly. For example, if you wrote:

- *Writing Is a Sedentary Activity*

You might then list the following reasons for your belief:

- Most writers I know are extraordinarily pear-shaped; they hardly ever play contact sports.

- To write, you have to sit at a desk or computer.

- Writers seem to go away from people to where it's quiet, to sit in their rooms and come up with great ideas.

- I saw a TV interview with Steven King and he claimed that to write . . .

After you have done this, try to imagine another kind of writer and another world of writing. List some reasons for your belief that show a new perspective; take the opposite stance:

- *Writing Is Not a Sedentary Activity.*

- In one of my English classes, I read the poet Gary Snyder, who wrote poems while he was working as a fire lookout.

- Biologists are writers, too. They take field notes; in fact, my backpacking catalog sells special writing pads for writing outdoors and my friend Susan writes reports *and* a journal in the field.

- Some writers like to write after walking.

- I bet a few writers tape-record their ideas while walking.

- Ernest Hemingway used to write standing at a desk.

- Writers write about active things—playing baseball, going to Mardi Gras, trying white water rafting; can't I consider the times when they gather material to write about as part of writing?

Our beliefs influence our visions of and understanding of other writers, and they can even influence our work habits and productivity. If you believe the best writing is produced under calm, quiet, orderly circumstances, for instance, and you know you live in a disorderly, chaotic household, you may prejudge your ability to succeed at a project you've taken on.

The activities that follow are based on your responses to the belief statements.

Explorations to Do by Yourself or with a Partner

1. Write out a fuller response to several of the belief statements that interest you most. Next, reshape these statements as questions and use them in an interview with a professional creative writer. Did that writer agree or disagree with your findings/beliefs? Did that writer's responses change your thinking?

2. List some other beliefs you hold about writing or writers or the creative act that aren't on my list. Then discuss each one.

Explorations to Do in a Small Group or as a Class

Try to assess the beliefs of your new writing classroom community by taking an informal poll of each person's circled, highlighted, or starred responses. Discuss those statements for which there is most agreement and disagreement.

Exploring Your Own Feelings

For most of us, writing isn't the easiest thing to do or the first thing we choose to do, given any other options. In fact, it's often a lot more fun to think about what we *could* write than to actually get down to work. Ellen found this out. She suggests that fellow creative writing students should realize that

> [I]n the beginning, things are generally slow. You feel as though you have to force everything from the back of your mind onto your paper. You see everything as it appears to the naked eye and fail to see what it could actually be. Don't worry. With each piece of writing, a new image arises, generalities become specifics. It will get easier.

It's easy to suggest that a writer relax and not worry. Still, most of us have strong feelings about our writing. Here are some statements that tap those feelings.[2] Again, read the statements and circle any that surprise you. Use a highlighter to mark any statements you want to argue with or that contradict your experience. Finally, put a star next to any statements about which your feelings are particularly strong.

- I avoid writing.

- I look forward to writing down my ideas.

- Taking a creative writing course is a frightening experience.

- Presenting my work to others makes me feel good.

- My mind seems to go blank when I start to work on a piece of writing.

- I would enjoy submitting my writing to magazines for evaluation and publication.

- I like to write my ideas down.

- I feel confident in my ability to express myself in writing.

- I like to have my friends read what I have written.

- I'm nervous about writing.

- People seem to enjoy what I write.

- I enjoy writing.

- I never seem able to write down my ideas clearly.

- Writing is a lot of fun.

- I worry about doing well in writing classes even before I enter them.

- I like seeing my thoughts on paper.

- When I hand in my writing I'm afraid I'm going to do poorly.

- It's easy for me to write well.

- I don't think I write as well as most other people.

- I don't like my writings to be evaluated.

- Discussing my writing with others is an enjoyable experience.

I suggest that, in your journal, you continue to explore your feelings about writing. Often, you can do this best by telling stories from your past. For instance, if you have remarked that you are undecided about whether you like to share your writing with friends, you might look into your writing past and ask why. Have you had both successes and failures when you shared your writing?

Perhaps a parent, teacher, or friend responded critically to your writing or misunderstood it? Or perhaps these individuals responded to you and not to your writing? Missy suggests that novice writers should not be afraid "to show your work to other people. It helps tremendously. You not only have your mind working, you have someone else's helping you work on the same thing (two heads are better than one!)." However, if you have had an experience that leads you to doubt or qualify Missy's statement, writing in a journal may help you understand that experience. Writers' journals are discussed more fully in Chapter 4.

Explorations to Do as a Journal Entry or for Small Group or Class Discussion

In a small group, share some of the experiences that have shaped your feelings about your writing by addressing the following questions:

I avoid writing.
- Under what conditions does this happen?
- What do you do instead and why?

I look forward to writing down my ideas.
- As a writer, what gets you excited? What gets you going?
- Do you enjoy writing about particular topics?
- Do you enjoy writing under particular conditions?

My mind seems to go blank when I start to work on a piece of writing.
- Try to describe this state even more vividly to your group.
- Also, what tricks have you used in the past to get out of this state?

I like to have my friends read what I have written.
- What do your friends do to make you feel this way?
- Do you approach them or do they approach you?
- Is the sharing experience enhanced if it takes place at certain times (for example, at mealtimes, the end of the day, right when you jump off the computer, and so on)?

I'm nervous about writing.
- How do you know and how would someone else know?
- Do you exhibit regular mental or physical behaviors that would tip someone off to your nervousness?
- How have you learned to get around your nervousness?
- What conditions make you least nervous?

People seem to enjoy what I write.
- How have you learned this?
- What can you tell someone else about learning to share their writing with others?

A few writers may relate some of their responses here to their experiences with writer's block. Throughout this book, we look at ways for writers to get writing and keep writing. Nevertheless, there are times when writers feel that nothing is happening. Jaren looks at it this way:

> Probably the worst nightmare of any writer is the dreaded writer's block. It is 11:05 P.M. on a Sunday night. You've got an essay or poem due at 8:00 A.M. Monday morning. Like any other student on campus, you have saved it all for the last moment, because, hey, let's face it, "There's no time like the future." The instant your pen hits the blue lines of emptiness, you panic . . . "AAAGGGGHHH!!" You can hear every tick of the round clock in the study room. Sweat drips off of your forehead and onto the desk. It's not a pretty scene to behold.
>
> Other writers have suggested keeping a list of interesting words on a scrap sheet of paper. When you get writer's block and you need a good idea, just look at the scrap sheet. This method is pretty good but I like mine better. My method consists of standing up, walking out the door, going to the nearest Rax Restaurant, and ordering a roast beef sandwich. BE OBSERVANT! Watch the people in the restaurant. There are usually some strange characters in fast food restaurants late at night that make great supporting characters in a short story. If this method fails, then open a dictionary up to any page and look at the first word you see. Now use this word in the first sentence of your paper. If this does not work, then write a paper on how stupid it was to save the paper for the last minute.

Like me, Jaren believes there are ways to avoid writer's block. In fact, some of us think that delay, and even procrastination, can be used by some writers to useful effect. Caroline explains, for instance, that

> [O]nce I get a writing assignment, I toy with different ideas solely in my head. And I can't even say when or where these thoughts begin, but I know it's not while I'm studying. For days, I mentally write and erase possible ideas or theses. And then, at some point, one idea keeps returning. And once this idea has occurred in my head a significant number of times, my mind stops thinking about the assignment. It's as if my brain opened up a decision-making compartment and the workers went out, formulated ideas, picked and eventually chose the best one, and then went back in and shut the door. A door that wouldn't be opened again until I sat down to write the paper. So interesting! To me, I mean, because I've *never* realized that my mind actually does this but it *truly does.*

Inspiration, writer's block, useful delay, and debilitating procrastination, are all important to writers. But, in order to fully understand these concepts, writers first need to understand their own writing processes and writing habits.

Throughout this book, you'll be developing a more and more sophisticated understanding of the interrelated nature of writing and not-writing. To help you begin, in the next section I introduce a writing process self-audit. Answering these questions will start you on the road to this understanding.

Completing a Writing Process Self-Audit

A self-audit can turn into a literacy autobiography, a memoir, or a self-study; it helps you see who you once were as a writer and who you are now. David and Michelle's explorations, taken from the beginning of their audits, show you that answering questions about your writing past and writing habits isn't simply a cut and dried task of listing.

> I never wrote stories as a child, but I did discover the ability to lie believably. A kickball game at camp became a third grader's equivalent of the 1969 World Series. I would spin the stories but never ink them. In high school I took a class in creative writing and discovered that the "junk" I scribbled during lunch hour was as good or better than stories my other classmates toiled over for hours. I had discovered something I do well.
>
> —David

> I remember winning a contest in the third grade for writing a story based on the characters in the "Betsy" books (don't ask me who wrote them or what most of them were about, but I did love them). I still have the story and blue ribbon in a box in my room at home (even after moving twelve times it was always saved from the trash bin). I used to write much more fiction and poetry when I was younger (I recently found a poetry compilation I did in the sixth grade. It included my own embarrassing illustrations, which prove that I am a much better writer than an artist—which isn't saying much.). I also used to write much more for my own enjoyment than for anyone else's. Once I got to high school, I began to learn how to write to please each particular teacher. I would find the "formula" and style they approved of and tailor my work to it. In retrospect, this seems to be the time that I began to write to receive the recognition for my writing, rather than just writing for my own satisfaction.
>
> —Michelle

By probing the past, writers begin to understand how their interest in writing developed and what persons and what events encouraged them.

Start your audit by answering the following questions. Your answers may be entered in a class journal, but they should certainly be saved. Days, weeks, or even years from now, you may find it useful to "revisit" your writing process self-audit to discover how you have changed (and how you haven't).

Self-Audit Questions

1. What is your first memory of writing? How old were you? What did you write? How did you like it? Who did you show it to? What did he/she/they say? Write this up as a scene.

2. Tell something of your own "history" of writing in school. Do you remember particular moments, pieces of writing, periods when writing was important, and so on? Write a short autobiographical piece that relates several of these moments.

3. In particular, what teacher helped you most with your writing? In what ways? Tell stories. Or write a character sketch.

4. Stand back from yourself and describe yourself as a character who reads. What does this character choose to read, when, where, why, how, and so on?

5. Who reads *your* writing? Do you like to share? Write a dramatic scene in which you share a piece of writing with someone else. What is it? What are the circumstances? What do you both say?

6. What do you think makes writing good? What does one need to be a good, successful writer? Can everyone be a good writer? Start this answer by listing your favorite authors and what you like about them. Write a short, imaginary letter to one of these authors, praising his or her work. Then, write back to yourself—an imagined answer from that author—giving advice on how to become a "good" writer.

7. Explain how you write by answering the following:
   a. Where do your most creative ideas come from?
   b. How do you get started?
   c. What keeps you going and/or what stops you?
   d. Where are you when you write your best and what are you doing?
   e. How much do you revise?
   f. Do your write drafts in longhand, on typewriter, at the computer?
   g. Complete the following sentences and expand on each answer with a few additional sentences; note, you don't have to use the same comparison/image for each answer although you might:
      i. For me, writing is like . . .

ii. For me, revising is like . . .

iii. For me, reading is like . . .

Use your answers to the self-audit questions in some of the following ways.

Explorations to Do by Yourself

1. "Revisit" these questions over time or as you progress through a writing course by writing new answers, or by expanding or annotating your old answers.

2. The next time you write an essay, poem, or story, keep an informal record of *your actual* composing process. What did you do, when, why, and so on. Then, go back and read your journal entry to see if the process you *remembered* is the same process you *actually used* when writing.

Explorations to Do in a Small Group

1. In class, share portions of your writing process self-audit. Have each member of your group read a sketch, dialog, or story, and then have the group share one of those pieces with the whole class.

2. Read answers to questions 7a–g. How are the members of your group similar as writers? Do any of you have habits that are very different from other members of the group? Be ready to report your findings to the class. Examples of actual notes taken for this type of group report are given in the two samples below; these reports were followed by a class discussion.

Group Notes: Sample 1

We formed these general opinions about writing:

1. Stare into space—zone out!

2. Brainstorming

3. Composing and editing (with breaks)

4. Writing with comfortable surroundings

5. Writing with food/drink/other

6. Creative writing is most favored.

7. Enjoy most writing about personal topics

8. Random composing works best.

9. Cosmic juice, good mood, imagination flow

[Notetaker's comment] I'm glad that I am not the only one who does all these things! I feel like I am more human now that I know about twenty other people who have had bad grades on papers, uncontrollable circumstances, writer's block, bouts with procrastination, and lack of motivation when it comes to writing.

Group Notes: Sample 2

The members of our group are surprisingly similar with respect to the way we write. Almost all of us do some form of formal categorizing. Some of us outline, some brainstorm, some write lists, and some of us just write. One thing remains constant among all six of us—we all procrastinate. I used to think I was a horrible individual for waiting until the last minute, but now I realize that everyone procrastinates—maybe we do it to actually "psych" ourselves up. We all preferred to write straight through with breaks only for their nutritional value. Most of us need quiet in order to keep up our train of thought but one of us (surprisingly) preferred lots of loud music. With regard to writer's block we agreed that the only way to beat it is to keep working. We all seemed to have a lot in common—at least where writing is concerned.

3. Interview another class writer and present an informal discussion of him or her as a writer. As a follow-up, write a comparison of you and that person as writers. The essay can take many forms— I've read, for example, imaginary talks between the papers of two writers as well as practical point-by-point comparisons of self-audit responses.

In the next chapter, we look more carefully at what is known about the writing process and discuss how such knowledge can help you as a writer. Before leaving the subject of beliefs and feelings about writing, though, it is worth looking at two issues that come up in writing classes over and over again.

Who Writes: What Is Good Writing?

You'll remember that the writer's self-audit posed the questions: What do you think makes writing good? What does one need to be a good, successful writer? Can everyone be a good writer?

As they began a writing workshop, David and Michelle each offered insightful but very different answers to these questions. David classified writers into three categories and then ranked those categories: "There are three types of writers that exist: those that see life in a unique way and share it with the reader; those who manipulate language to create beautiful flowing manuscripts; and those who do both. Good writers are the first two types, great writers are the last." Michelle felt good writers were those who had a command of craft and technique but who were, foremost, great readers, able to analyze the needs of their potential audiences.

A writing class never resolves but always engages these complicated issues, and as you develop as a creative writer you can expect to consider them from a changing viewpoint. Eventually, I think, you will learn that each of us defines "good" somewhat differently; when we agree that someone has produced a "good" poem or a "great" painting, we are agreeing *as a social group* about *implicit* and *explicit* criteria, often after some serious negotiation. Equally, our evaluations are influenced by our expectations. At the least, we are influenced by:

1. *Audience expectations*—our poem for our mother may be given a better reading by our mother than by our biology teacher; our attempt to write a forceful argument in a letter to the editor will be influenced by our understanding of the types of people who inhabit our community.

2. *Our own expectations for and experiences with form*—we don't expect a best-selling adult novel to sound like a book for preteens; we do expect poems to utilize certain techniques.

3. *Values current in our culture*—we may be moved more by fiction that deals with particular ethnic groups or environmental issues; we may feel that writing that earns authors big bucks can't possibly be as "serious" as that written only for "art's sake"; we may find it impossible to give a fair reading to advocates of lifestyles that seem morally or ethically problematic to us, and so on; also, members of our "student" culture may value some things that members of our "work" or "education" cultures don't value.

The following excerpts from student writings discuss "good writing" and "good writers," and the differences between "novice" and "professional" writers and between "art" writing and "regular" writing. They reflect the breadth of this topic, and I follow them with questions for discussion and suggestions for writings with which to explore these questions. The exercises can result in poems, stories, and dramatic scenes. These issues are worth tackling as a class, in groups, or on your own in journal entries.

Discussion 1: Gale

The Hemingway interview only served to confirm several opinions of the man I've heard. He does say a few things that don't come as a surprise but still lend to the notion that one has to force oneself to sit down and write on a very regular basis if one expects to achieve anything. I had heard this before, but I either didn't think that I could do it this way, maybe because I tend to write better when I've already formulated an idea, or maybe because I've never had the time to be so methodical about it. And that's another thing. Writing, methodical? I guess I've always had some romantic notion that a great writer uses the process only when a brilliant idea has hit. No mistakes. No forcing. Just pure, fluid, creativity that comes out after many sleepless nights of type—type—typing into a work of genius that any publishing company would die to print. That is, if the author already has made a name in the world. I do know that it is much harder to get something published, or even read, if the writer is unknown. But, I never really thought about, oh, say Jessica Fletcher getting up each morning and going through a certain ritual to get the written word down on paper.

Questions and Writing to Explore

1. What do you imagine are the working habits and writing behaviors of some of your favorite authors? You might want to sketch humorous possibilities. Write a poem or story in which two unlikely authors meet and discuss writing.

2. Read some interviews with writers in which they describe their working habits (see the reading list at the end of Chapter 2). What percentages of work and inspiration do they report? What are the habits you might borrow? What habits amuse, horrify, or surprise you? Imagine yourself borrowing the habits of some of these authors; predict the results in a story.

3. Why do "unknowns" have trouble getting published? Does that mean they aren't good writers? Imagine you are trying to support the writing of an excellent but unknown writer who just happens to be one of your good friends. Compose a letter to the editor of a literary journal, requesting that she print this author's work. Explain why the writer hasn't yet become famous or widely read and why the editor should risk publishing this unknown writer's work.

Discussion 2: Caroline

What are the differences between novice (inexperienced) writers and professional writers? This is a really good question because I (personally) don't see a lot of differences aside from the obvious—professional writers are paid and published whereas novice writers just write. I believe that many novice writers write for their own enjoyment and betterment of themselves while many professional writers write for fame and fortune. Novice writers write for fame and fortune, for fun, for emotional release and various other personal reasons, but many don't even know if they're good enough to be taken seriously. However this hypothesis can be contradicted by professional examples like Emily Dickinson who never knew she was worth reading (by the public) and probably never wanted anything but self-satisfaction from her writing even though her writings received a lot (how much is a lot?) of fame and fortune. Writers both novice and professional are very different but nonetheless, they're both writers, they just have different motives.

Questions and Writing to Explore

1. Who are your different audiences? Do you change your work when you write for these audiences? Revise one piece of your writing to suit two of your most different audiences.

2. Would your writing become "better" if someone paid you to produce it? Write an imaginary journal entry for a day in your life as a famous screen writer. You've been given a $100,000 advance, and the 200-page draft is due next week. Think aloud about the connection between money and writing.

3. Do you agree that novice and professional writers have different motives for writing? Write a dialog between you and one of your writing idols—each of you should talk about motives.

Discussion 3: Sherri

As I started looking back through my journal, I had to laugh when I came to question #7 response from the handout you gave to us the first day of class. Question #7 was: What makes a good writer? And to think I only wrote a paragraph answer on this question, when now I (along with many classmates) could write a few pages, or more. Even during a few tense discussions during class, which I enjoyed, we never all agreed on a clear and precise definition of what exactly makes a good writer. Some of us argued that some people just have a special "talent" when they write, like a singer or a sportsperson, and that some people write well—but not as well as those who have the "talent." Most of the class thought that with a lot of practice almost anyone could be a good writer. This of course had to do with "what exactly is a good writer and how do you know if you are *good*? I never really came to a set answer in my mind, and maybe that means something. Maybe a good writer is whoever that someone reading the work thinks is good. For example, I could think the piece of writing stinks, when other people may feel as though it is wonderful.

Questions and Writing to Explore

1. Think of a piece of writing that made you say to yourself, "_____ is a talented writer!" What is it, precisely, about the writing that

makes you say that? List as many synonyms for *talented* as you can. Exactly what is writing talent? Turn this into a strong opinion essay.

2. How do you know when one of your pieces of writing is good? Do your readers always agree with you? Are there criteria for judging good and bad writing? If so, who sets those criteria? Do the people you respect for their good taste ever disagree on the quality of a piece of writing, a movie, or any other piece of art? Write a poem praising a piece of art that you admire that you know a friend doesn't like.

3. What does it mean if we can't agree on a definition of good writing? Write an essay defining good writing from the perspective of three very different fields—say, the humanities, the social sciences, and the natural sciences—or three types of writers—say, a literary novelist, a political speech writer, and a gossip columnist —and draw some conclusions about good writing.

Discussion 4: Fran

Dispelling the Myth That Writers Are a Special Type of People   If we are to accept the definition of a writer as one who writes, we must accept the fact that writers are not a special type of person. Those who write might be of any age, shape, background or interest. They may produce a technical manual or a provocative essay or a piece of artistic prose. The one thing they hold in common is the use of language.

Following this premise, we can even include among writers those who do not have the physical ability to pick up a pencil. Certainly a paraplegic who dictates his innermost thoughts and feelings about his limitations—or any other subject—to another must be considered a writer. Writing can even be performed by a scribe of some sort—human or mechanical.

The distinctions that must be drawn if we are going to look at the specialness of writers include the purpose for writing and the degree of skill or artistry desired or required. If I write a letter to my friend, I am a writer. If I submit a term paper of the same caliber of technique [written as informally as a personal letter] to a committee judging my dissertation, they might dispute whether or not I am a writer! Perhaps writing, like beauty, is in the eye of the beholder.

On the other hand, I can consider myself a writer if no one beholds that I write. Emily Dickinson certainly was a writer during her lifetime, not just after the discovery of her wealth of poetry. Whether the authors of colonial diaries ever considered themselves writers is questionable. Yet today, their works are included in anthologies. The first grader who tells in scrawled words and pictures of the arrival of a baby sister should be encouraged to call herself and be called the writer of that piece.

Perhaps by widening the definition of writer and dissolving the aura of specialness as a prerequisite, we might better encourage possible writing artists to give it a try. Ah-ha! Now there is another category—the writing artist. All writers won't enter that category, due to lack of talent, or dedication, or luck or some mysterious something that can't be pinned down. But with a recognition of a larger pool of writers as those who write, we are more likely to find among us those who write well.

Questions and Writing to Explore

1. Does an author have to actually write or type the words to "create" a piece of writing? Compose a scene set in a futuristic world in which composing and creating take place in an entirely new way.

2. As in the case of Emily Dickinson, who was published rarely in her own lifetime, evaluations of writing, including definitions of what is good or valuable, can change over time. How can that occur? What does the fact that it *does* occur mean for you as a writer? Write a letter from Emily Dickinson to a classmate; Emily should dwell on the subject of writing in general or fame in particular.

3. Can we consider ourselves good writers or does it take an audience or public to make us good? Sketch the feelings of a world-famous writer who is suddenly cut off from her or his audience by loss of the physical ability to write, by isolation, or by overwhelming writer's block. Does she or he still feel like a writer? Will she or he write again?

4. What is the difference between a writer and a writing artist? Write a short short story about a writer who works harder than any other writer in the world. What are the results of his or her efforts?

5. If we widen our definition of *writer,* what is lost and what is gained? Sketch life in a world where everyone is a fluent writer and an eager reader.

Who Writes: The Scene of Writing

Imagine the best writer in the whole world. Where is this person? What is the person doing? Is the person male or female? What is that person writing?

Think about "scenes" of writing that you have read in books or seen in movies or on TV. Is the writer furiously scribbling a master piece? Is the hard-boiled male writer sitting in a small, shabby room, pecking at a typewriter with two fingers and blowing cigarette smoke into the air? Does the writer move from the impoverished but serious garret room (one high window, birds, gray rooftops) to lively nights at The Ritz with piano bars and wealthy patrons?

For some of us, my request "Imagine the best writer in the whole world" immediately evokes stereotypical images such as these. And like all stereotypes, these images are true *to some extent*. For instance, published "art" writers have, for several centuries, often been men. Expatriate American writers did live in inexpensive Paris rooms in the 1920s and 1930s and haunt the Parisian cafes at night. Also, like Americans in general, writers used to smoke, and before the computer, most relied on a No. 2 pencil or battered Underwood typewriter. A few writers still even hold to these habits despite growing concerns about lung cancer and the advent of word processors and electronic mail. We all like romance, and these romantic images linger on.

For some of us, though, this persistent image of the lone writer is troubling. Consider—a young female vegetarian who writes plays in collaboration with her sister; a black male poet who performs his poetry to jazz and "composes" and presents his work in video, working with a production crew; a once-heterosexual, now-gay, older woman who shapes her best-selling romance novels on the screen of a 386 PC on the days she isn't taking care of her young granddaughter and working at the local NOW headquarters or discussing revisions with her editor; the white male academic who writes and then tapes "radios" for a national radio network—these individuals are more likely to be today's "average writer," and yet the romantic image of the lone writer in the garret is still with us. For modern "composers" of language, this image can be a problem since they may find the traditional scene of writing to be conservative and limiting. When mentally we evoke the writer in the garret each time the word *writer* is mentioned, we put many modern writers at a disadvantage.

We put ourselves, as writers, at a disadvantage too. Whenever we hide ourselves away in a spare room, sit at the kitchen table after everyone else has gone to bed, or go alone to a weekend retreat and try to compose, writing becomes immensely intimidating. On paper like this, in scenes like this—we are sure—all the best authors in the world have written their glorious prose. And at that moment, as we evoke our favorite, most intimidating models, we ask ourselves to perform *as well* as those models—and we ask this before we have taught ourselves to perform *at all*. Our expectations are simply far too high.

Poet William Stafford is famous for offering the practical advice to "lower your standards." In essence, he is suggesting that writers should demystify the scene of writing. To do this, writers need to start by interrogating their own "scene." The following exercise is intended to help you to begin this project.

Scene of Writing Exercise

Directions   Write, following the prompts that your teacher or a friend will read to you; if you're alone, read them to yourself. Write without censoring yourself and keep writing until the next prompt changes your direction. Whoever is reading the prompts should allow at least ten minutes for section A and at least five minutes each for sections B and C. Longer time periods would be even more helpful.

A. (minimum of 10 minutes)
   1. Where are you?
   2. Who is there?
   3. What do you want?
   4. What are you risking?
   5. What are you writing?
   Stop. Read what you have written. Circle the most unexpected sentence. Now, begin again.

B. Choose one of the following four options. You will write a minimum of five minutes on the option of your choice.
   1. Relocate your scene of writing.
   2. Describe an "ideal" scene of writing.
   3. Describe a communal scene of writing, one in which you are not writing alone.
   4. Write a scene of writing but adopt the opposite gender.
   When you are finished, read what you have written.

C. Now, write for five more minutes to describe what it was *like* to complete this exercise. Your teacher or group members may ask you to share parts of your writings. You can read directly from what you have written. Leave material out if you feel more comfortable "editing" your spontaneous writing, or paraphrase by telling in general what you wrote. It may be useful to read several individuals' versions of section A, then section B, then section C.

Explorations to Do as a Journal Entry or for Small Group or Class Discussion

1. How influenced are you—as an individual, group, or class—by the "traditional" scene of writing?

2. What is the point or value of relocating scenes of writing?

3. What keeps individuals from attaining their "ideal" scenes of

writing? Are we always sure we know what scene would be most conducive to writing, or are we fantasizing about hoping to write?

4. To what degree can a scene of writing actually be communal?

Although many of us will draft scenes that feature that expected image of a person in a room, alone and writing, most of us do not write in isolation. We read to understand other writers, and we talk over our writing with friends and family. Writers are human beings with complex personal histories that influence the way they think and feel about things. Writing process self-audits, for example, show how teachers influence writers, as do almost all experiences with reading and writing.

I'll end this chapter by asking you to think about placing the scene of writing and the writer in the wider world of readers. That is, although we may begin to write alone and for ourselves—or within a family, peer group, or classroom—the movement many writers follow is outward, toward larger, more public audiences. Amy realized this when she wrote the following advice for students starting a writing class:

Dear New Student,

The first day you enter your creative writing class, don't worry. You will not recognize any faces and they may be intimidating; they are probably as nervous as you. If your teacher shows you his/her list of demands for that semester, don't think stressful thoughts, you have four months to work on it. Relax, take the class slow, but pace yourself.

The student who enters a writing class has already gone public, and for some very good reasons. Most writers—workers with words—like to share their writing. We all want and need audiences, and we all need experiences that help us to move from being our own audience to having wider and wider public audiences.

The following activity may help you better understand your own audiences.

Audience Exercise

Directions Take five minutes and list the audiences who shared your writing *before* you enrolled in a writing class. You may want to "draw" a writing audience map or sketch out your history over time. You can be elaborate (draw a roadmap of whom you've shared writing with) or sketchy (use circles to diagram overlaps), or you can simply write a paragraph that explores your development with audience. To clarify your paragraph, you could also sketch out a brief flowchart. For instance, my audience memory list would include:

> Girlfriends in high school, parents, sisters (sometimes), my English teacher, my grandparents (sometimes). More public, a poem in a high school literary magazine, a verse printed on the card at my father's memorial service. Even more public—in college, my first writing class, teacher, and peers. Soon after, my first submission to a campus literary magazine, being read by editors and contest judges, still my family, still my friends. First publication and an award in a regional contest. Travel and work abroad—that expatriate writing group in Nigeria. Publication in an anthology and a poem on a calendar; my current co-author and writing cohort . . .

As you can see, most writers' audiences ripple out from the self-as-writer-and-reader (as found in private journals) to family, to school, to a local writing community, to a national writing community, and so on. The number and variety of audiences is almost infinite—religious communities, readers in the workplace, and on and on.

By this point, you should have gained a fair understanding of your own beliefs about writing and of your feelings about being asked to write; you should also have some awareness of the ways in which beliefs and habits can slow or support your writing, and of whom you write for. Chapter 2 discusses what we already know about writers and connects these insights back to your work in a writing workshop. At this point, you may want to move ahead to the chapters on invention, drafting, or revision, or you may want to continue following the chapter progression and consider "writers' worlds" for a little longer.

Notes

1. Many of these statements are adapted from Frank Smith's essay "Myths of Writing" found in *Language Arts* 58 (October 1981): 792–798, and also reprinted in a volume of his essays, listed below.
2. These statements are adapted from Michael Miller and John Daly's study of writing apprehension. See Daly's article listed below.

Sources and Readings

Brand, Alice G., and John Chibnall. "The Emotions of Apprentice Poets." *Empirical Studies of the Arts* 7 (1989): 45–59.

Daly, John A. "Writing Apprehension." *When a Writer Can't Write: Studies in Writer's Block and Other Composing Process Problems.* Ed. Mike Rose. New York: Guilford Press, 1985. 134–165.

Dillard, Annie. *The Writing Life.* New York: Harper, 1989.

McAndrew, Donald. "Writing Apprehension: A Review of Research." *Research and Teaching in Developmental Education* 2 (1986): 43–52.

Murray, Donald. "The Essential Delay: When Writer's Block Isn't." *When a Writer Can't Write: Studies in Writer's Block and Other Composing Process Problems.* Ed. Mike Rose. New York: Guilford, 1985. 219–226.

Plimpton, George, ed. *Writers at Work.* Third series. New York: Viking, 1967.

Smith, Frank. *Essays into Literacy: Selected Papers and Some Afterthoughts.* Portsmouth, NH: Heinemann, 1983.

Chapter 2

Discovering a Writer's Moves

When you are first given an assignment, go home, get at your desk and write out your first ten ideas, then ball up the paper and throw it out. After that get up, eat 8½ Oreos, play some Nintendo, and then go back to your desk. And start again. This will ensure your ideas are new and different. Always remember if you have an idea which is a bit odd or different or simply bizarre, go for it. Just do it. It is always easier to get forgiveness than permission. Be bold and different. There is no right vs wrong way to write.

—CHRISTOPHER

Writers like to tell others about the way they composed a piece of poetry, fiction, or drama. Their stories are always interesting because creative writers are individuals who have given themselves permission to take necessary chances; they pursue the odd, different, productive writing direction. And, like most storytellers, writers are selective, telling what strikes them as memorable, true, or useful. Some tell the story of how they write as they would like it to appear—a brilliant, inevitable, controlled activity—and some tell confusing or contradictory tales. Because writers differ, their stories about how they write may hide some of the very information that would be useful to a newcomer to the field. To gain insight into the writing process, this chapter looks both at how writers say they compose and what writing researchers know about the composing process in general.

Creative Writers: Composing Stories and Writing Rules

When they are identified as experts and asked to share their processes and advice, writers often fall into the trap of offering rules—sometimes seriously, sometimes tongue in cheek. These rules can be expected to help in *certain* situations. Red Smith's often quoted suggestion, "There's nothing to writing. All you do is sit down at the typewriter and open a vein," is a rich metaphor but not a wise rule, and Winston Churchill's observation that "the short words are best and the old words are best of all," would eliminate the work of journalist Tom Wolfe and severely inhibit a writer modeling her prose on the luxuriant sentences of novelist Virginia Woolf.[1]

Creative writers describe complicated parts of complicated processes, each from his or her own illuminating—but limited—viewpoint. Gathering their advice together, we find consensus and contradiction. That's not surprising if we remember that a writer's views on writing will change not only with each piece written but also across a writing career, as the writer develops and thrives.

Since you are currently investigating *your* life as a writer, it is useful to explore the composing rules that you work by.

Explorations to Do as a Journal Entry or for Small Group or Class Discussion

1. List all the "rules" for writing that you can remember hearing from teachers or peers. For instance, "Always start an essay with a thesis statement" or "Never start a sentence with a conjunction such as *and, or, so, but, for, yet.*" Try to remember some rules for writing poetry, fiction, or drama; common ones might include: "Always use a title," "Don't shift point of view," "Avoid clichés," and "Try to create 'round' not 'flat' characters," and "Show don't tell." You can shape this into a list poem about rules; tell a reader how to (or how not to) write a poem, story, novel, and so on. List writing is discussed more fully in Chapter 3.

2. By yourself, in a group, or in class, list the reasons you can imagine for the invention of an often-occurring rule. Why do we have rules for writing? In what ways are rules productive and counterproductive?

3. Take some of the professional writers' advice/rules that I quote throughout this chapter and write a journal entry that supports or argues against the writers' statements.

Here are two student writers taking different positions on the same quote by writer Tim O'Brien: "Writing doesn't get easier with experience. The more you know, the harder it is to write."

Keith's Response

I disagree with this [O'Brien's] statement for various reasons. The more you know, the easier it is to write. The more organization techniques, grammar, and revision you are familiar with, the easier the paper is to write. Most importantly, the more vocabulary you know, the better your writing will sound. All of these things you learn with experience.

Writing becomes easier as you mature also. A writer learns to manage time for a more effective paper. I feel this quote is totally wrong. Writing well takes time, hard work, and most importantly, experience.

Tyrene's Response

I agree with the quote above by Tim O'Brien. As you learn more about writing and as you write more, it becomes harder and harder to write. You are constantly comparing your writing to works of others or even your own.

There are many different kinds of audiences to write for. As you begin writing this is not very important, but as you become more experienced it is more important. You realize the fact that you may be writing to just one audience, but want to reach different kinds of people.

As a writer becomes experienced he has more ideas to write about. Deciding between the different ideas or sorting through them makes it difficult to choose a topic or even take out parts that are not really needed. Writing becomes harder as the writer gains experience because he has more experience in writing well and more ideas to write.

4. Think of a time when "writing rules" stifled your writing or kept you from writing. Informally, in a journal entry, try to tell that story and explore what obeying rules and breaking rules mean to you as a writer.

5. Perhaps a more profitable way to look at rules is to consider them "useful advice," information that may help but that also may be ignored given your own situation. Below, you'll find the advice that student writers were willing to offer to those just beginning a writing workshop.
   a. What advice recurs?
   b. What piece of advice tells you something you didn't expect to hear?
   c. At the end of your own writing class, come back to this advice and write a journal entry discussing the usefulness or validity of these writers' rules to someone taking a writing workshop.

Laura's Advice

- Don't panic! Everyone in the class is in the same boat.

- Conference, conference, conference! Talk to the teacher.

- Break a rule. Show the teacher what you can do.

- *Always* revise!!

- Don't think of your work as "stupid."

- Don't think of anyone else's work as "stupid."

- Don't listen to anyone who calls your work "stupid."

- Read your work out loud. "What looks good on paper . . . "

- Criticize, don't ostracize.

- If an idea doesn't work one way, save it for another format.

- Try different points of view, images, style.

- Anything can be made into a poem or story.

- If something sounds bad, make a copy, then tear it to shreds.

- If nothing works, take a break and then get back to it.

- Read so you can write.

- Your past is an untapped resource; use it.

- Save discarded fragments of prose or poetry. Maybe another story or poem can be created from them.

Tony's Advice
Buy a word processor—you're dead without one.

Jeannie's Advice
- Dust off your brain.

- Get out your favorite pen and notebook.

- Watch the world around you.

- Write what you see.

- Know the rules.

- Break the rules.

- Steal from other writers.

- Write, write, write.

- Keep a journal by your bed for middle-of-the-night inspiration.

- Notice little things as well as big things.

- Write what *you* want to write about.

- Play with new forms of writing.

- Expect to do a lot of reading.

- Expect to do a lot of writing.

- Expect nothing but the best of your writing.
- Don't be afraid to write.
- Love what you write about.
- Get ideas from other writers.

These days, we don't need to rely solely on hunches, rules, and observations, as illuminating as many of these can be. Writers' knowledge should never be discounted since it takes us to places researchers' observations can never take us, but we can increase our understanding of composing by looking at recent developments in writing research.

Research and Writers' Knowledge

Early researchers in composition studies began by studying writers' drafts and final written products and explored a model of writing that included three stages: prewriting, writing, and rewriting.

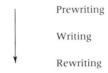

Prewriting

Writing

Rewriting

However, this model is linear and derives from products—written texts. In 1971, Janet Emig used her work to expand earlier categories of prewriting, writing, and rewriting by observing and interviewing writing students. She discussed the recursive nature of the composing activity, exploring, for example, the ways in which writers use planning in the prewriting *and* in the writing stages.

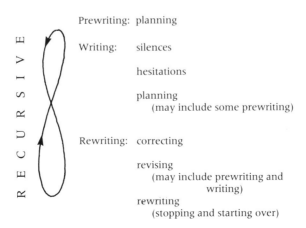

R E C U R S I V E

Prewriting: planning

Writing: silences

hesitations

planning
(may include some prewriting)

Rewriting: correcting

revising
(may include prewriting and writing)

rewriting
(stopping and starting over)

Emig's research findings are echoed in the observations of professional writers. Andy Rooney humorously touches on prewriting as planning: "If I have an idea, I sit down and start typing. If I don't have an idea, I sit down and decide to have one" (135). John Haines claims: "So I guess you could say that I generally have some idea of where I'm going, of what I want to *say*, and I more or less follow this hunch. . . . A writer needs to know when to abandon an idea and take up another" (146). For Haines, planning is complicated and recursive. Grace Paley makes a strong argument for counting a writer's thinking as part of prewriting and reminds us that writing doesn't have to take place at a desk:

> I have a basic indolence about me which is essential to writing. It really is. Kids now call it space around you. It's thinking time, it's hanging-out time, it's daydreaming time. You know, it's lie-around-the-bed time, it's sitting-like-a-dope-in-your-chair time. And that seems to me essential to any work. Some people will do it just sitting at their desks looking serious, but I don't. (Todd 50)

In her teaching, writer Kelley Cherry focuses on the recursive nature of writing: "It's crucial to stress the process of draft, critique and revision" (Bunge 22). Clarence Major's rewriting stage includes revising, rewriting, even planning: "I think it's possible to do a first draft, for example, and put it away. . . . I'll put it away and look at it six months later, three weeks later, sometimes two years later, so that I can see what is there in a way that I wasn't able to see in the beginning. . . . I go back and I try to reshape it and impose a kind of order upon it and focus and direction" (Bunge 59).

After Emig's work appeared, researchers continued to investigate the composing process, observing writers and often asking them to think aloud while composing. This research generated more questions about the writing process, questions like some of those we looked at in Chapter 1: What are the differences between basic and expert (or professional) writers? What are the steps in the revision process? What keeps certain writers from becoming more successful in their composing?

Mina Shaughnessy explored the problems experienced by writers with inadequate or unproductive writing processes. Such writers, she found, usually work within a rule-governed system. Their mistakes are often the result of mis- or overapplying rules in their writing. She explained that mistakes can be productive—they are necessary steps in a writer's progress toward fluency and control.

Shaughnessy's work shows why rules we explored earlier in this chapter can prove disastrous if applied by writers to every type of writing occasion. The unsuccessful writer, in fact, may be trying too earnestly to apply the expert's "rules." When writing isn't working, it is useful to examine inherited rules. Keep in mind that such rules are culture-, genre-, and context-based. Modify any that inhibit your creative explorations.

Some researchers explored the differences in composing strategies among writers. Sondra Perl found that more proficient writers worry about audience and listen to what she termed a "felt sense," which helps them negotiate the demands of their writing-in-progress by choosing to weave a metaphor throughout a text, deciding that an intended audience wouldn't understand a term and including a strategic definition, or imagining that an especially ironic passage would be judged flippant rather than effective. These decisions are made when writers are able to scan their partially completed texts and make effective choices for the words that will be added.

Creative writers often discuss a composing state that appears similar to Perl's "felt sense"; they mention listening for direction or being taken over by the text. Erica Jong explains how work turns to inspiration:

> You sit down every morning and push that pen across the page, and you have to get from one point to another. You know that you have to move your character to a certain city and out again and you must do it that day whether you feel like it or not. You don't always *start out* inspired, but as you work your way into the scene, things start happening. You begin pushing that pen along, and then maybe after two hours you're really going. Things you hadn't expected are happening on the page. (Packard 179)

When writing researchers began to focus on revision, they found that expert writers use many strategies to improve their work—adding and deleting material, for example, but also reordering a text and thinking about its structure and meaning in general. Inexpert writers, on the other hand, speak primarily of cleaning up their writing; they have few strategies for revision; often, they just don't revise enough.

Not unexpectedly, many creative writers have commented on the need for scrupulous revision. Ernest Hemingway explains that he rewrote the ending to *Farewell to Arms* thirty-nine times because he was working on "getting the words right." James Michener observes, "I can never recall anything of mine that's ever been printed in less than three drafts." For such authors, rewriting is exciting *and* generative; it leads to larger vision. Clayton Eschelman says, "I rewrite, splice, and try to only present what is taut and vital. I work on this poem, then that poem, then I see suddenly that I like this part here and that part there and move them together to see if they actually work as a piece." He explains that his goal truly is to achieve something new through revision: "That is really a hard thing to learn—revision as a way to open up material and draw more edges into the material, as opposed to sanding the material down so that you end up with something smooth, polished, and featureless" (Bartlett 51).

Research and writers' practices show that writing is about choices, large and small—choices that can't always be discovered by looking at a finished text. Sometimes we can learn only from watching the writer as she works with words. As Kelly Cherry explains:

> [T]here's a kind of inevitability about the ending that fools everyone into thinking that it [the text] is indeed inevitable. The writer is up here with starting point "one," recognizing there's an infinite number of choices and that because it's Monday or because it's Tuesday, he chooses "two," and then "one" and "two" together narrow that infinity. So there's an infinity that's slightly smaller for "three." He makes this jaggedy path down and it's a good thing he does too; otherwise there would be a limited number of works that could be written. Because you can go any way you want, every story can be different. The writer is highly conscious of this tricky way of getting through to the end of the story and conscious of all kinds of accidents that contribute to his route. (Bunge 28)

Because writing is a complex activity, the demands of the writing workshop are great. Students are asked to write, to revise, and to write and revise some more. Always, creative writers agree that more writing leads to improved writing. "One of the things you have to do is simply submit to the time in front of the typewriter or desk every day," Wallace Stegner warns would-be novelists (Bunge 120). Flannery O'Connor finds that her process involved *readiness:* "Every morning between 9 and 12 I go to my room and sit before a piece of paper. Many times I just sit for three hours with no ideas coming to me. But I know one thing: If an idea does come between 9 and 12, I am there ready for it" (Murray, *Learning* 51).

Maya Angelou claims similar rituals, "I go to work everyday about 6:30 in the morning. I keep a hotel room and I go to the same room each day" (Todd 61). William Hazlitt notes, "The more a man writes, the more he can write." This is true for women writers, too, of course. All writers thrive when they analyze their writing habits, set reasonable writing goals and deadlines, and find real audiences, such as supportive writing work groups.

Recently, Barbara Tomlinson reviewed the published interviews of over 2,000 creative writers and noted the metaphors they used regularly to discuss the writing process in general and the revision process in particular ("Cooking"). Tomlinson found writers using four major metaphorical stories to discuss their composing: cooking, mining, gardening, and hunting or fishing. When a writer chooses one of those metaphors, he or she is projecting a certain way of looking at writing. For instance, the metaphors of *writing is cooking* or *writing is gardening* are craft-oriented—writers can mix elements and form a whole or nurture an idea—whereas *writing is mining* or *writing is hunting or fishing* are more inspiration-driven—writers discover the vein or capture an elusive ideal. Tomlinson found that writers also use metaphors to describe the revision stage of writing: They compare the process to refining ore, casting and recasting (a metal), sculpting, painting, sewing and tailoring, tying things off, fixing things, and cutting ("Tuning").

Writing metaphors can help us increase our understanding of the writing process. The following are some images of writing and revising that have been collected from writing students and writing teachers. To develop their metaphors, these individuals completed the "Writing is like" and "Revision is like" statements found in the writer's self-audit in Chapter 1.

Writing Students' Images of Writing

- Writing is like painting a picture with words and lots of detail.

- Writing is like giving birth, conception of an idea, delivery of the idea onto paper (strain, stress, pain, and anxiety) and completion (relief and joy), leaving one empty and exhausted yet elated with the product and anxious for its future.

- Writing is like talking; it should be entertaining.

- Writing is like therapy; I sort things out in my brain; it makes me feel organized and a better person, in a happier mood, satisfied with what I've done.

- Writing is like freedom; I can give voice to any kind of strange bizarre thought that enters my head. It doesn't matter because I don't have to show it to anyone, unless I choose to.[2]

Writing Students' Images of Revising

- Revising is like diluting an original brew, working on an assembling line for twenty years, going through labor again to bear the same child.

- Revising is like dwelling on past mistakes with a chance to set things right.

- Revising is like a secret; I hide all the stupid things I wrote (when I was obviously not myself) the first time.

- Revising is like cleaning the house.

- Revising is like a neverending story; it's hard for me to leave my work alone. I always find some sort of problem or something I want to change.

Compare these students' images with the following teachers' images.

Writing Teachers' Images of Writing

- Writing is like driving fast down a dark road without headlights. I have to rely on instinct to get me there.

- Writing is like running. It's hard to get motivated, but once I get going, it picks up momentum until I reach that "high."

- Writing is like trying to build a boat when you're already dog-paddling in the water. Once I get something hammered together to *stand* on, I do okay.

- Writing is like spelunking with no light. I bump my head real hard, then change directions. Sometimes I draw a little map of what the cave is supposed to look like, but I always lose it a few feet into the darkness.

Writing Teachers' Images of Revising

- Revising is like finishing getting dressed.

- Revising is like turning on the headlights. I can now see where I've been and what's in front of me.

- Revising is like weeding, making decisions about what goes, what stays, what to transplant.

- Revising is easier than writing, but harder to get started.

- Revising is like having a second chance. I wish I could revise each day before I let it go. But if I could, I would probably still be in junior high right now.

- Revising is like the whittling done as a cub scout on a bar of soap. You carve an initial shape, a whale, and keep carving until you have a minnow.

Explorations to Do as a Journal Entry or for Small Group or Class Discussion

1. In this small sample of images, are there any commonalities and differences in the students' and teachers' accounts of writing and revising?

2. How do these images compare to the images you wrote down in your own self-audit? Do these images enlarge or change your understanding of writing and revising?

   Now, to help you gain a clearer understanding of the commonalities in writing processes, you might complete one or more of the following exercises.

Composing Models Exercises

1. On a sheet of plain paper, sketch out your own composing process. To do this, you may want to focus on your image of composing: "Writing is like . . . ." Figure 2.1 is a student sketch that compares writing to making a sauce.

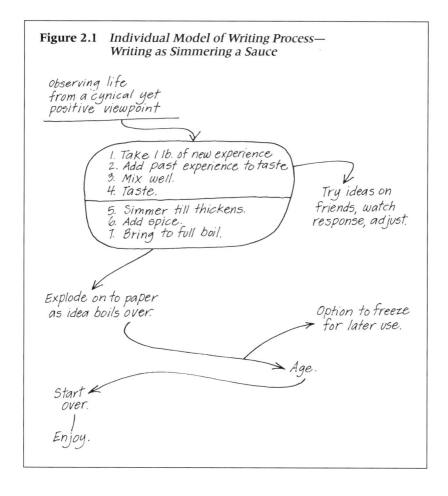

Figure 2.1 *Individual Model of Writing Process— Writing as Simmering a Sauce*

observing life
from a cynical yet
positive viewpoint

1. Take 1 lb. of new experience
2. Add past experience to taste.
3. Mix well.
4. Taste.

5. Simmer till thickens.
6. Add spice.
7. Bring to full boil.

Try ideas on
friends, watch
response, adjust.

Explode on to paper
as idea boils over.

Option to freeze
for later use.

Age.

Start
over.

Enjoy.

2. Form into groups; your teacher will give each group a large sheet of butcher paper. Use the drawings of the composing process of everyone in the group to find an image that encompasses all your methods of composing. Together, sketch out a group composing

model. Figure 2.2 is a group sketch that compares writing to brewing coffee.

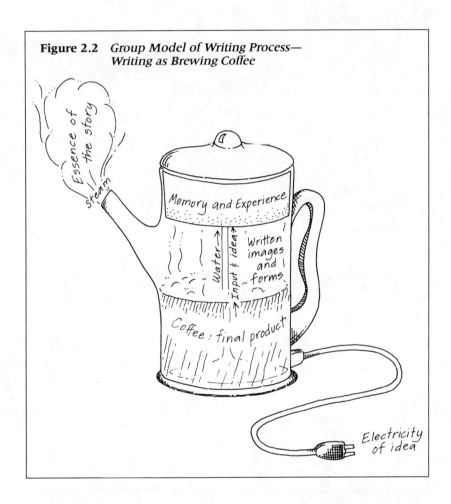

Figure 2.2   *Group Model of Writing Process— Writing as Brewing Coffee*

Essence of the story

steam

Memory and Experience

Water →

Input & idea →

Written images and forms

Coffee: final product

Electricity of idea

3. Each of four groups can sketch out one of Tomlinson's writing metaphors: Writing is cooking, mining, gardening, and hunting or fishing. Decide if parts of any group members' processes are left out of the metaphor. Show your drawings to the whole class, and take a quick survey to see who identifies most with which of the four illustrated metaphors.

Writing Is . . . Exercise

Drawing models of the composing process makes us look at the world of writing just a bit differently. But most writers like to write about the experience of writing as well. At their worst, these pieces are derivative, uninspired, academic, but at their best—the kind you hope to create through this exercise—writings about your composing process can be both insightful and humorous.

Directions

1. Your teacher will list the following prompts on the board:
   - "Writing is a . . . "
   - "Recipe for . . . "
   - "Why write?"
   - "To my ideal reader . . . "
   - Choose your own beginning.

2. Pick one of the prompts, and write freely for at least ten minutes.

3. After ten minutes, stop, read what you have written, and circle or mark the most interesting section.

4. Pick a *different* prompt, and again write for ten minutes.

5. Stop, read what you have written, and circle or mark the most interesting section.

6. Volunteers can read their favorite piece to the class.

7. At home, for your journal or for sharing with your group during the next class, shape this freewriting into a more formal piece. The following sample is a draft from this exercise.

Strawberry Shortstory

Heather Jordan

1 qt. fresh strawberries, nurtured in a fertile patch of inspiration

2 cups experience, well sifted

2 tbsp. spirit

3 tsp. imagination

1 tsp. humor

½ cup plot

2 eyes

Wash berries well, then pick them over. Weed out clichés, shortcuts, and hackneyed expressions. Add about 1 cup pressure and meditate at room temperature to the taste.

Heat workroom to comfort level—make sure brain is hot. Gather fuzzy socks, security blanket, cool drink, and paper. With favorite pen in hand, stir experience, spirit, humor, and imagination. Cut in plot, scraping bowl constantly to ensure an even mixture. Blend in eyes, stiffly beaten for detail. Spread dough on 2 or more blank sheets, 8½ × 11″. Sprinkle with organization. Bake 20 min. to 1 hr.

Place first draft on final paper after cooling with grammar. For a less crusty shortstory, spread first draft on second (and third, if necessary) blank paper. Add ½ cup more grammar and organization, each to taste. Sprinkle well-polished berries over all and serve warm with plain or whipped readers. Savor reviews. Unlimited servings (Bishop 33).

Discovering a Writer's Moves

It's all very well to look at complete processes; we have them, we use them, we need them, we are often worried about them. But for most of us, discovering a way to get started is the biggest challenge of the entire creative act. Often, we participate in writing workshops or organize informal writing groups primarily for the pressure that peer groups provide. We know that in such groups we will be asked to write and to invent our selves; we will become practicing writers, working seriously with words. Invention activities—such as the exploratory "Writing Is" piece you've already completed (and a number that will be discussed extensively in Chapters 3 and 5)—can help us discover what we mean to say. We will learn a writer's moves.

In a writing workshop, we also start to consider what prompts us to write—from what sources come our desires to express ourselves and share those expressions. The following exercise allows you to explore your thinking on the topic of inspiration.

Muse Exercise

Directions

1. On a sheet of paper, list the people, places, things, situations, moods, and occasions that prompt you to write. For instance, I seem to generate writing ideas when I go running, go shopping, read other writers, and so on.

2. Next, share these lists with others in your group. If you want, compare your lists with this one (drawn up by a group in one of my writing classes):

   dreams; the past; books; people I catch glimpses of; clothes; photos; staring at maps; listening to language; eavesdropping; traveling and eating strange meals; watching people—friends, relatives, family; newspaper articles; post cards; family objects; powerful moments considered later; the muse; wanting to send a message; being upset but not knowing why; to show off; from being hungry; from things I'm dying to say.

Draw up a master list that represents all of you, and share it with the class.

3. On your own, you might borrow some ideas that you find interesting from all these lists. For instance, I like the idea of using the prompt of staring at a map to help me write some travel pieces I've been avoiding.

4. For your next class:
   a. Read this brief definition of the muse: "MUSE. One of the nine Gr. goddesses who preside over poetry, song, and the arts, traditionally invoked by poets to grant them inspiration."[3] (You may also want to read about muses in an encyclopedia or in a book like Edith Hamilton's *Mythology*.)
   b. Read the student muse pieces that follow (Bishop 64–67).

On the Muse

Luis R. Amadeo

I have a muse who comes and goes freely as she pleases. Sometimes I'll be walking down the sidewalk and she'll go "Hey, look at that!" while she pokes me in the arm. Then I have to run and get pen and paper to write with, so this idea won't escape me.

If it comes, it comes, and if it doesn't, I force it out. But when the muse is there, the writing froths up from the keyboard and smacks me in the face, saying, "Here, write this down." And, how can I refuse?

This muse is oh so undependable. She loves to sleep late, and won't get out of bed those early mornings when something is due. Stress just scares a muse away, I guess. Strong emotions are good, but I have to write them down, and then finish while I'm calm.

Confessions of a Male Muse

Jennifer Wasileski

I am late,
I see
her pen is poised.
An eager erection,
of sorts.

Face twisted in ignorance.
She's not hearing me,
I'm not there.
Or am I?

"Bastard!"
She's thinking.
"Sunning himself somewhere!"

"I am fashionably late
my dear"
I announce
throwing open our door.

"Well look what the cat
dragged in."
Says she.
"I almost started without you."

5. In class, read these muse drafts aloud (or read others provided by your teacher). Compare the traditional "image of the muse" with these modern re-creations. How have these writers made the muse relevant to their writing? What do their versions of the muse tell us about their writing processes and beliefs about writers and writing?

6. In class, begin your own muse piece:
   a. Take out a sheet of paper.
   b. Write for ten minutes, without self-censoring, beginning with one of the following prompts:
      - "To my muse . . . "
      - "In the _____, she (he) comes to me."
      - "Dear _____:"
      - Choose your own beginning.
   c. Share a few of these; read them out loud and enjoy them.
   d. At home, shape your uncensored writing into a "Muse" piece. Your teacher may ask you to share this with a group or with the whole class, or to save it in your journal. You may find it interesting to "revisit" the muse around the time of your last writing class. Write her (him) a letter or invoke her (him) again, and you may find yourself viewing inspiration in new ways.

Often it's more interesting to talk about the muse or insight or inspiration and ignore the problems of actually writing to a task. But, in fact, that's the writing most of us do most often: We write for a particular purpose. All writers give themselves assignments, to get the writing in motion on those mornings or evenings when it just isn't flowing. Professional writers write by commission: Novelists write screenplays, poets write librettos, and most writers turn out reviews and criticism as well as original work. In addition, much well-regarded writing through the centuries has been social writing

—that is, writing done to observe certain ritual occasions: to celebrate marriages, to mourn the deaths of children or statespersons or celebrities, to memorialize wars and uprisings, and so on. There is nothing crass about taking on any writing assignment or project. There is nothing dishonorable about writing without waiting for the muse to strike up a conversation. Wallace Stegner says, "People learn much writing to order" although he goes on to add, "but they learn more writing what they want." For a beginning writer, writing to some order—using class activities, for example, to prompt writing—always helps illuminate what *can be* written.

To show you how the private assignments of writers develop into public work, the next chapter presents a series of invention exercises that you can return to again and again. Discovering a writer's moves through invention is like learning a new dance: Try, watch, listen, try again. Pay attention but stay relaxed, and, above all, give yourself permission to attempt each turn and to take productive chances.

Notes

1. Authors' quotes here and following are taken from Murray's works—especially *Expecting the Unexpected, Learning by Teaching,* and *A Writer*—unless otherwise noted. Recently, Murray has published a collection of these quotations titled *Shoptalk.*
2. Portions of the discussion on writing research and students' images of writing and revising are adapted from Bishop, *Released into Language,* Chapter 2.
3. Preminger, 533. The muse pieces of professional writers, such as James Laughlin's "My Muse" and Ted Kooser's "Selecting a Reader," can be found in the appendix to Wallace, *Writing Poems.*

Sources and Readings

Bartlett, Lee, ed. *Talking Poetry: Conversations in the Workshop with Contemporary Poets.* Albuquerque: U of New Mexico P, 1987.

Bishop, Wendy. *Released into Language: Options for Teaching Creative Writing.* Urbana, IL: National Council of Teachers of English, 1990.

Brande, Dorothea. *Becoming a Writer.* Los Angeles: J. P. Tarcher, 1981.

Bridwell, Lillian S. "Revising Strategies in Twelfth Grade Students' Transactional Writing." *Research in the Teaching of English* 14 (1980): 197–222.

Bunge, Nancy. *Finding the Words: Conversations with Writers Who Teach.* Athens, OH: Ohio UP, 1985.

Emig, Janet. *The Composing Processes of Twelfth Graders.* Urbana, IL: National Council of Teachers of English, 1971.

Flower, Linda. "Writer-Based Prose: A Cognitive Basis for Problems in Writing." *College English* 41 (1981): 19–37.

Flower, Linda, and John R. Hayes. "A Cognitive Process Theory of Writing." *College Composition and Communication* 32 (1981): 365–387.

Haines, John. *Living Off the Country: Essays on Poetry and Place.* Ann Arbor, MI: U of Michigan, 1981.

Hamilton, Edith. *Mythology.* New York: Signet, 1969.

Lakoff, George, and Mark Johnson. *Metaphors We Live By.* Chicago: U of Chicago P, 1980.

Lakoff, George, and Mark Turner. *More Than Cool Reason: A Field Guide to Poetic Metaphor.* Chicago: U of Chicago P, 1989.

Madden, David. *Revising Fiction: A Handbook for Fiction Writers.* New York: New American Library, 1988.

Murray, Donald. *Expecting the Unexpected: Teaching Myself—and Others—to Read and Write.* Portsmouth, NH: Boynton/Cook, 1989.

———. *Learning by Teaching: Selected Articles on Writing and Teaching.* Upper Montclair, NJ: Boynton/Cook, 1982.

———. *Shoptalk: Learning to Write with Writers.* Portsmouth, NH: Boynton/Cook Heinemann, 1990.

———. *A Writer Teaches Writing.* Boston: Houghton Mifflin, 1968.

Packard, William, ed. *The Poet's Craft.* New York: Paragon House, 1987.

Perl, Sandra. "The Composing Process of Unskilled College Writers." *Research in the Teaching of English* 13 (1979): 317–336.

Plimpton, George, ed. *Poets at Work: The Paris Review Interviews.* London: Penguin Books, 1989.

———. *Women Writers at Work: The Paris Review Interviews.* London: Harcourt, 1979.

———. *Writers at Work.* Third series. New York: Viking, 1967.

———. *Writers at Work.* Fourth series. New York: Viking, 1976.

Preminger, Alex, ed. *Princeton Encyclopedia of Poetry and Poetics.* Enlarged edition. Princeton, NJ: Princeton UP, 1965.

Rooney, Andy. "A Few Thoughts About Writing." Reprinted in *Writing Your Way* by Peter Stillman. Upper Montclair, NJ: Boynton/Cook, 1984.

Shaughnessy, Mina P. *Errors and Expectations: A Guide for the Teacher of Basic Writing.* New York: Oxford UP, 1977.

Sommers, Nancy. "Revision Strategies of Student Writers and Experienced Adult Writers." *College Composition and Communication* 31 (1980): 378–388.

Tobin, Lad. "Bridging Gaps: Analyzing Our Students' Metaphors for Composing." *College Composition and Communication* 40 (December 1989): 444–458.

Todd, Janet, ed. *Women Writers Talking.* New York: Holmes & Meier, 1983.

Tomlinson, Barbara. "Cooking, Mining, Gardening, Hunting: Metaphorical Stories Writers Tell About Their Composing Processes." *Metaphor and Symbolic Activity* 1 (1986): 57–79.

———. "Tuning, Tying, and Training Texts: Metaphors for Revision." *Written Communication* 5 (1988): 58–81.

Turner, Alberta. *Fifty Contemporary Poets.* New York: Longman, 1977.

Wallace, Ronald. *Poems on Poetry.* New York: Dutton, 1965.

———. *Writing Poems.* 2nd Ed. Boston: Little Brown, 1987.

Waldrep, Tom, ed. *Writers on Writing.* New York: Random House, 1985.

———. *Writers on Writing.* Vol. 2. New York: Random House, 1988.

Chapter 3

Uncovering a Draft

List things that have happened to you or that you wish happened or anything you can remember from your childhood. All these bits of information can be used, either in your writing (part truth, part fiction or poetry) or to trigger new thought and images.

—TIFFANY

Over time, writers have developed some simple techniques to get them writing. You may have encountered these techniques in other writing classes—cubing, looping, freewriting, clustering—or you may have picked them up on your own—list making, asking the reporter's questions of who, what, where, when, why, and how. You'll find a chart listing basic invention techniques later in this chapter. Here is Missy talking about one—clustering:

> A technique that I've found helpful is clustering. You sit down, take your pen and write down everything that comes to mind. Grandma Metz, her old swing, Anthony, times at the beach, Clermont Lanes, Millstream Estates with Brian, homecoming, prom, and on and on. You don't stop writing until your page is full, full of possibilities. Never discard this. This can be a pool of resources for your writing for years to come. You then take one thought and cluster on another sheet of paper, everything you remember about that specific event. You'd be surprised how many things you can remember that you can use in your poem or story.

Clustering offers a writer a method for *expanding* and *adding* detail as well as for *focusing in* on a topic in subsequent, related clusters.

In Figure 3.1, Tina uses clustering to help her develop a poem. (Remember, though, that this activity could just as easily have led to a piece of prose.) Tina's clustering was followed by a first shaping of her poem, "Liquid Emotion." The partial draft that follows is in the form of a list.

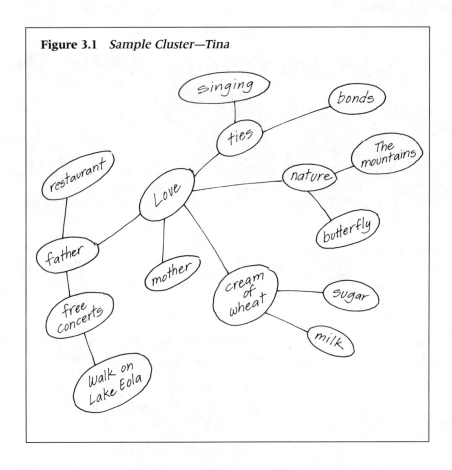

Figure 3.1   *Sample Cluster—Tina*

A walk with papa on Lake Eola with the purple,
    green, and blue florescent fountain.
Hot cream of wheat with sugar and milk on a
    cold December morning.
Singing in unison "You've Got a Friend."
A honeysuckle in bloom with a hummingbird
    sipping its sweet syrup.
The Suwanee that flows and currents
    supporting the manatee.

When we begin writing, most of us base our first writings on our own experiences. Often, however, we have to push ourselves to explore those experiences more fully. Invention techniques can act as triggers to our memory. They ask us to dredge up *particular* details although we may also fictionalize and shape memory later by changing, heightening, and expanding on that memory. In the following piece, Missy, now at the end of her writing workshop semester, talks again about invention techniques:

> When I first started to write, I would sit for hours trying to think of something worthwhile to write about. So many things passed through my mind but not one seemed important enough to write about; nature, animals, helping others, and love were only a few topics. All of these topics are so broad, but I, as a young writer, thought I could tackle them. I didn't know then that I could never give these subjects justice unless I broke them down and wrote about specifics in each.
>
> Now I see things as I walk to class and say "That would make a great poem." A squirrel rummaging to find something to eat; the way the rising sun makes the dew on the green lawns glisten; the leaves changing color, dying, and falling to the ground; all great starting points for poems. You will see that as you do mature in your thinking as well as your writing, how much easier it is to find subjects for your works. Actually, they seem to find you.
>
> As I think back on all the times I sat clueless of what to write on, I realize I thought of a million things to write about. Now I wonder if I'll ever have enough years in my life to write about each one in my own way.

Let's look at how invention techniques can help you develop the specifics that writers like Missy find so important to their work.

To begin writing an autobiographical piece, for instance, Angela used clustering, listing, freewriting, character sketching on individuals from her own past, and first-paragraph exploration. First, Angela *listed* descriptions of twelve people from her past who were memorable or interesting. Here are three individuals on Angela's list:

> *Grandpa G.*—tall, old but young in spirit, sparkling blue eyes, wrinkles, retired. St. Johns, north bay, jeep, knows all plants and animals, boats.
>
> *Ingrid F.*—stepaunt, yuppie, rich and expensive tastes. Impulsive, dress for success, witty, attractive, travel agent, tennis.
>
> *Stacy G.*—individual, nonconformist, skinny, responsible, modern, nontraditionalist, actress.

This listing activity helped Angela to draft a character sketch:

> The first thing a person realizes about Stacy is that she is thin, skinny, bony. Some would even go so far as to call her emaciated. She's

really not though; she's just plain thin and because of her hair (it is cut very short sometimes) people mistake her for a boy. . . . Stacy liked to experiment with new styles and ideas. One time she bleached a pair of pants and left them soaking too long. The fabric became weak and ripped. She also colored her hair. I'm not sure what color her natural color is. Her hair was always a shaded reddish orange during the year I knew her.

During another invention exploration, Angela worked to construct her personal history by completing an autobiographical freewrite. Here is a section from her in-class freewrite about being a foreign-born American.

In order to explain my life I must start from the beginning. I was born in Wiesbaden, West Germany, the daughter of a DODDs teacher and his wife. DODDS is the Department of Defense Dependant Schools. It is a school system set up to teach the children (dependents) of military service members stationed overseas. Because of my father's job, we moved quite often as I was growing up. By the time I was two, I had lived in Germany and two different towns in England. I lived in Wisconsin for three years and then my family moved to Japan. That was the only time I ever lived in the U.S. until I came to college.

This freewrite is filled with facts but with few particulars. Her autobiographical clustering exercise (Figure 3.2), though, helped to develop and focus her autobiographical writing. In this cluster, Angela develops her original view—comparing the changes in her life when she stopped being an expatriate American and became an American college student. She contrasts the snow of Germany with the heat and humidity and swimming pools of Florida. She starts to explore her new culture, composed of Winn Dixie supermarkets and southern accents, malls and American consumerism.

Next, Angela started a more formal draft of a possible first paragraph, using her freewrite and clustering to help her develop an idea:

The first thing I had to get used to was the heat. Back home in Germany, the heat was almost never a problem. It was usually mild. We had no air conditioning because we didn't need it. We would just open the windows. Windows have screens in the U.S. Another change for me. With the heat comes an entirely different way of life. Because it is warm, people spend more time out of doors in Florida than we did at home. . . .

Angela is still working through the changes that seem so vivid to her, yet are so hard to communicate to others. As a reader, I wasn't engaged until Angela shared her observation about screened windows in the United States. For me, that is the type of detail that evokes the string of large and small surprises and adaptations she is

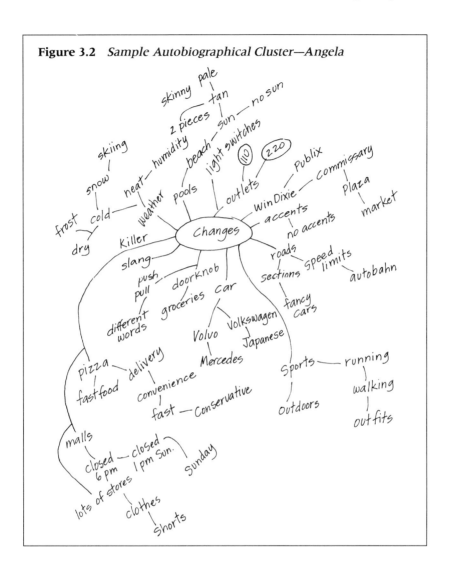

Figure 3.2 *Sample Autobiographical Cluster—Angela*

going through. Looking back through Angela's clustering, it is possible to guess where that detail came from. In her cluster, she lists light switches and outlets (110 and 220) as being different in German and U.S. houses; most likely, that discovery led her to a discussion of screens and air conditioners. In fact, Angela focuses the rest of her paragraph on the way the different climates in Germany and Florida result in different architectures and lifestyles.

Invention techniques alone won't always lead you to your best work, but they certainly help you get started when you're stumped or even when you have too many ideas. Not everyone uses the same invention "tools" in the same way. Bill explains:

In class, we have discussed the creative process in our writing, which led to the creation of a toolbox. All of our methods, and ideas, writing tools, etc., all neatly arranged in a box, ready for us to pick and choose from it at our leisure. As the class progressed, I realized that I don't have a toolbox. Mine is a bag. It's like a pillow case tied to a stick carried by a hobo, with all of his belongings, few in number, tossed haphazardly inside.

The basic invention techniques in Table 3.1 might become some of the basic tools in your writer's toolbox. Use the list to let you create and explore, in a haphazard or orderly manner, depending on your style. You may be a writer who finds great comfort in the habit of clustering or listing and planning before undertaking each piece of writing; you may find these techniques free you from self-censoring and allow you to relax as you write. Or, like Tina you may discover:

As a new writer, I do not have any true "tools of the trade." Mainly, I try to have a ballpoint pen and small pad of paper near when I am attending an unusual function such as a homeless march, a performing arts show, or any other event. One other thing that I find helpful is writing down something when it is really upsetting to me. Traumatic, angry experiences are easy to write about because they affect my mental state and cause conflict, which always needs release, and paper takes the beating well.

I've learned from experience that writers choose different invention techniques for different purposes and that most benefit from experimentation with these techniques. Remember, fluent writers avoid writer's block by developing alternative strategies to help them get started and to keep them going. Invention techniques may provide you with strategies *and* help you to look at your world(s) from new angles.

The invention exercises that run throughout the rest of this chapter are intended to support your writing explorations and are illustrated with student drafts-in-progress. Although these exercises are intended, generally, as in-class activities—with your teacher reading prompts or directions and acting as orchestra conductor to the class composing symphony—you can almost always adapt them for individual writing outside of class. Also, when you read through the writing of notable authors, you can sometimes see that their drafts may have been started from exercises much like these.

Exploring Language:
Clichés and Metaphors

Often, in the creative writing workshop, we have discussions about avoiding clichéd language and about developing effective

Table 3.1 *Basic Invention Techniques*[1]

FREEWRITING	Write about anything for a set amount of time (five or ten minutes). Don't stop writing or reread. If you get stuck, repeat the last word you wrote until the boredom of doing so unsticks you. When freewriting at the computer, turn your monitor off and type rapidly, speeding your thoughts. Stop your freewriting, reread it, and circle the most interesting discovery.
GUIDED FREEWRITING	Same as above; however, you start writing in response to a *particular* prompt. For example, write something autobiographical; write a letter to your muse; envision a person who means a lot to you and start writing about him or her.
LISTING AND BRAINSTORMING	When you get ready to go to the market, you often make a list of all the things you think you need. Do the same with your writing. Quickly write down short notes related to your topic, or brainstorm a topic by listing everything you're interested in/concerned with at that moment.
GROUP BRAINSTORMING	Several individuals dictate ideas to a recorder. Or, all the individuals in a group write about an agreed-upon topic and then compile a master list. Or, you may read something you've written to a group and ask them to help you add ideas, details, and so on.
THE REPORTER'S FORMULA	Alone or with a group, ask who, what, where, when, why, and how about your topic or subject. Freewrite your answers to each question and then use your discoveries to start a draft.

Table 3.1 *(continued)*

CLUSTERING	Alone or with a group, list a core word or term in the center of your paper or on a chalkboard. Brainstorm related networks of concepts, events, details. Use connecting lines to indicate relationships.
CUBING	Alone or with a group, take six perspectives on a topic or subject: describe it, compare it, associate it, analyze it, apply it, argue for or against it. Freewrite your answers to each perspective and then use your discoveries to start a draft.
LOOPING AND CENTER-OF-GRAVITY SENTENCE	Freewrite for ten minutes; then stop, reread, and circle the most important sentence. Next, begin with that circled sentence. Write ten minutes more. Stop, reread, and again circle the most important sentence. Start with that circled sentence and write again. Complete three or more loops, finding several center-of-gravity sentences. A computer can help your invention process; use the cut and paste function to move center-of-gravity sentences and then start typing again.
WRITING ABOUT INVENTING	After invention drafting, write for five more minutes about what it felt like to complete that writing. Do you prefer to invent on paper or at a computer screen? Did the piece come easily? Did you encounter some hitches, dangerous spots, difficulties? Did you sense that this was a useful technique for you? Did you feel you should do the activity again soon? Explore and explain. In your next draft, try starting with that dangerous or difficult material.

metaphorical language. When you work language seriously, you will always be urged by your teacher and peer readers to use the most exact, evocative, and interesting words you can find. All of us have particular word hoards—useful terms, favorite phrases, regional and slang words, and basic and intentionally acquired vocabularies. We also have different registers—levels of diction—for different occasions—informal to formal speech or scribbled notes to formally written, almost sculpted, texts. Whenever we speak or write, then, we are constantly choosing the appropriate word.

When we work words quickly, we may fall back on "filler" phrases, easy ways of saying things that let us draft quickly or that just let us talk quickly. Choosing to move quickly through language is a productive strategy. However, when we write creatively, we usually expect to spend more time, to pick and choose and experiment with and alter language. Since precisely chosen language is an attribute of a creative writer, filler words or phrases—when used at the wrong time—are counterproductive. Clichés are formerly useful ways of saying things that became too popular, and so overused. Clichéd language no longer conveys a precise, vivid idea or image to the listener or reader.

However, clichés can be used humorously or to personify a character. Some people really do talk in clichéd language or use large dollops of regional sayings. To capture the flavor of a character, writers may pay attention to the "expectedness" of that character's language. Also, clichéd language can be used to make fun of characters; clichés can help make a situation parodic or ironic. Whenever writers use clichéd language this way, however, they need to make sure the use is justified and that they don't unintentionally mock a cultural group or a regional way of speaking.

One of the best ways to heighten your sense of clichéd language —both the unproductive and the productive aspects—is to write an intentionally clichéd piece.

Cliché Exercise

Directions

1. Before your next class, collect at least five clichéd expressions or phrases. You may take them from your own writing or ask friends to suggest the most overused sayings they can.

2. When the next class begins, each class member writes his or her best (that is, worst) clichés on the chalkboard. Here are some I've collected and used in the past:
   - dark as a dungeon
   - hot to trot

- cold as ice
- crazy as a loon
- high as a kite
- as fast as greased lightning
- blind as a bat
- the apple of my eye

Before long, the chalkboard should be crammed with clichés. If you forgot to collect some, seeing these, you should be able to add a few of your own.

3. Next, read through the following example of clichéd writing.[2]

Trite

Ken Waldman

It was Saturday night. She was standing there pretty as a picture and I was drunk as a skunk and hot to trot. Yessirree, Peter Van and the Econolines were playing the rockin' rhythm and blues—you had to see them to believe them. The drummer pounded away nuttier than a fruitcake. The bass player looked crazy as a loon. The guy playing lead guitar, Peter Van, well, his fingers moved fast as lightning and the sounds coming out of that thing hit you where it hurts. All in all, though, the harmonica player was the one who really turned me on—the guy knew his business. You could really tell he had a rock and roll heart.

Anyway, she was standing by the bar cute as a button, and by the way she was moving it was plain as day she wanted to dance. Like I say I was higher than a kite, so, sharp as a knife I made my way across the room. Quick as a wink I said, "Hey baby, you wanna dance?" Light as a feather she took my hand. Then we looked into each other's eyes.

She was gentler than a lamb, I thought.

It was Christmas come early, I thought.

I must be in heaven, I thought.

I felt like I was floating on cloud nine while we danced. I looked around and for a split second I saw everything as clear as a bell. I'll never forget that moment for as long as I live. Everyone else looked stiff as boards while me and my partner moved smooth as silk. I felt as happy as a lark. If anybody I knew had seen me, they'd have said, "Mac, what's with Mac? He looks like a million dollars out on the dance floor, hey."

The fast song ended and another began. It was a slow, gut bucket blues. I held her tight like I'd never let her go. I was prouder than a peacock, feeling her leaning against me—all warm as toast. For a minute we danced like that. I began to whisper sweet nothings into her ear.

But then—from warm as toast, to cool as a cucumber, to cold as ice. What? What?? Had the bubble burst??? A guy bigger than a house was running across the dance floor.

"Elmo!" she shrieked.

I knew it! Her boyfriend!! I knew I had smelled trouble. The guy looked madder than a hornet and strong as an ox.

The band stopped playing, and the bar grew as quiet as a grave. You could have heard a pin drop.

I could see what was about to happen as clear as glass.

His right fist met my left temple like a ton of bricks.

The room went dark as dungeon, then black as night, then I saw stars.

I woke up with a crowd surrounding me.

"Is there a doctor in the house?" I heard someone shout.

"Doctor, my ass," I said. "Get me a beer and I'll be good as new." I got up and wiped the blood from my lip. I felt fit as a fiddle and free as a bird. "Get me a beer," I repeated. "I'm as dry as a bone."

I drank the beer and ordered one more. Inside me I knew that something special had happened and this was the first day of the rest of my life.

4. Clichés can be collected in thematic clusters. Some writers choose sports, dating, love and fairy tales, parental advice, and so on. As a class, choose several areas that lend themselves well to clichés (weather, sports, politics, love, time, seasons, particular types of work, and so on). List clichés under each category.

5. Each class member chooses one of these category lists and freewrites the beginning of a cliché piece before leaving class.

6. At home, begin to shape this freewrite into a more formal piece of writing.

Workshop Suggestions   Group members read their cliché drafts to each other, working to make them better—or is that worse? Suggest eliminating some clichés and adding others. Help the writer get the necessary best punch line.

For writers working from similar categories and lists of clichés, share drafts to see the variety of directions those pieces took.

Follow-up Activities

1. Go through your old writings and find the clichés. Where do they work and not work? What are your war-horses, your tried and true favorites? Do you still need anyone to explain to you that "Today is the first day of the rest of your life" is a cliché? If so, find an explainer on the double.

2. Go to a campus bulletin board and try to create a cliché piece from

the overused language you find in the memos and bulletins there. Or, look at posters and album covers and try to do the same.

3. In class, as a group, or in a journal entry, discuss why and how clichés work in popular songs.

4. Have a class contest to create the best clichéd piece of writing. What are your rules and your criteria for choosing the winner? You might want to look at two anthologies of bad verse called *The Stuffed Owl*, edited by Wyndham Lewis, and *Pegasus Descending*, edited by James Camp and others.

5. To write an even more unusual cliché piece, mix and match "normal" clichéd phrases. For example, try versions such as "hot as a hedgehog" and "deep as a light blue sea" and "a penny saved is a penny saved" and "let the good times pour when it rains." Try to invent offbeat clichés or sayings or parables and then use them in prose or poetry.

Now that you've written into clichés and come out on the other side, seeing when they can be effective—sometimes—and when they aren't—often—you might want to replace your stale language with something new: metaphors. Most writers describe by analogy. They see, and then say that something they perceive is like something they already know, but just a bit different. Using similes—that is, comparisons that include the words *like* or *as*—or metaphors—essentially, comparisons that insist one thing *is* or *is equal to* another thing—writers interest, shock, and illuminate with their language choices. Through effective observation and carefully chosen metaphors, our language reflects our reality and illustrates our visions.

Once writers make careful, detailed observations, though, they have to evoke them for listeners or readers. It's one thing to be told: "Use fresh, vivid, interesting similes and metaphors." But actually doing so takes a certain amount of relaxation, experimentation, and exploration. The following exercise is intended to help you start to explore with metaphors.

Metaphorical Character Exercise

Directions

1. Close your eyes and visualize a person you know and about whom you have strong positive or negative feelings. Open your eyes and write the individual's name or a code name for the person on the top of a sheet of paper. This could be a color, emotion, nickname, and so on.

2. Write responses to the following prompts, which your teacher will read. The prompt reader should move through the prompts fairly rapidly to help force you to make jumps, analogies, and unexpected comparisons. It doesn't matter if you skip one of the prompts, but try to respond to as many as you can. This section should take twenty to forty minutes of writing time.
   a. Think of this person as a landscape. What landscape would he or she be?
   b. Describe this person as a kind of fruit. What would the fruit taste like?
   c. If this person were a metal object, what would he or she be?
   d. Describe this person as a time of day.
   e. If this person were a period of history, what period of history would she or he be?
   f. This person is what piece of clothing?
   g. Name all the things that go into this person.
   h. Name all the things that come out of this person.
   i. Place this person in her or his favorite location.
      i. Have him or her speak.
      ii. Bring someone else into the scene and let them talk together.
   j. What does this person always say?
   k. What are this person's dreams?
   l. Tell some lies for this person.
   m. Who is this person most like?
   n. What would this person like to say but never will say?
   o. If this person were a car, what car would he or she be?
   p. What job should this person never have?
   q. What emotion is this person?
   r. What weather is this person?

3. At home, shape this freewriting into a portrait of the person. You don't have to use his or her name unless you want to. Add to your freewriting but try to retain the most unexpected and original way of viewing your familiar character that you gained through this exercise.

Here is a short poem written through this exercise.

Owed to Mom

Ashley Bristow

She is a desert—barren, hot, and rocky
Speckled with prickled cacti
    Yet she comes to life with a little rain.

She is a black wrought iron gate—elaborate and strong
Locking some out
    But opening to those who have the key.
She is a wool sweater—moth-eaten and scratchy
The collar is a little tight
    But it's the warmest and most comfortable sweater you have.
She is an artichoke—tough unless cooked just right
Her thorns can prick your tender fingertips
    But the heart is well worth the effort.

Ashley's note on this poem says: "Originally, this piece (in the freewriting stage) was very negative—my mother and I were in an argument. However, I feel this [more positive version] sums everything up." Like Ashley's, your work will probably change with subsequent revisions.

Workshop Suggestions   Metaphorical character pieces develop from odd juxtapositions and describe individuals for whom the authors hold strong feelings. As a listener, it may be difficult at first to respond to a classmate's character piece. One of the best ways to respond is to tell the writer what image of the person the writer has conveyed to you: "This makes me imagine a person who . . . " Or, you might try to identify the overall tone of the piece: "I feel like the person is warm and friendly, always making people feel good," or "You've created an angry portrait when you compare this person to . . . " Finally, you might tell the writer which metaphorical comparison is the most unexpected and why, and which is the most interesting and why.

    In your group, you might want to spend a minute identifying similes and metaphors to be sure you all understand those terms since they're used often in workshops; they're also defined again in Chapter 9.

Follow-up Activities

1. Metaphorical prompts can be reordered, expanded, and grouped in interesting ways. You can complete a different version of this exercise by asking, simply, what persons, places, or things your character is like or not like. You can speak *for* this person or *as* this person. You can move this person through time. After trying the original set of prompts, which I borrowed from several metaphorical description exercises, you could choose other prompts—ones that stretch your analogy-making capabilities—and complete the exercise again for another individual. You can also type these questions into your word processor and answer them through

rapid freewrites, one after the other, creating unusual character sketches.

2. This exercise can be adapted to describe animals and places as well. It's a riskier exercise but fun for all the risk—how many great portraits of boa constrictors have you read lately? What metaphors can you find for the Grand Canyon or your local dismal swamp?

Exploring the Material World: Objects and the Senses

One of the simplest descriptions of a writer might be that he or she is a person who translates and transforms personal experiences through language. The writer resides in the same world as other human beings, but she watches it particularly closely, using all her senses—taste, touch, sight, smell, and hearing.

Most of us rush through the material world. We drive to work or school or run across campus to get to a classroom on time. Or we spend more hours than we like sequestered from the pleasures of landscape and climate as we watch computer screens, meet other individuals, and keep the machineries of existence in order.

A writing workshop gives participants permission to get out, roam around, watch, enjoy, observe, and feel. The following exercises are intended to encourage you to get back in contact with your senses. Jeran describes how careful attention to the astonishingly complex details of the material world provides him with a wealth of writing opportunities:

> Well, the most powerful tool [for a writer] that I have come up with is to be more observant. Watch squirrels running through the tree-tops on your way to work. Look at the designs of the buildings around you. Observe the color of your friends' eyes, clothes, and shoes. Don't limit yourself to one sense. Listen to the sound of the cars racing along the street. Smell the pine trees at the local park. Taste the deep tangy taste of Key Lime Pie. Feel the heat from a burning candle. Watch, listen, smell, taste, and touch the things around you, no matter how minor or unimportant they might seem. Sometimes the most remote detail can add that final touch of reality you are looking for.

The following exercises should help you feel just as optimistic about finding an abundance of detail to share with your readers.

Paired Object Exercise

This exercise requires a set of interesting objects: two per writer. The objects can be intentionally paired articles of clothing—hats and shoes—for instance—or can be randomly paired objects—silver spoons and woven belts, an old framed family photograph and a homely coffee mug, a carved African mask and a trophy. Your teacher may supply some of these objects from her own hoard; the local used clothing store can present you with interesting variations on hats and shoes. Or, you will be asked to bring a hat and a shoe or two unique objects to class. As the exercise begins, the objects are placed together on a table in the center of the room.

Directions

1. Each writer picks an object from the table that intrigues him or her. (If you have contributed objects for the exercise, always write about the objects contributed by others. When using intentionally paired objects, like hats and shoes, all writers work with one object from that pair—hats, for instance—and later in the exercise work with the second object of that pair—shoes.)

2. Freewrite for ten minutes about that object, creating a character that suits the object you have chosen.

3. Now everyone returns the object to the table.

4. Writers choose a second interesting object and write for ten minutes about this new object, creating a character that suits it.

5. When the two character sketches are completed, write for another ten minutes. In this third directed freewrite, each writer puts his or her newly created characters into a scene together. Have them interact, talk, and, if possible, come into conflict.

6. Freewrites can be shared after each character is created and/or after the final, created scene. It is also interesting to have one writer share his entire set of freewrites.

   Here is a freewrite that I completed, writing with my students one day in class. This character sketch developed from my first object (step 2):

> This is a purse but one unlike any I use. Seven inches by four inches by one inch does not describe its kidney bean shape. The coarser fabric is covered by a delicate lace overlay, woven in a raised monotonous flower pattern. The flower garlands flow away from a pierced net-like center medallion. Color: tan. Not much wear will fray such loosely woven stuff. Closed with a loosely sewn plain silver snap; a matching thin fabric handkerchief breathes within.
>
> She walked out of the Goodwill store on high green spike heels with a greasy near-mink boa slipping down one freckled arm. The grocery bag shifted under her arm as she sat on the Wonder Bread emblazoned bus bench. From a small but ornate tan bag, she tapped out a

cigarette lighter the size of a match box. She lit two cigarettes and dropped the gun metal grey lighter into the lacy bag. She relaxed—all her purchases and bags adrift on the brightly painted bench. Her arms moved mechanically, drawing first from one and then her other cigarette, as if the right bus would never come.

Workshop Suggestions   Your character sketches and scene can be shared and examined in an unfinished state. With a bit of work, though, you can also turn this draft into a prose poem or short short story. You may discover a character that you didn't know before who is so intriguing you use him in your next piece of work. And don't feel limited to fiction—your characters may show up narrating or becoming part of a poem.

Follow-up Activities

1. Collaborative composing: As a self-challenge, a writing group can share their characters and each member can write a story in which the group's characters figure.

2. Natural objects can replace manufactured objects, and the tone of the sketch and scene will change. The writer's challenge will be to create a character who might have picked up that rock or shell or leaf. Or, try mixing natural and manufactured objects together.

3. Working from photographs of individuals, create, in the first freewrite, a personal history for one person. In the second freewrite, use a second photo to create another imaginary life. Finally, turn the photos over, reread your sketches, and move these newly invented individuals into a scene.

4. Go to a location that is unusual for you—a bus stop, a bar, a skating rink, a courthouse. Observe one person and write a character sketch. Go to a second, very different location; observe one person and write a character sketch. Place these characters together in a scene, but use a third location for that scene, again one that is real and unusual for you.

Often during revisions of this type of writing, one of the original objects or characters can disappear as the invention turns into a piece of writing that you value. Object writings work because humans invest their possessions with so much meaning—the way an object is cared for and shaped by wear often provides insight into the life of the owner.

Talismanic Object Exercise

Your teacher will ask you to bring to class one object that has particular meaning for you. This may be a family heirloom or sentimental keepsake or anything that you feel is invested with special significance. This exercise can also be completed by using an object you carry with you that has special significance. Most of us have a favorite earring, watch, lucky coin, dog tag, and so on.

Directions

1. Place your talismanic object before you, where you can see it while you write.

2. Write for the first five to ten minutes to describe it in detail so that someone who has never seen it will be able to visualize your object perfectly.

3. Write for another ten minutes to explore the significance of the object; remember, you want to share this significance with a reader.

4. Write brief answers to these prompts:
   a. What is the humor of this object?
   b. What is the secret of this object?
   c. What is the weakness of this object?
   d. Who is the rightful owner of this object?
   e. Who wouldn't want this object?
   f. What is this object most like? Most unlike?

5. Reread all your freewriting and circle your discoveries.

6. Share sections of your freewriting.

Workshop Suggestions   These freewritings often shape into moving poems and prose pieces. In poetry, you may focus on evoking the image of your object and its meaning for you. In prose, the object may trigger a personal or family narrative that you can fictionalize at will.

Follow-up Activities

1. Complete the same exercise but use a class member's object instead of your own object. That is, exchange objects with a neighbor.

2. Write about the object; then exchange freewrites with the object's owner. Read each other's work and write for ten minutes in response to your neighbor's freewrite.

3. Instead of talismanic objects, use mundane objects like paper clips and pencils and white-out and lined notebook paper, and so on. Try to get at the essential "thingness" of your common object. Set the object before you and freewrite at the computer.

Audio Exercise

One of the best ways to get in touch with the material world is to go out into it, to observe, to sketch, and to come back and shape. It is also possible to bring that world into the classroom for sharing, as in this audio exercise.

Directions

1. A teacher or class member will make a short tape of environmental sounds (jungle birds and rain, for example), music (Gregorian chants), and "canned" noises, such as doors slamming. Tapes can also be contributed by class members. Libraries often have "canned" sound-effect records in their collections. Or, someone may take a tape recorder around for a day and tape sounds: car doors slamming, morning bird calls, the dishwasher, a typewriter or dot matrix printer.

2. If possible, dim the classroom lights a bit. Play sections of the tape, stopping after each audio stimulus. Writers then freewrite, imagining characters, scenes, emotions that help them respond to what they have just heard.

3. At the end of the exercise, play each sound again and have class members read their response/interpretations.

4. Writers should plan to develop a piece of prose or poetry from their notes to share during the next class.

It is also interesting to follow one writer through the entire in-class exercise, sound by sound. Or, to compare several writers' responses to one sound.

Workshop Suggestions   Decide in your group that each member will develop a scene based on the same audio prompt. Compare the directions you took.

Read the entire set of revised "audio writings" and discuss the function of the prompt. Can you still "hear" the original sound or has it disappeared as your poem or story direction developed?

Annie Dillard talks about this experience of a disappearing prompt when she discusses revision. She says: "The part you must jettison is not only the best-written part; it is also, oddly, that part which was to have been the very point. It is the original key passage, the passage on which the rest was to hang, and from which you yourself drew the courage to begin" (4).

In the pieces you are responding to, if the prompt did not disappear, should it?

Follow-up Activities

1. Try writing in response to music rather than environmental sounds. Turn off the lights, turn on your computer and the music, and type your thoughts rapidly. Expect to revise this material a great deal.

2. Put yourself in a noisy environment and try to describe that place—a bowling alley, an airport, a rock concert, and so on—in great and precise detail.

Sensory Excursions

The audio exercise just detailed provides only a sample of the many guided environmental excursions you can take. Your excursions may be simple: walking across campus, for example, intentionally looking for things to write about. Or they may be more complicated: blindfolding yourself and having a friend walk you around campus, and then trying to recapture the sensations you felt in words the minute the blindfold is taken away. You'll be able to expand on the following list of sensory excursions. In completing these exercises, respond in writing during or right after the activity.

Options

1. You are asked to close your eyes and listen to a story. The narrator's job is to get you halfway into a scene, location, or event and then strand you. At that point, you open your eyes and start writing, completing the story in your own way.

2. Include as many fragrant and smelly items as you can in identical brown paper bags—an orange, a handful of spices, some wet leaves, garlic, a harmless but fume-filled powdered chemical. Pass the bags around the class. Not looking inside, each writer smells the scent and then writes.

3. Describe the growth or construction of a natural or man-made object: a plant growing quickly over several weeks, a house going up, a child's play area being elaborated and festooned, a sandcastle being sculpted. Then, write a piece about this coming together.

4. Describe the decay of a natural object over time: observe fruit ripen and decay, a flower bloom and die, an ice cube melt. Write about the object several times as you carefully observe it during an hour, day, or week. Then, write a piece about this coming apart.

Exploring Your Personal World:
Autobiography and Personal Archeology

Of course, the most engrossing object in the material world, for many writers, is the writer herself. Through writing, we uncover important insights about the world around us, but we also uncover ourselves. This uncovering requires care; some areas of our experience can be painful or dangerous to explore. And, too, those who read our work won't always care. They will tell us they are looking for our art—the way we work the language—not for the mundane secrets of our hidden selves. Still, storytellers have always been valued members of all societies because humans need to share significant aspects of their lives. In a writing class, then, we learn to shape personal knowledge carefully, remembering that when writing autobiography we begin to understand those people, places, and events that have influenced us since we were born. And we share our discoveries when they represent common but important experiences.

Guided Autobiography Exercise

To begin this exercise, it is valuable to list important life transition periods on the board. This can be compiled when every class member writes out a list of the "big events" in his own life, and then everyone agrees on those that are mutually shared. In American society, for instance, birth, christening, first day of kindergarten, high school graduation, and so on, are all important cultural rites of passage. Other moments are culturally shared also—first kiss, first trip alone without parents, first car, and so on. It is helpful to discuss how these "firsts" are different in different cultures and in different regions.

Directions

1. To help writers, keep the list of cultural, maturational "firsts" on the chalkboard.

2. The teacher also writes the following prompts on the board:
   a. When I was born . . .
      When I was six . . .
      When I was sixteen . . .
      But now I am sixty-five (or any larger age) . . .
      When I'm in charge (of the world . . .)
   b. Or substitute ages agreed on by the class, or writers insert the ages they wish to use based on their own "big events" list.
   c. Freewrite for twenty or thirty minutes total, responding for a few minutes to each of the prompts in this autobiographical frame, remembering that the primary focus of this exercise is to move the self as a character *through* time.

3. Take the sketch home and revise it into an autobiographical work. Please note: Feel free to "change the story" to make it more effective; in fact, your readers may feel that you need to do this.

These prompts lead to widely varying responses, as shown in the work of the next two writers.

Miller

Pam Miller

When I was first born, my parents brought me home in a bright red Ford convertible. Their apartment was in the upstairs of a carriage house which had been built by my great-grandmother Duffy. At that time her estate was separated from downtown Cleveland by miles of farms and well-kept residential neighborhoods. The houses had been lost from the family's holdings along with everything else when her will was torn up. But the building had special meaning for my father; it was still family.

For my mother, once I arrived, the modest apartment was merely inadequately heated and cramped. The stucco and brick house, crowded between apartment buildings, faced a narrow street paved with wooden bricks. A wooden street! From the time my father first pointed it out during one of his innumerable Miller family history tours of the city, I always found it fascinating. During junior high I roller skated over its uneven surface. My friend Roberta lived around the corner on Hessler Street where I went to my first street fair during my freshman year of college.

By two, we moved to Buttternut Lane in Warrensville Heights. While my mother breast-fed my brother Paul and dressed my father's mother Ahben, I stuck a barrette in the electrical outlet under the stairs, and still remember the surprise of having the scalloped edges of the blue bow melt around the metal clasp. My father fondly recalls tucking me into bed at that house and my insistence on reading the book about mammals. He quizzed me about which was an opossum, a cougar, a marten. Though I don't remember those early lessons, he believes it was the beginning of my interest in biology.

By the time I hit six, I lived in a three-story house on Derbyshire Road in Cleveland Heights, and my youngest brother Peter was already one. My father had lived across the street in a white house smaller than ours during his elementary school years, and partly for his sentimental memories had chosen our new house.

But only one year since we had moved, my father no longer lived with us. I have a hazy memory of his first moving from my mother's room to the back bedroom. I've been told that Paul helped my father load up the convertible, three different times in all, but I likely disappeared to my room, closed the door, and tried to act as though this was just what happened to everyone. I decorated and rearranged my seven foot long, three-story dollhouse constructed of wallpapered cardboard boxes. I talked with my 6-inch tall dolls about the new furniture I would make them, though I didn't play with the dolls as much as I moved things around the house. I never wanted a Barbie doll like my friend Susan had; her sexy shape was too embarrassing and unreal. I read voraciously in the evenings while my mother watched old movies with Paul, and often finished three "Snip, Snap, and Snur" books during lunchtime. We went to my father's apartment on the west side of town once. It felt strange, even though he tried to make us comfortable by having games there for us to play. I preferred to read.

At 16, I fit in for the first time in my life, and had my first love, in the Wind River mountains of Wyoming during a five-week summer mountaineering course. Waiting for our bread to bake nestled in the coals, watching the constellations, I lay with "Q" as he sang " . . . If I were a miller, at a mill wheel grinding, would you still love me? . . . " I was still skinny, wore two long braids, and was terribly self-conscious. Yet as I learned the names of the peaks and the alpine flowers, to use an ice-axe and glissade through ass-deep snow in July, I found my own voice. Many years afterward, my brothers agreed that it was the best thing that ever happened to me, and to them, since I stopped harassing them with the shrill voice of a mother they didn't need. As one of only two women in the group of ten, I found myself in a minority, a pattern often repeated since then.

For most of high school I immersed myself in playing flute: practicing over an hour a day in my room so that I could maintain my second chair in the orchestra; dreading marching band practice in the early fall mornings (I wanted to put peace symbols in the tubas for parades). While I still often found myself curled up in my big white easy chair on Saturday nights, reading the diaries of Anais Nin, I didn't spend as much time reading. Roberta called "Hey Miller" down the school hallways to include me in things. I drank hot cocoa while my friends drank coffee and smoked cigarettes after concerts. I went with Roberta on a bus to a protest rally in Washington, D.C., one of the massive ones against the war. Everytime I saw a TV camera I backed away, sure that my father would see me in the evening news.

Right now, I'm typing in the small log cabin in the woods where I live alone. The rest of my family lives far away and does not understand why I choose this northern life. Peter struggles in Hollywood, editing other people's lousy movies and realizing that he'd rather be a writer. The others are still in Cleveland where I could never live again having known the wildness of the west. My mother lives alone, only four blocks from my brother Paul, who has two children. A whole new family fills my father's expansive brick house.

Everybody thinks I will never get married. Both of my brothers married when they were below the average national age. My father has been married four times. But my mother never remarried, though she was wilder when I was still at home than I realized then. Perhaps I am overly skeptical of marriage because all I have really known was divorce.

When I'm 36, perhaps I will be married. But somehow I can't envision myself at 76 looking over to my husband in a rocking chair. Instead I hear my good friend Sally, or my niece Kristen cooking dinner in the kitchen.

When I'm in charge, fathers will cook more than french toast and no one will eat peanut butter sandwiches for lunch after the age of ten. Third graders will love apples more than McDonalds. Unborn children will meet snow leopards and condors won't live in cages. My family will all live in the same part of the world, but in the places we all want to be. Biologists will spend all year walking the rivers, tundra, and hills and still have their reports and papers get written. Congressmen won't be bought and sold like drugs, and the people who actually do the work will make the decisions. And Fairbanks would have 12 hours of daylight on the winter solstice.

A Letter to My Best Friend

Van Mong Trinh

You were the groom and I was the bride
Two small kids on the balcony
Banana shoots were our food
Cut-up paper dolls were our children

When I was five, you were six
Walking together to the same school
Butch, "The Bulldog," pulled my pigtail
All because you were my friend
You pushed and fought with The Bulldog
And warned him to leave me alone

When I was eight, my imagination blossomed
And asked my mom if I could open a business
You went home and asked your dad
If you could join me in my wild fantasy
We sold hot peppers, lemons, and parsley
Just as we had dreamt many years ago

When I was nine, we moved away
Your sad eyes engraved in my mind
Good-bye my play husband,
shining knight, business partner
You truly were my very best friend

Workshop Suggestions Since family stories are somewhat sensitive topics (it's okay to criticize your own family, but let someone else try and . . .), it's important to remember that we should respond to the story and not to the writer.

Sometimes it's effective to "swap" stories. Each writer reads his redrafted autobiography piece and group members freewrite for five minutes, telling a story the writer's story triggered. These swapped stories can then be shared also.

One way to help all writers distance themselves from "true stories" is to declare all stories up for grabs and to have the next writing exercise be a "stolen" story. Writers take the best elements of all the autobiographical writings they have heard and create a character that tells a whopper of an autobiography.

Finally, classmates may simply want to respond informally, saying what they like best. Each group member can then write a follow-up entry in a journal, describing what it felt like to hear these personal tales.

Follow-up Activities

1. Combine an object exercise with an autobiography exercise by choosing a family heirloom, describing it, and telling the family story it evokes. The challenge is to make this very personal writing accessible to and interesting for your unknown, public reader.

2. Tell the story of your name. Elaborate on this story; fictionalize it until you become a character in your family story.

3. Write in response to one of the autobiographical writings I've included in this chapter.

4. Personal archeology: Find a photo album or scrapbook (your own or one from someone else's family). Write a story that tells about the life and times of one person in the album or book. Use real, specific details from the photos, prom dance cards, graduation announcements—any of the artifacts of family life—as you develop your narrative. Visit other "sites" for personal archeology; attics, a former bedroom at home that still looks as it did when it was yours, personal letters, old diaries, and other sources can provide powerful writing prompts.

5. Revisit your current living space as a stranger. Try to describe the person who would inhabit such a room *based only* on the artifacts you find there.

6. Use the mirror and write *an honest* self-portrait. Or, observe a close family member and write a clear, detailed description of him or her. Then interview that person, asking questions about his or her

past, using, if you would like, the prompts from the autobiography exercise. Write a portrait of that individual, including descriptive details and interview dialog.

Transforming Familiar Forms: Lists, Letters, Advice, Directions, and Found Pieces

Think of the kinds of writing you did before you entered a writing workshop—perhaps list making, giving directions or advice, writing letters. Most of these familiar forms can work as triggers to help you transform the ordinary into effective creative pieces. Since you've already internalized some of the demands of these forms, drafting *through* familiar forms allows you to worry about one less skill. Your "form making" mind goes on autopilot, and your invention potential can soar. Remember, too, that since these forms are familiar, they are easily accessible to your readers, who enjoy the way you choose your words to give the predictable a new twist.

List and Repetition Exercise

List making is not only an old device, it is also a powerful one, especially when the lists you make play with repetition, because the repetition of words, phrases, and clauses is the basis of sentence building. Repetition and list making also function as memory aids. Some of the earliest known poetry—chants, hymns, and epic verse—used repeatable, memorized units as building blocks. In *Writing Poetry*, David Kirby traces list poems to Old Testament psalms. Lists are also found in New Testament writing such as the Sermon on the Mount, and list writing was used by Sei Shonagon in 9th-century Japan.

In imitation of Sei Shonagon, one of my writing students, Elaine, wrote a "Things That Are Unpleasant" list poem using Shonagon's title but her own, Alaskan imagery: "[Things that are unpleasant] finding that the squirrels have shredded your entire winter supply of toilet paper/waking on a minus fifty-degree morning with the fire gone out in the stove." Later she matched it with a "Things That Are Pleasant" poem: "a big, bull moose in the yard when you thought you'd be eating fish casseroles all winter/the black expanse of night ablaze with the Milky Way as you stand small and alone on the frozen lake." Both of Elaine's Alaskan poems were published in the local newspaper.

List/repetition poems—and list/repetition prose such as Robert Coover's fiction—allow you to explore linguistic links; rhythm; line length; alliteration, repeated consonant sounds; and assonance, repeated vowel sounds. See also the work of poets like Allen Ginsberg, who imitated Walt Whitman's extravagant list making.

Directions

1. Think about all the reasons you use lists: for grocery shopping, to remind you not to forget tasks, and so on.

2. As a class or group, share some artistic, possibly humorous, uses for lists: for telling someone you love them, for a self-portrait, for giving advice, for an ecological petition, for . . . . Put these uses—list topics—on the board.

3. In class, write for ten minutes on one of the list topics from the board.

4. Share some of your lists.

5. Add to the list topics.

6. Repeat steps 3 and 4.

Workshop Suggestions   Share list pieces with your group or the whole class. Look at two issues in particular:

1. Identify items that don't seem to fit or identify gaps—places that need another item.

2. Help the writer achieve closure, a sense that the piece is finished. List pieces tend to feel stopped, as if the writer ran out of gas, rather than finished. Share ideas about making effective endings. To do this, you may need to read the pieces aloud and brainstorm alternate endings.

Here is a list poem that imitates both Ginsberg and Whitman.

Steadily Depressing . . . Construction Site Blues

Sean Carswell

When the time comes, I pack up
my DescartesEliotKantKafka
and even my Ginsberg
and stack them next to
my guitar and ponderings of what
makes poetry and what exists
and put on the same pair of torn-seated nylon shorts
that I wore every day last summer

and I tie the same nailholed dried sweat filth Babcock apron
around my waist,
slide the Hammer-of-a-Man in its dead leather holster
hook the Stanley 25 footer onto my hip
and try to keep those nylon shorts pulled up so that
I won't have a tan down to my crack again this year
and I walk across the sugar sand onto
the hardening foundation
watch the mist rise from dew
inside and outside my mind
think about the girls who'll pass me in the Jiffy Mart saying,
"Ooh, look how dirty he is,"
think about my hands on the last day of tenderness
think about Big Don, who'll tell me,
"You gotta believe in God in a foxhole, but here, you just want
        to get your hands on the Bastard."
think about the morning I hammered five-hundred nails and
slept through lunch
think about the Dr. Pepper I'll drink by the 44 ounce jug
and my sawdusted lungs
and Gary, who'll tell me,
"Ain't no damn sense in going to college. You're a carpenter.
        Face It!"
think about lifting walls
tar paper melting on the soles of my shoes
my nose peeling shades from Georgia clay to purple
four sheets of plywood on my back
wonder if Greg will come back this year to shoot
more nails through his toes
learn how toast feels
hate the sun yellowing my eyeballs burning color out of my
        hair
think about my shingle dented knees
my wear-once-then-burn socks
the three million times I'll hear "Black Dog" on Orlando's
        home
of classic rock and roll
and maybe later on,
when I get used to the 6 AM alarm
and my rubbery spine
and my M*A*S*H rerun evenings
I'll read one or two of Gary Snyder's poems
and tell myself,
"I was a poet once."

Follow-up Activities

1. Move from list pieces to more formal list and repetition forms like the sestina (discussed in Chapter 5).

2. Write a prose paragraph that uses listing and repetition.

3. Take some of Sei Shonagon's 9th-century titles and write modern list pieces using her titles and your vision:
   - Things That Have Lost Their Power
   - Embarrassing Things
   - Things That Give a Hot Feeling
   - Rare Things
   - Things Without Merit
   - Things That Fall from the Sky

Letter Writing Exercise

Many of us write letters fairly often. The letter form lends itself to both poetry and prose and to autobiography and created characters. Letter pieces have an implied, eavesdropping reader, as well as an author who addresses someone in particular (a relative, friend, famous character, statesperson, and so on). The mix of public and private voices found in letter pieces usually creates a complex texture. Here is a letter poem that offers an unusual look at love as well as a statement about letter writing.

Post Script

Mark Winford

Dear Sam:
There are some things
you need to know
and get used to
there are also a few things
you need to do.
Scratch her back when
she wants you to—
she likes that.
Fix her oatmeal lumpy,
her toast light,
keep the eggs a bit
runny—but not too runny,
if they hold form they're just
right. She likes to listen

to the yodel and twang of country music—
the same Dwight Yoakam record
all day—over and over,
it seems like sonic
torture at first
but you get used to it.
When you sleep with her
pull the covers up tight
to her chin. Then roll over
away from her, she kicks
like a mule once she falls asleep.
When she cries
just leave her alone,
anything else just makes it worse.
Late at night when she
whispers those catchy
three words in your ear
ask her just what she means
and she has a spot on her
left breast and when you touch it—
you probably know about that already.
    Sincerely,
    Jack

In creating this persona of Jack, writing to an ex-friend Sam about an ex-wife or girlfriend, Mark used the letter form to build a full and vivid story about a love affair, reversing our usual expectations about who would be writing to whom and why. "Memorandum" by Karen Janowsky delivers a serious message in an unusual format.

Memorandum

TO: Dad
FROM: Your Daughter
DATE: March 12, 1991
RE: My visit to Boca Raton last December

Tonight, the thunder is bellowing
And I have nothing to say to you.
We sit in your Republican living room
on overstuffed flowered furniture,
your face is flaccid, your muscles
limp underneath the plush gray robe,

me in a "Jane's Addition" t-shirt
and blue jeans, my hair
tightly pulled back, fraying
over my neck like black yarn.

Raindrops kamikaze the fuchsia flowers
and tropic-green palm trees outside;
the pool overflows into the crack
between the glass door and the living room
floor. The dog is licking the puddle on the
tile. He cowers each time lightning strikes.
He snarls at the red beach ball floating
underneath the patio furniture outside.
It is as if the stormclouds have entered this room.
But you fail to notice any of this.
You are only interested in my grades (but
not what they are in) and how cold it
must be in Tallahassee.

Your pupils are dilated
from staring at a computer terminal(ly)
every day in a gray three-piece suit.
I look past them to the lightning
through the door as I answered your questions.

What I'm trying to tell you
is this: I have no feeling around you.
When you tell me I ought to consider
studying accounting, that my concern
for the future ought to be wealth, it
makes me wonder about the time when
you were twenty and wanted to be an artist.
What kind of colors did you see then?
Why did you change your mind?
When I'm with you I want to turn your head
towards the window and focus
your eyes on the dark wet sky
that will be dew on the grass in the morning.

Directions Choose a person you know fairly well, someone you've
shared several experiences with or have known for a few years and
would like to write a letter to.

Freewrite a letter that touches on most or all of the following:

1. The weather, both where you are and where they are.

2. Your relationship; ask questions about the past or the future.

3. Say something you have always been afraid to say to this person.

4. Share a wish that you have.

5. Share something you are doing nowadays.

6. Remind your correspondent of a shared moment.

7. Set the record right about something.

8. Predict one of his or her responses to your letter.

9. Tell how you have changed—physically and/or emotionally.

10. Tell about one of your dreams.

11. Explain your most important recent discovery about you or your correspondent or your relationship; if possible, use a metaphor for doing this.

12. Stop the letter promising to tell more about _____ next time.

Now, take a minute and jot down the strongest feelings you have about this person. Finally, use this invention material to write a letter poem, letter essay, or letter short short fiction. Break out of the letter form if you feel you need to.

Workshop Suggestions   In pairs, exchange letter pieces and write a letter back, responding "in character" to the letter you have just read. With the author of the original letter, revise your two pieces into a collaborative exchange.

If letters are shared in a full-class workshop, classmates will want to think about and react to the letter writer's voice. This will not necessarily be the student writer's voice; that is, the writer may have adopted a *persona*, an assumed personality, as in the two preceding examples. Look for inconsistencies in the voice and also look at the use of clichéd or colloquial language. Suggest ways in which the writer can maintain the tension between "real letter" style and "art letter" shaped language.

Follow-up Activities

1. Try writing an exchange of letters among several characters or a series of letters over time from a single character that, taken together, tell a story.

2. Take a current event and write letters from the viewpoint of several individuals who are involved, or whom you can imagine being involved, in that event—for instance, the last San Francisco earthquake or the argument over the new, local shopping mall.

You may need to conduct some research in order to create realistic characters.

3. If you keep your own letters on computer disk, interweave sections from these into a composite letter. This should create a multiple-voiced collage since you probably use different voices when talking to different people. See Chapter 5 for a discussion of collage writing.

4. Write some outrageous letters—letters from aliens to earthlings, Elvis writing from the grave, and so on. In this, combine a persona piece, speaking for a character, with a letter form.

Advice and Directions Exercises

The longer we live, the more advice we have (and want) to share. We can combine letters and advice and write a Dear Abby type advice column. We can offer younger brothers and sisters advice from our place at the top of the heap. We can use advice to help others avoid pitfalls or to bully them into being smarter than we were. This type of writing may depend on irony or humor. Some advice writing works by negation; that is, it tells you what to do when really you shouldn't do such things at all.

Directions

1. Some entertaining advice and how-to pieces have already been written and make excellent prompts for your imagination. The story that follows was written after the writer read stories by author Lorrie Moore. Moore's short story collection, *Self-Help*, contains unusual directions, including "How to Become a Writer," which offers a serious *and* tongue-in-cheek look at our field. Other story titles include: "How to Be an Other Woman," "The Kid's Guide to Divorce," and "How to Talk to Your Mother."

    Before or after reading some of Moore's work, write a how-to piece explaining to someone the way to do something that you already do well—build a harpsichord, cook an obscure dish, sing a foolish song. The more unusual your subject choice, the odder it will seem to the reader to receive your detailed directions.

2. Or, give directions for doing something unexpected. A model for this would be Charles Simic's poetry, Russell Edson's prose poetry, or W. S. Merwin's poetry and prose pieces. See, in particular, Merwin's poem "Unchopping a Tree." Unexpected directions can free writers' imaginations, allowing them to explore difficult or impossible actions. For instance, once chopped, we assume a tree stays chopped. Try unbuilding a house. Try creating a world without gravity.

Here is a sample—writing advice in the form of a short short story.

Typewriter Foreplay

Jean M. Clements

Answer the telephone panting because you just got into the shower and had to run down the hall and around that pile of dirty clothes that have been begging to be washed for a week now. Say hello in an angry voice and change your tune abruptly when you realize it's *him* on the other end. Can he borrow your typewriter to type a thousand-word essay that is due at 9:05 in the morning—yes, of course, no problem. Can he type it at your place if it won't be an inconvenience—yes, of course, no problem. Say good-bye in a sweet yet alluring voice and hang up. Run to the stereo and put on some good tunes like that group with the name having something to do with eye movement. Run to the closet and grab your black turtleneck right off the hanger. Watch the hanger swing back-and-forth in your empty closet because all of your clothes are dirty. Look for your grooviest jeans and scream above Michael Stipe because they're in the pile of dirty clothes. Make a quick decision and ferret through the pile hoping they don't smell. Find them and give them a quick shake to get the wrinkles out. Look at the clock while you jump around trying to get your jeans over your butt. Pull hair back in a pony-tail because you didn't get to wash it. Pour on the Giorgio to cover the smell of the jeans.

The door rattles when he knocks on it. Are you ready? Of course not but who said life was fair and open the door with a big smile on your face. Is he early? No—of course not. You've just been sitting around waiting for him to get here. Show him where the typewriter is under your bed and drag it out and hope that nothing else comes with it. Blow the dust off and set it all up for him on the desk that you spilled Dr. Pepper on.

Ask him if you could type it for him. Say okay when he says he'll do it himself. Sit on your roomie's bed and remember what happened on it two nights ago when her boyfriend was here for a visit. Watch him use two fingers to type his thousand-word essay and think about how you could get him into your bed and repeat the action from the other night.

Listen to the boring click click clatter of the typewriter and fall asleep with your mouth open.

Workshop Suggestions   As with any advice or set of directions, you'll want to evaluate these for consistency. What else might be included and what has been left out that is needed? You're looking, of course, for a different type of consistency since you're not expecting a reader to actually undertake "typewriter foreplay" or to unchop a tree. Check, in particular, for the right tone. Does the author start with Road-Runner and Wiley Coyote type slapstick humor and then lose steam? Or does the piece start quietly—you can't tell if it's real or a put-on—and then have you laughing at its inexorable absurdity?

Follow-up Activities

1. Try writing your own advice column. Be as absurd as you want. Compose advice to lovelorn dogs or produce an imitation of National Public Radio's "Ask Dr. Science," where an individual who is hopelessly unscientific gives crackbrained explanations of the universe to his happily gullible audience. It could be fun to work with a partner on this one, trying to top each other's questions and answers. This could also be a full-class project, with each class member writing a question and an answer once the personality of the Dear _____ or Ask _____ individual is agreed upon.

2. Instead of the letter format, try a community column in which you, the star columnist, offer strange but arresting advice and observations. Dave Barry, who writes for the *Miami Herald*, might be a fair model here to be emulated or topped.

3. Look for existing advice and shape it to your purposes. The "simple" directions for setting up a prefabricated picnic table can actually be so complicated they feel as if they've been written in ancient cuneiform. The directions for cooking found in an haute cuisine French cookbook can be adapted surrealistically for a college dorm room hotdog dish. What you're playing with here is a humorous translation of the language and jargon of one field to another incongruent or mundane field or subject.

Found Poem Exercise

The final proof of our environmental wealth is the found poem or prose piece. In its purest form, the found poem results when an observant writer takes words already available in the material world and reshapes them to make a statement. Often, the statement is about language *and* about a subject. Here is a small word sculpture.

Found Poem

Elaine Bernard

Chapter One
Fundamental Concepts of Algebra
What is Algebra?
Real Numbers
Exponents and Radicals

Algebraic Expression
Fractional
The Binomial Theorem

Found poems like Elaine's are created when you notice and save natural juxtapositions. For instance, Elaine noted the odd "voice" in the title and subtitles of her algebra textbook. Found poems, then, are created when you cut and paste already existing texts together, saving some of their original intent while you form a new meaning or a commentary upon that intent.[3]

This type of cutting and pasting occurred when I created a found poem from my father's V-Mail letters, written when he was stationed in Iceland during World War II. Reading his letters, I was struck by the number of times he repeated formulaic phrases (often about weather and the act of letter writing). Also, hidden among the letters was the thread of a story about my parent's marriage, and by analogy, about the state of relationships among individuals separated by time, distance, and war. I typed phrases and sections from the V-Mail letters into my word processor and began to sculpt this poem.

from V-MAIL

Wendy Bishop

Passed by Base 083 Army Examiner
Somewhere in Iceland
1940–1943
Today
TWO YEARS AGO AT SIX IN THE MORNING I BROUGHT THE
FIRST WORKING PARTY ASHORE IN ICELAND. WE WENT OVER
THE SIDE OF THE TRANSPORT ON LANDING NETS AND USED
LANDING OR HIGGENS BOATS TO COME ASHORE. IT WAS IN
POURING RAIN AND WAS ONE OF THE MOST UNCOMFORTABLE
DAYS I HAVE EVER PUT IN.
TODAY IS CLEAR AND THE SUN IS SHINING BUT THE WIND IS
COLD.
TODAY IT IS RAINING LIKE THE DEVIL.
TODAY IT IS SNOWING AND RAINING AT THE SAME TIME.
IT IS RAINING PITCHFORKS TODAY.
IT IS A VERY DEPRESSING DAY ANYWAY, DARK, AND
RAINING, AND THE RAINY SEASON IS HERE AGAIN SO WE WILL
PROBABLY REVERT TO BEING DUCKS.

TODAY I START MY THIRD YEAR IN ICELAND.
I HAD HOPED TO HAVE A LETTER FROM YOU TODAY.[4]

Directions

1. Before your next class, collect one of the following:
   a. A set of letters
   b. Several dictionary definitions of a word that interests you
   c. A set of work or school memos
   d. A collection of random posters off an abandoned bulletin board
   e. All the magazines in your room
   f. The written operating instructions for every machine, electronic component, and/or appliance you own

2. In class—alone, in pairs, or as a group—fashion a found poem from one of these sets.

   If you use letters, try to juxtapose them so you create a subtext, a second way of seeing the information; create a story behind the literal words.

   With a dictionary definition, try to manipulate the stiff language to illuminate and define your word. Sculpt a poem that explores the meaning of your word; the word may provide the poem title. Use the cut and paste function on your computer to repeat key phrases.

   Using memos, posters, magazines, or instructions, make a collage—from the words you find there—that comments on the language of those materials. Memos may illustrate the redundancy of bureaucratic language. Posters may illustrate the culture of a place or time—from yoga and spiritual enlightenment to 1940's movies and rap performances. Magazines may prompt you to fashion a social commentary, while the written operating directions for a machine may allow you to lead the reader through an absurd Orwellian maze that also comments on our "plugged-in" society.

Workshop Suggestions   After drafting, bring in several photocopies of your piece, as well as scissors and tape. Let your group help you make your found piece even better by cutting, adding, and reshaping. Everyone in class can make copies of their final found (or environmental) creation to share with class members; compile a class book of found/shaped language sculptures. For optimum effect, be sure to read these aloud and discuss the "reading voice" required for some of these appropriated jargons.

Follow-up Activities

1. Extend your found pieces to include artwork and collage.

2. Use your own previous writings as found text. This is especially fun if they are already on your word processing disk. Try interweaving your old words with new lines, cutting and pasting, and even eventually adding illustrations.

3. Use spare copies of class members' pieces that were prepared for any full-class workshop and make a found class piece by weaving lines from everyone's work into a new whole.

The inventions you've tried in this chapter should get you ready to share work in a writing workshop format. The ins and outs of sharing your writing—from sharing with yourself in journals to sharing with a class in a critique session—are covered in Chapter 4. Chapter 5 returns for a while to invention, discussing ways you can develop your own self-challenges and ways you can experiment with your writing.

Notes

1. A wealth of information on invention techniques can be found in Neeld's text *Writing*. Peter Elbow popularized freewriting, looping, and center of gravity sentences. See *Writing Without Teachers* and *Writing with Power*. A recent book by Belanoff, Elbow, and Fontaine reviews the classroom use of freewriting. See Rico for more on clustering.
2. Writing samples by Waldman, Miller, and Winford, and parts of the letter writing exercise are reprinted and adapted from Bishop.
3. See Ron Padgett's text for more information on found pieces and list poems.
4. This poem appears in its complete form in *American Poetry Review* 17 (1988): 7–8.

Sources and Readings

Barry, Dave. *Dave Barry's Greatest Hits.* New York: Crown, 1988.

_____. *Dave Barry Slept Here.* New York: Random House, 1989.

Belanoff, Pat, Peter Elbow, and Sheryl I. Fontaine. *Nothing Begins with N: New Investigations of Freewriting.* Carbondale: Southern Illinois UP, 1990.

Bishop, Wendy. *Released into Language: Options for Teaching Creative Writing.* Urbana, IL: National Council of Teachers of English, 1990.

Camp, James E., X. J. Kennedy, and Keith Waldrop, eds. *Pegasus Descending: A Book of the Best Bad Verse.* New York: Macmillan, 1971.

Coover, Robert. *Pricksongs and Descants.* New York: Dutton, 1969.

Dillard, Annie. *The Writing Life*. New York: Harper, 1989.

Edson, Russell. *The Reason Why the Closet-Man Is Never Sad*. Middletown, CT: Wesleyan UP, 1977.

_____. *The Wounded Breakfast*. Middletown, CT: Wesleyan UP, 1985.

Elbow, Peter. *Writing Without Teachers*. New York: Oxford UP, 1973.

_____. *Writing With Power: Techniques for Mastering the Writing Process*. New York: Oxford UP, 1981.

Ginsberg, Allen. *Collected Poems*. New York: Harper, 1984.

Kirby, David. *Writing Poetry: Where Poems Come From and How to Write Them*. Boston: The Writer, Inc., 1989.

Lewis, Wyndham D. B., ed. *The Stuffed Owl: An Anthology of Bad Verse*. London: J. M. Dent and Sons Ltd., 1930.

Merwin, W. S. *The First Four Books of Poems*. New York: Atheneum, 1975.

_____. *The Miner's Pale Children*. New York: Atheneum, 1970.

Moore, Lorrie. *Self-Help: Stories*. New York: Knopf, 1985.

Neeld, Elizabeth Cowan. *Writing*. 3d ed. Glenville, IL: Scott Foresman/Little Brown, 1990.

Padgett, Ron, ed. *The Teachers & Writers Handbook of Poetic Forms*. New York: Teachers & Writers Collaborative, 1987.

Rico, Gabriele L. *Writing the Natural Way*. Los Angeles: J. P. Tarcher, 1983.

Shonagon, Sei. *The Pillow Book of Sei Shonagon*. Translated and edited by Ivan Morris. Baltimore: Penguin, 1971.

Simic, Charles. *Selected Poems, 1963–1983*. New York: Braziller, 1985.

Whitman, Walt. *Leaves of Grass*. New York: Modern Library, 1940.

Chapter 4

From Private to Public:
Journals and Workshops

I thought I was the only one who felt nervous about sharing my work with my peers but now I know that everyone feels some sort of apprehension and that knowledge helped me through all of the group work. I trust my peers to help me revise and go through my writing. It's very important to me now to have the opinions of at least two other people my own age who will tell me the mistakes I've made and hopefully help me fix them. Before this class, I didn't trust anyone to read my stuff because I was afraid they would laugh at me.

—SHERRI

You gain many benefits by sharing your writing more regularly with yourself in a journal and by sharing your writing in workshops with small peer groups or the entire class. By showing you in this chapter selections from student journals as well as a workshop transcript, I hope to encourage you to share your writing more freely than you might have otherwise. By discussing problems encountered by previous students and including their advice for developing effective workshops, I hope to encourage you *to work* to become a more supportive class member.

At first, sharing your writing may feel like taking a plunge into a lake or swimming pool of unknown temperature. You're sure it will be too cold, but once in, you find the temperature is just right— something you were craving—and the uneasiness leaves your body. The next time you get ready to dive, expect to feel similar hesitations, but work from experience and the knowledge that sharing will benefit you. The more you learn to identify these benefits, the more quickly you'll be able to discern them in action in your own writing life.

Saving and Sharing:
Your Writing Journal or Notebook

> *Keeping a journal is the best habit any writer can have; indeed, most real writers probably couldn't function without their notebooks, whatever form they take or however they are kept. Notebooks can serve as cradles, which is the way Henry James characterized his jottings—scraps of conversations, speculations about one image or another, sketches of characters, plot ideas, etc.*
>
> —Anne Berthoff (11)

Journals exist under many aliases: notebooks, daybooks, diaries, almanacs, calendars, monthlies, logs, dialog journals, field books, thinkbooks, travel journals, pillow books, commentaries, accounts, ledgers, sketchbooks, taped logs. Journals have been used by travelers and prisoners, pioneers and artists, scholars and students—all of whom have valued them for the ways journal writing helps to focus and clarify thinking. Each writer, though, is sure to have different reasons for beginning a journal and for continuing to follow the discipline of making regular entries.

In the writing classroom, journals are valued because they encourage productive habits, especially writing regularly, and because they encourage exploration and experimentation. In journals, student writers feel free to explore without evaluation. Jill explains how this worked for her:

> One of the most beneficial aspects of this class is writing in a journal. I have learned to effectively transform my emotions into words on a page. I can remember many times that I have sat and stared at a blank page and tried to figure out a way to express myself. However, it was not always feasible and it led to nothing but frustrations. Yet, writing in a journal has strengthened my expressive side. I think that knowing that it wasn't necessary for me to have perfect structure, correct spelling, or faultless punctuation helped me to write better and with more honest feelings than I would have otherwise.

In addition, journals, as Anne Berthoff points out, have traditionally been used to collect and focus materials that the writer might otherwise feel were scattered and unusable. In journals, writers often keep track of their writing process itself—how they write—as well as store materials for writing: sketches, ideas, lists, titles, pictures, and quotes. Journals have been particularly significant for women writers:

> The diary was, after all, available to them [women] for expression in centuries when their attempts to practice other forms of literature—say, produce a play—were considered presumptuous or silly. Japanese women were confiding their emotions to "pillow books," kept in a slipcase and away from a husband's eyes, for centuries before there was anything like a tradition of diary-keeping in the

West. The history of women is being written as much from diaries as anything else. (Mallon 19)

The diary or journal is probably appealing because it is a fluid form, one in which the writer sets the rules. One of America's most famous journal writers, Henry David Thoreau, found this to be true *and* useful:

> As he sought in the journals to comprehend the world, and to simplify and perfect his place in it, Thoreau frequently meditated on the proper balance of the concrete and the abstract. He wants the "daily tide" to "leave some deposit on these pages, as it leaves sand and shells on the shore," but he worries that he sees too many details at the expense of wholeness. . . . The solution, at last, is not to banish facts, but to get the right ones down. . . . Thoreau tells us on February 18, 1852, that he keeps one notebook for facts and another for poetry, but that finally he has trouble keeping them separate, "for the most interesting and beautiful facts are so much the more poetry and that is their success." (qtd. in Mallon 79)

Finally, even writers who don't think of themselves as "regular" journal keepers still keep clippings, files, thought folders, places where they save the bits and pieces of exploratory thinking that are a necessary and fruitful part of any creative process. In an interview (part of which is included here), poet Gary Snyder explains that much of his composing takes place in his head. However, he admits, when pressed, that his short- and long-term memory is often aided by notetaking of some sort:

> **A:** I write by hand when I write. But before I write, I do it in my mind many times—
> **Q:** *The whole thing?*
> **A:** Almost the whole thing . . . I have learned as discipline over the years to avoid writing until I have to. I don't put it on the page until it's ripe—because otherwise you simply have to revise on the page. So I let it ripen until it's fully formed and then try to speak the poem out. . . .
> **Q:** *How long does that ripening process usually take?*
> **A:** Anywhere from a day to a half a year. I have several things that I've been holding in my mind now for five years.
> **Q:** *Only in your mind? You don't write down even a line?*
> **A:** Well, I must confess I have a few notes on them, but the greater part of it's in my mind.
> **Q:** *Do you keep a notebook?*
> **A:** I keep many notebooks—many notebooks and many useful files. (qtd. in Packard 271)

In the writing workshop, then, the journal serves as a storehouse. Here are some of the various uses you might make of your academic journal.

Use a class journal for self-exploration and/or values clarification. You can keep sections on autobiography, dreams, friends, emotions, unsent letters, dialogs, portraits, and freewriting.[1] You, your friends, or your teacher may pose values-clarification questions: "You are invited to a party that will be attended by many fascinating people you've never met. Would you want to go if you had to go by yourself?" or "You discover your wonderful one-year-old child is, because of a mix-up at the hospital, not yours. Would you want to exchange the child to correct the mistake?"[2] These questions can lead to class discussions and exercises in fictional character development.

Use a class journal for self-analysis. You can respond to class readings and class activities; keep a section for class notes and questions, a section for drafts, a section for pursuing a long-term writing project, and so on.

Use a class journal for drafting, sketching, collecting. You can keep class exercises in one section and self-assigned exercises in another section; both sets may include invention activities, observations from life, experiments, and lists. Or, plan to keep two notebooks: a small one that you always carry with you and a larger one into which those materials are transferred and where they are further explored. You may want to include photos, drawings, and other art work.

Use a class journal for dialog. Keep a public and a private section. Plan to read aloud from your journal entries and share your public writings with peers and your teacher. Entries may be exchanged at the beginning of each class so that readers can write and respond on them, or you may supply the entire class with a copy of an entry in order to start that day's discussion. For a dialog journal, be sure to leave a wide right-hand margin; your teacher or classmates may write there. You can plan to write commentaries on your own commentaries, too, rethinking your earlier attitudes and opinions.

Explorations to Do as a Journal Entry or for Small Group or Class Discussion

1. Share your own history of journal keeping. Have you been a life-long recorder or have you only experienced bouts of journal keeping? What helps you keep journals? What slows down or stops your journal keeping?

2. In the past, who have you shared journals with? Whose journals have you ever read and why?

3. If you've ever been required to keep a journal in a class before, discuss the format and that experience.

4. What would prompt the following individuals to keep a journal? What would they probably write about and what benefits would

they find in collecting their ideas this way? Write a set of imaginary entries for one of these people.

a. A prisoner
b. A news photographer assigned to political hot spots around the world
c. A novelist (be specific and imagine writing this for your favorite author)
d. The mother and father of two young children, ages 3 and 6
e. A politician
f. Your parents or siblings
g. Your teacher
h. You

8. Look for published journals of some of your favorite authors. Read and enjoy some of these and try imitating their style in some of your own entries.

In *The Journal Book* Toby Fulwiler lists the attributes of productive journals. The more a journal exhibits these attributes, the more successful it probably has been for the writer. A productive journal, he finds, will have several important characteristics. It will be written in an informal style and use the first person pronoun, I. It will use informal punctuation and punctuation for effect—dashes, underlining, exclamation points; it will follow the rhythms and patterns of everyday speech. A successful class journal usually shows experimentation; consists of frequent and long entries; includes entries you initiate, usually in chronological order; and, overall, both explores and informs (Fulwiler 2–4).

In analyzing his own daybooks, Donald Murray finds that his include the following: observations, questions, lines, notes, plans, titles, leads (beginnings), quotations from other writers, outlines, diagrams, drafts, ideas for pieces, discussions with himself, postcards or pictures, paragraphs from newspapers, chunks of drafts that haven't worked, titles of books to read, prewriting, notes on lectures, and so on (*A Writer* 69). After you keep a journal for your writing workshop, you may find it useful to complete just this sort of self-inventory.

I looked for some of Murray's collection techniques in several of my own, fifteen-year-old travel diaries. In looking over my own habits, I found I included newspaper clippings—several of which developed into parts of poems I wrote—quotes from books I was reading, lists of books I should read, interesting vocabulary words and their definitions, and so on. I was collecting language in order to better shape my own words. In addition, as a student, I completed a dialog learning log that I shared with peers in my class. We swapped journals, took them home, commented in the margins on what the writer was saying, and returned them.

Journal writing, in my experience, leads to more journal writing, which helps raise the consciousness of all class participants. The following samples are from the journals of writing students. In the first, Ray looks particularly at his changes through enrollment in the class.

Sample: Ray's Journal

1–21

I have a friend with whom I am always sharing my work. I always thought that this person was the one who has helped me the most with my writing. Yet now as our class moves on and I am realizing so much more about my writing, I feel this person is more of a detriment than aid to my writing. Although we share a common bond in our creativity, I feel that there is also a very strong sense of competition between what it is that we write. We no longer are allies in writing but, as I see it, more like enemies. Much too judgmental and much too critical, instead of being much more supportive and helpful to one another.

I'd hate to see you lose friendship but I'm glad to see you gain insight. It's also profitable and possible to turn others on to what you're learning (even just by your actions).

In this class I really feel the need and desire to write, knowing that my endeavors will be supported. I feel good about writing and am able to analyze what, how, and in what direction writing is taking me. I think I have talent in writing and I really hate unnecessary criticism which I feel stems from a lack of knowledge about writing by my friend. Granted he is a very talented writer, but I really don't think his understanding of the reasons for writing are clear. He writes every piece as if it were going to be viewed by an audience as a masterpiece. He doesn't realize that all I want out of my writing is to create in a way that makes me feel proud. Makes me secure in my abilities. And if the day ever comes when my work is ever considered great . . . then wonderful. What I think I am trying to get at is that I don't like the added pressure of great expectations.

Most of us don't need that pressure. The demands of fine crafting are high enough.

2/26

Toward the beginning of this class I had notions of my writing, what I was doing and what I want to accomplish. These ideas have changed greatly. I now understand my writing and understand what it is that moves me to write. I think I was misleading myself for a very long time. I had so many grand ideas about writing that I had forgotten that you have to write to be a writer. I had set so many preconceived notions in my head, grand notions, that I never could of expected to live up to them all.

I have realized that just by sitting down and writing, many different ideas just pop into your head. It is as if you turn on a hose that has been lying out in the sun. You expect cold water to come out & then are amazed that you get scalded by the water that has been heating in its length.

writing has become a generative process — writing to learn.

I am glad I have been doing this, because I am leaving in a few months to go backpacking through Europe. I expect some of my greatest writing yet to come from this experience. It takes something as unexpected and new as this trip to really get my mental juices flowing. I can hardly wait. I have decided to keep a daily journal and a book to write stories in.

Great! I'm envious. I did this at 18, 22, 27, and 30 and never regretted my wanderings or my writings.

This class has really, if nothing else, taught me to tighten my belt, bite into my lip, and just sit down and write. I only wonder how I am going to do separated from my computer for so long? God I'll miss him.

3/30

As a way of revitalizing my journal, I have gone through and read it in its entirety. It's sometimes hard for me even to believe, I wrote some of the things I wrote. I was amazed by the way I allowed myself the freedom to spontaneously write any feeling that had occurred to me, at the instant I was making an entry. I have to admit it was nice though to have that record of my progress throughout this class. The journals are a definite asset for learning your own techniques and styles.

Another important realization that I have made, is the bounds by which my opinions have changed about writing. I am more aware of my process now than I ever have been before. Also, I feel that because of this, I am writing better and thus am less apprehensive about sharing my work.

One of my first entries showed me the deep seated fear I had with writing. Even though I really love to write, I was holding back because I feared criticism and any denouncement of my writing. I had angry feelings toward teachers of the past schools I have attended. I refused to accept any hint that writing and understanding writing is essential. I was holding on to the belief that all of my writing had to be perfect. This year alone, this semester for that matter, I feel I have become a more competent writer. I have dismissed the reactions I have had from my teachers of the past. I have realized my own writing process and have tried to master it, and I have pursued writing just for the sake of writing, good or bad.

I must tell you though, in all honesty, that I have now actually begun to discover the difficulty and determination it takes to become a well-developed writer. It is much more difficult than I had ever imagined it would be. But it is also challenging, and a joy to attempt for that reason. If you were to ask me where my writing will be in 10 years, I in all honesty could not tell you. But I must admit, that if I keep up with it, hopefully it will reach a point that I am truly happy with. So far I am overwhelmed by its progress.

What a neat entry and great growth. Send me a postcard this summer!

Explorations to Do as a Journal Entry or for Small Group or Class Discussion

1. In these selections, to what uses did Ray put his journal?

2. Do you think he'll keep writing in a journal as he travels? Why or why not?

3. How do you feel about the teacher's comments? What purpose do they serve? How should outside readers respond to journals? Should anyone else read them at all?

4. Do journal writers ever write just for themselves?

The next journal sequence is part of an extensive set of entries representing a poetry-writing student's semester-long analysis of his work. The writer, John, shares many particulars of his composing process in these entries.

Sample: John's Journal

1/22 [First poem]

My first poem for class was "The Whales." The way I ended up is sort of weird. To shorten the story, I was absolutely nowhere as to getting the poem done, so I took it to the W.C. [writing center] where Ken and John helped me. The problem was that I knew what I wanted to write about, but simply didn't know how; it was my first one, and I guess I had "poem fright."

1/25 [Second poem]

My out of class poem is called "Herman Gets His Dinner." . . . I've been working on it a lot, and am satisfied with its present incarnation (for now, at least) . . . I learned quite a lot about poetry from this poem alone. Let's see, what did I learn? The most important thing I learned was condensing the poem and deciding what stuff I don't need. As I look at earlier drafts, I can see quite a big difference. What originally took me 25 words to say took 10 in my most recent version, without eliminating any pertinent ideas.

2/5 [After a class workshop during which John's second poem was discussed]

One idea that came up during the [class group] critique was that the way I read the poem did not correspond with the line breaks. Now that I think about it, this is quite true; the most change will take place in the third stanza. I think this stanza should be changed to:

> "you slowly
> pass it
> with a flick
> of your gilded tail."

I also think that the first line of the fourth stanza should be broken up so that it reads:

> "I pity you,
> waiting for death."

I'm not sure why but I think these changes in the line breaks make more sense than the way the poem is now.

3/15 [After a class workshop that discussed John's third poem]

I noticed that the class was really divided during critique about my poem. . . .

The first problem with this poem was its title. The title gave the content away and made it too predictable. . . .

The second problem with the poem is that it was too ordinary—the events were too expected. From the feedback I got, "Solitude" was *very* predictable, which sort of surprised me. I know that loneliness is a "poetic" topic—depressing, sad, etc.—just right for the "sensitive" poet. Although I try to avoid these poetic topics, I thought I'd give loneliness a go, because I could identify with the guy in the poem; I've written letters to about 4 friends of mine back East and haven't got a reply in almost 2 months. . . .

Some of the written comments that I really like (and I got several that were similar) are ones that said that "Solitude" reminded the reader of "Fool on the Hill," or "Eleanor Rigby" by the Beatles. As I think about it, the sort of loneliness that those songs so effectively evoked is the sort of thing I was trying to get at. So, since *some* people seemed to see what I was getting at, I think my poem *did* work to some extent.

4/15 [Final self-evaluation]

I sort of see this semester divided into two parts, the division just happening to be about mid-semester. In the first period, I was just learning about how to write poetry, the different types and forms, the kinds of poems that there were, and so forth. Since I had never written poetry before that point, I was pleased with the poems that I managed to wrestle onto paper. Just getting ideas and putting them down was enough for me to do. Then, roughly at mid-semester, I became fairly confident with my poetic ability; my writing wasn't anything spectacular or particularly original, but I knew that if I had an idea, I would be able to write it down without leaving the reader out in left field. Once I reached this point, I thought that it was about time that I learned what good, effective poetry should be, so I started reading others' poetry and trying different forms, subjects, tones, etc. in my own poetry. That's where my problem began. You see, I had ideas of what makes poetry work, and some of the pitfalls to avoid; I employed these observations as much as I could, yet wasn't especially pleased with what I ended up with. I'd write something, knew that it could be better, but didn't know just how. I'm still in this "phase," if you will. As I noted in my learning log, I think that simply being aware that my poetry can be better is half of the battle. I sort of see it as getting all the "bad" poetry out before I can write "good" poetry. (I'm not saying my poetry is necessarily bad—I use "bad" as a general term.)[3]

Explorations to Do as a Journal Entry or for Small Group or Class Discussion

1. In what ways does John's journal differ from Ray's journal?

2. What portions of each journal seem most valuable to you?

I hope that these sample journals have shown you some of the many ways journals can work for you as a writer. Journals provide a safe place for thinking and exploration. Journals also create a place where discovery can be tempered by your observations *about* writing. For many writers, much of the learning that can consciously be traced in their processes will be stockpiled in the journal and draft folder—a pile of rough drafts from two to fifty or more that make up the thought-journey of a piece of creative writing, from inception to production or abandonment.

On the first day of workshop you will learn whether journals will be a formal or informal part of the class requirements, but take the practices of successful writers of the last several centuries as your example: You don't have to wait for anyone's directions or permission to start keeping a productive journal on your own.

Sharing Within a Writing Workshop

The small groups are fun. I attend every time. I like to show my poetry around; I offer what I know, which isn't always on the same level or proportion as the other people—and rightfully so. I think that's great that in workshop for example you get 16 pages back of comments on your poem. Where else but class would you get that amount of feedback, and unbiased, by other poets? It's very enlightening.

—Paul

Traditionally, the writing workshop has followed this general format: Students write, copy their writing, and submit those copies to class members. Class members prepare for the workshop by writing comments on the copies before class. They share their oral evaluations during the workshop, suggesting changes by offering interpretations of and responses to the piece under discussion. Workshops are generally conducted by a teacher who mediates the discussion, sometimes focusing on a certain issue such as point of view or line length, and sometimes offering only opening or summarizing remarks. Often the teacher is also the timekeeper, with the power to linger over texts of interest or to speed up discussion so that all class members share a piece.

Today, a great deal of time in many creative writing classrooms is devoted to small-group experiences. In groups, your writing will be shared with only two or three classmates instead of with fifteen to twenty-five. The small group is beneficial since it allows more time for peers to discuss your piece of writing and it provides a smaller audience for you to adjust to. In addition, in workshop groups we often share ideas (by brainstorming before writing), early drafts (by reading drafts aloud), experimental work or revisions (by bringing in different versions for other writers to consider), and final versions (by editing work you plan to submit to the teacher in a final class portfolio).

Before discussing workshop alternatives in the next section, it is worth getting a feel for a full-group response workshop. The following pages present a slightly edited—I've removed some of the *um*'s and *uh*'s—transcript of the first section of a workshop, which was considering the first of four student poems. I comment on the progress of the discussion, explaining what I think the teacher is doing and the writers are learning. I also try to point out missed opportunities since these exist in any impromptu experience. In this workshop, the writer of each poem was asked not to talk until the response session was completed, and then he or she was invited to respond to the discussion. Although I was present at the workshop, I wasn't always able to identify speakers when transcribing the tapes later, so I've numbered the speakers and identified their gender and, when possible, given their names.

A Poetry Workshop

DONNA (INSTRUCTOR):	Alright, let's take out the poems. Let's do them in this order: "Cape Breton" first, "Daddy's Girl" second, Josh's [untitled poem] third and "Nothing Is Black and White" fourth. [pause]
DONNA:	Alright, let's take a minute to refresh ourselves with the poem and your comments on the poem and then we'll start talking about it. "Cape Breton" first.

The teacher, Donna, sets the order for discussion.

Cape Breton

Linda Douglass

Craggy Highlands
Gannets nesting on rocky cliffs
Oceans of blue
　　　　blue
　　　　blue
Pounding waves
Threatening fishing boats
Lobster traps.

May Day Sunday
Ferry boat ride
Whales are scarce
Plenty of seals
and the best scallops
Outside Digby Neck
　　[an imitation of poet William
　　Carlos Williams' style]

[long pause]

Donna invites students to share responses.

DONNA:	Alright, let's start talking about it. Who wants to start?
FEMALE STUDENT 1:	I like how she has blue . . . it reminds me of a deep color blue or a deep ocean and I think it had really good descriptors, words like "threatening." The words that you

This student helps set the discussion in motion.

used were really good; I really liked it a lot.

DONNA: Can you pick some out? Besides "threatening"?

FEMALE STUDENT 1: "Threatening" and let's see. The "pounding waves" and "nesting on rocky cliffs." I liked that a lot.

Donna pushes for more particulars.

FEMALE STUDENT 2: I liked the images that make me think. I also liked how all the words here were so important. In helping you see the image.

She asks for support for an opinion based on the text, the poem under discussion.

DONNA: Can you pick some out? Pick the images out that you think are really sharp?

FEMALE STUDENT 2: I like the craggy highlands, that and the pounding waves. I like the last few lines a lot "and the best scallops/Outside Digby Neck."

FEMALE STUDENT 3: Hey!

FEMALE STUDENT 2: That's great [class members laugh in agreement].

Students share opinions outside of class.

FEMALE STUDENT 3: We were talking about this poem on the phone last night.

DONNA: Is that what you were going to say?

FEMALE STUDENT 3: Yeah! I haven't said anything about the poem.

DONNA: Okay. Okay Rosalyn come on.

ROSALYN (FEMALE STUDENT 4): I just don't see how whales are scarce and plenty of seals . . . the best scallops. The rhythm and the way . . . I don't know. It just doesn't fit there. Like there's a bit of action going on and you just throw it in. I just don't see how whales are scarce and plenty of seals go in with ferry boat ride. And then you're talking about the best scallops.

This student prompts discussion by adding what she likes and then she becomes the first person to raise a question — even if it isn't completely articulated.

LINDA (AUTHOR): Okay.

ROSALYN:	And maybe it's the rhythm of the words you got . . .
DONNA:	Yeah, What might she do there? Do you have any suggestions?
ROSALYN:	[laughs] Well . . .
DONNA:	Okay. Alright.
FEMALE STUDENT 5:	To me, they're talking about humans which is maybe why the whales are scarce. There's actually plenty of seals and . . . to me the whales are scarce and the threatened fishing boats are now going to go after the seals and the scallops because the whales are scarce.
DONNA:	Okay . . . I didn't read it that way either. Go ahead Jill and then Brian, Chris, . . .
JILL (FEMALE STUDENT 6):	I liked the "blue, blue, blue" because it just made me think of a blue sky and blue water. I mean, everything was really blue. I just imagined a day without clouds and I really like it. The reason I didn't find anything wrong with it about the whales scarce and plenty of seals was because wherever this is I know it's like an island, and so, is it? Can you answer? [Author shakes her head.]
	And if you're there and are looking out on the water you might notice those things. It's excellent. I mean, it's just . . . I really like, the way that she described it.
BRIAN (MALE STUDENT 1):	I see what she's saying when she says whales are scarce and plenty of seals. I just think it's choppy. It's descriptive and it fits and it's choppy; it's . . . it's just like that, the rhythm, it just changes . . . because . . .

Donna asks Rosalyn and the class for help.

Another student offers a slightly different interpretation.

Jill changes the subject and points out a particularly effective device but then returns to the trouble spot.

Brian defends the author — interprets the poem but critiques a different aspect (rhythm rather than logic).

DONNA: What could she do Brian? Do you have any suggestions?

BRIAN: Other descriptive words that would help smooth it out or perhaps try and break it up in a different manner. Try to . . . *the,* the whales were scarce to make it smooth, instead of . . . because the rest of it—May Day Sunday, ferry boat ride, whales are scarce, plenty of seals and the best scallops outside Digby Neck. I like that, I like the sounds, but I think the poem could be a little more smooth. I have no idea how.

ROBIN (FEMALE STUDENT 7): I like the language a lot, like Digby Neck and craggy highlands and all that, but I thought that there were too many images and maybe you can try to like . . . see how it's lobster traps and then it's May Day Sunday? And then you're going to go on a ferry boat ride. Maybe you could try to get images that have something in common . . . you know, something that can tie them all together. But really I like it. You can see the place . . . but if they all had more in common. May Day Sunday kind of threw it for me.

Robin offers a global remark about the overall effect of the poem.

DONNA: Okay. Pat—did you want to say something?

PAT (MALE STUDENT 2): I want to say something about the repetition of the word blue. I think it reinforces that pounding of the waves . . . and I was wondering if you meant to do that or if you were just trying to emphasize blue. [Class laughs.] But to me, I thought that's what it was for. It kind of had a double purpose there.

I was just thinking in the second stanza, perhaps, getting

Pat refers to an earlier part of the class discussion, makes an insightful craft suggestion, but doesn't force the author to accept his version.

the same type of rhythm going as in the first stanza with the "blue, blue, blue" something like that and combining some of those lines. Now I like the images—but combining some of those lines and bringing in that rhythm again and making that second stanza consistent with the first. I'm not sure if you would want to use oceans of blue blue blue again, but you could say something to the effect . . . you could keep them flowing the same.

DONNA: Josh—did you want to say something?

JOSH (MALE STUDENT 3): I just liked the language a lot. Because you're right, it reminds me of going up north, the craggy highlands, a lot of the words are typical New England words: gannet, craggy highlands, lobster traps, scallops, Digby Neck.

DONNA: Okay. One thing that I thought she could do with "whales are scarce" is just get rid of the verb. There aren't verbs in the poem. Right? And then keep the rhythm; [it] would be—Ferry boat ride, whales scarce—and then do something with the "plenty of seals." I don't know what—give an image of seals rather than plenty of seals? One word that would give us the same meaning of plenty of . . . I don't know what the word is. Right? [laughs] But that's the only thing I thought you could do. The closure at the end I think is wonderful and . . . I wanted to know where it was . . . because [laughs] I liked it, I want to be there. Interesting words, Digby too, Digby Neck is really interesting. The only criticism,

The teacher, Donna, brings the discussion to a close, offers her responses, reviews some student comments as she does so, and then refers to the most perplexing issue . . .

let's see. First, I'm on a ferry boat
ride looking at the whales and
then it's like the scallops are on
the ferry boat, and I'm not sure if
the scallops are on the ferry boat
or just somewhere at Cape Breton.
So that threw me off a little bit.
But interesting word, gannet. Isn't
that an interesting word? I want
you to find a more unique word
for pounding and for craggy.
  Okay, let's pass them in
[return critiqued copies to the
author]. Okay, let's look at
"Daddy's Girl" next.

"... and finally offers some revision directions."

[workshop continues]

Explorations to Do as a Journal Entry
or for Small Group or Class Discussion

1. Look at my comments on the workshop transcript and agree, dis-
    agree, or expand on my interpretations.

2. After your first full-class workshop, reread this transcript and
    decide how your workshop was different and/or similar.

Workshop Formats

There is no "best" workshop method. However, there are
things students and teachers can do to make each workshop more
productive. The following summaries and suggestions can help your
class develop its own best format.

One-to-One (Partner) Sharing

Often, especially at the beginning of a writing class, you will be
asked to work with one other writer. Together you will share early
drafts, explore an issue and report to the class, and perhaps compose
and/or revise a piece of writing.

Benefits

1. One-to-one sharing can be less intimidating than group sharing.

2. Sometimes, two people can accomplish more than a larger group because only you and your partner have to agree.

3. Quieter individuals with good ideas often share them more freely when they are working with only one other person.

4. Working in pairs helps writers really get to know another class member.

Drawbacks

1. If you're paired with someone whose learning style (introverted versus extroverted) or values (Republican versus Democrat) or work habits (meticulous versus freewheeling) are different from yours, some time can be lost as you learn to agree and compromise.

2. Sometimes other partnered pairs seem to be working more smoothly or having more fun; this is the "grass is greener" syndrome.

Activities

1. On the first day of class, you may be paired with another class member. Briefly interview that person as to his or her writing past and class interests. Find out several odd, unusual, or interesting things about the individual. Find out how the person received her or his name. You'll be asked to introduce your partner to the class.

2. After one of the invention activities that you write in class, you may be asked to share your writing with a partner. Listen to each other's freewrite, identify the parts that are most interesting, and give your partner several ideas for expanding that freewrite into a piece of writing that he or she can share for the next class.

3. You may be asked to revise a workshop piece based on suggestions made during a class response session—either group or full class—and then to share both the original and revised versions with a partner. Analyze the success of the changes you each made.

4. Near the last class, you may be asked to help a partner edit final drafts that he or she is getting ready to turn in as a writing portfolio. Read each draft carefully, making notes of changes that you think should be made. Then, talk to your partner about each piece.

5. At midsemester and/or on the last day of class, you may be asked to exchange portfolio writings with a partner. Your task is to compare in a few paragraphs your writing style and class development with your partner's style and class development.

To Become a Productive One-to-One Partner

- Whenever you work with a new class partner, take a few minutes to introduce yourself and find out his or her interests and goals for the activity.
- Be up front about your own biases. Try to adapt to your partner's style and clue your partner in to your own.
- Be as honest and open as possible. If you don't think your work together is progressing, try to express this and make a change right away.
- Be supportive and praise your partner for work accomplished.

Small-Group Sharing

Small-group sharing among three to six members is becoming more and more common in the writing workshop. Groups may work together for an extended period of time, for a few weeks or for a semester, or change membership each time they convene. There are benefits to both formats. When you work with the same individuals for a long period of time, you come to know their strengths and weaknesses and you become comfortable with them. At the same time, sometimes you become too comfortable and forget to challenge each other to work to the best of your abilities. When this happens, or when one member gets restive, it is useful to have one member from each of the four or five class groups "travel" to another group. He or she will be glad of the opportunity to move on, and your group will welcome a new member, and that member's new perspective.

Benefits

1. When groups are small, you can spend more time on each writer's work.

2. Some writers are more likely to speak up in a small group of peers than they are in a full class when they know the class and teacher are listening to what they say.

3. Members of small groups get to know each other and each other's work, and become informed respondents and, often, friends.

4. Discussion in a small group may be more supportive and less critical than that in a large group, where students are trying to display their knowledge for the teacher.

5. The teacher can only "visit" groups, so he is not as likely to impose his own taste and ideas on class members.

6. In groups, you are more in charge of your learning and you can partially set the pace.

7. You may decide to continue to work with your group members after the class is over or outside of class hours. Often, these individuals form a valued writing community with you.

Drawbacks

1. If group members aren't prepared, nothing gets accomplished.

2. If some group members are too competitive, other members start to withdraw from projects and nurse grudges.

3. If group members don't remember to invite the teacher into some of their conversations, they may lose her expertise.

4. If groups allow one member to dominate by talking too much, imposing her ideas, or slowing down the work by going off on tangents, little will be accomplished.

5. Group work can take time since each member has a voice and understandings and agreements must be negotiated.

Activities

1. Try a fishbowl exercise to explore the strengths and weaknesses of writing groups. Choose any piece of student writing in this book. One class member volunteers to be The Writer. Four class members volunteer to be the group. The Writer reads the piece aloud to her group and asks members to respond in the following three ways:
   a. Members should tell The Writer what was most successful in the piece.
   b. Members should tell The Writer at what point(s) in her text they became confused and/or wished they had more information.
   c. Members should tell The Writer what she or he should do to improve the piece when redrafting.
   Finally, The Writer summarizes what she learned from group members and asks them questions of her own regarding her writing.
   At the end of this mock response session, class members who have been observing discuss what they saw. Class members should mention what was most useful in the session and suggest ways the group members and writer could have supported each other even more fully.

2. As a group, conduct a response session, using both a piece of writing from this book and a piece provided by a member of your group. Each group in class should do this. First, one member reads aloud the textbook poem or prose sketch and then the group takes ten minutes to respond. Next, the group responds to the

writing of the group member. Compare your responses to the two pieces. How did the group respond when the writer was absent? How supportive and how critical were the remarks? How did the group respond when the writer was present? How supportive and how critical were the remarks? How can you, as group members, adopt the best response styles of both sessions?

3. Your group may be asked to respond to early drafts of each other's work.

4. Your group may be asked to share journal or reading responses and report to the class. Be sure to ask your teacher how much time you have to complete your work.

5. Your group may be asked to compose or revise together. See Chapter 5 for collaborative writing exercises.

6. Your group may be convened regularly to respond to successive revision drafts of group members' writing.

7. Your group may be convened to listen to and offer advice on group members' potential submissions for a class book. You may help a group member edit work for a portfolio and/or help the member decide which of several selections would be best to submit.

To Become a Productive Group Member

- Work with people you don't know—don't try to always get in a group with a best friend, romantic partner, people of the same gender, and so on.

- Be meticulous about *your* part. If you need to read class materials the night before group work, be sure to do so; don't rely on others to do your work for you. If you need to prepare materials for the group to review, have the copies ready and available on time.

- Be on time. If you always slip into your group late, you force group members to waste time reexplaining the group activity to you.

- Keep track of your participation. It's worth asking yourself if you're talking enough *and* if you're talking too much. It's worth trying to change your group's habits, starting with your own.

- Realize that groups need to have members perform specific roles. At a minimum, you'll need a *timekeeper* to ensure that each member's work is discussed. Also, you may need a group *historian* to take notes on a discussion and share them later with the full class. Last but not least, being a *general group member* means helping to facilitate all these activities. No one should always take the same role; exchange roles and expand your capabilities.

- Share your feelings. If you feel your group is unproductive, try to bring up issues that are bothering you. If necessary, talk to your teacher about ways to improve your group's work.

- Help keep your group on task. It's easy to slip into small talk. Groups need to catch up and become reacquainted each time they start a session, but a group that talks more about the school's football team than about writing is wasting every member's time.

Now that you've learned about useful group participation, consider these students' comments, questions, and suggestions on group work.

Writing Student A

I was very encouraged by meeting with my "response group" on Friday, when we revised, or helped revise each other's creative writing. The information/suggestions/ideas they gave me were truly worthwhile. I felt like they were really interested—like "we're all in this together" so they took the time to give me some useful advice. What's funny to me about revising after an "outsider" has given me advice is that I almost feel guilty about using it—like I'm cheating or something. I remember in high school when my Mom and/or Dad would read my papers and give me suggestions, I wanted to use what they said, but I felt I was being fake. And now I'm having those same feelings. I *like* what my group suggested and I *want* to make a few additions that they specifically mentioned. Is it wrong to use them? Am I being weird and this is a usual occurrence among writers and their editors? I wonder.

Writing Student B

One of the main things I learned from this class that I found important is that the comments made by my peers were meant to be helpful not to be cruel and insensitive. I am a very sensitive person and I feel bad and get depressed when I feel people do not like something I have tried hard to do. I realized the criticism was constructive and I finally began to benefit from the remarks. I am glad I finally realized that because I have come to accept criticism better, not only in here but in other areas as well, and I believe that will be beneficial to me for the rest of my life.

Writing Student C

The peer responding to papers was pretty much a bust, I'd say. First of all, what an insult that people didn't bother to show up. At least we had five out of six there—but then one didn't have a paper, and others [papers] were in such rough shape they weren't ready for much critiquing.

I mean, I got disinterested just because they were in such rough shape. . . . Am I wrong to think that real writers—as this class seems to think of themselves to be—would be the ones most interested in non-graded but helpful critiques?

Actually, I think we just needed a lot more practice in this. People really didn't seem to know what they were supposed to be about. Generally, there was a lot of silence and a lot of talk about weather-level subjects. But even the amount of practice that might make us more adept at knowing what to look for would not have overcome the fact that the basic criterion—a complete draft—was ignored.

Questions

1. What do students A and B tell you about successful group work?

2. What would you have done in student C's place to make the group more successful?

Full-Class Sharing

In any creative writing workshop, much of your time will be devoted to full-class sharing. Although some students seem to prefer one or the other—small-group or full-class sharing—there are beneficial aspects to both, and most teachers try to strike the best balance. Here is John discussing small- and large-group sharing.

> I really never feel comfortable talking in a large group. Blame it on shyness, some weird hang-up of mine or whatever, but I really do not do well in large groups, in ANY of my classes. I do think I do well in small-group workshops, though, or working with one other person. . . . I think the most valuable aspect of class, for me at least, is (paradoxically) the full-class critiques. Even though I keep fairly quiet in them, all of the different views and opinions that I get about my poetry helps me a lot.

Without exception, writers seem to feel that critiquing the work of peers is difficult but ultimately rewarding, and that doing so as a full-class activity is particularly difficult. For instance, there are often tense moments at first: "It felt like when everyone was waiting for someone else to start the critique, I was always the one to open her big mouth. I could only think of how awful I'd feel if it was my story and no one had anything to say," said one writer to explain why she made herself break the ice and start to respond. Another observed, "I like the whole-class workshops because getting other readers' opinions helps me to understand the poems I read in the critique sessions. It also helps to hear how the poets read their own poems instead of just reading them myself."

Benefits

1. The greater the number of responses you receive, the greater becomes your ability to understand your audience(s) and discover revision directions.

2. Usually a full-class response session raises conflicting views and asks you to resolve them, encouraging you to think more deeply about your writing and writing goals. It is hard to remain complacent and overly content under such scrutiny.

3. When your teacher orchestrates the full-class session, she can ensure that important points are covered, that each writer receives attention, that no writer dominates the discussion, and that her expertise is shared.

4. By listening to and participating in full-class sessions, you have a chance to discover which class peers you are most comfortable with so that you can seek them out in group work or out of class.

5. Full-class sharing makes efficient use of limited class time. Instead of seeing what only a few peers in a group are writing, over time you get to respond to the wealth and variety of writing that comes from fifteen or more class writers.

Drawbacks

1. Only a few pieces of writing can be reviewed at each session, and often even those are not reviewed in great depth.

2. The responses you receive may be highly contradictory and unsupported, making it difficult for you to respond to any of them.

3. Your teacher may allow certain vocal students to dominate the discussion or she or he may dominate it. You may feel you have no voice or don't dare say anything.

4. Response may become overly critical, each student trying to top the remark of a previous student.

5. It may be expensive or complicated to copy and circulate the required samples of work for each workshop.

6. You don't get to know your teacher and your peers as well as you might wish.

7. The teacher generally sets and controls the workshop agenda.

Activities

1. As a class, draw up rules for your ideal full-class workshops. Questions to consider:

- How often will each class member get to share work?
- Who will moderate the discussion? Remember, class members can successfully share the moderator's role and learn a lot by doing so.
- What are the logistics of copying and sharing work? How do you ensure that each class member contributes? Orally? With written comments?
- How should the class deal with members who are constantly unprepared?
- How should peers phrase their responses to class members' writing?

2. How will you ensure that workshops don't become too critical? To decide, you might want to read and discuss the responses of the next two students to the questions: How did you feel after your first poem was critiqued in class? Did it change your writing? Why/Why not? How?

Writing Student A

In a way, I felt that after my first poem was critiqued I made a breakthrough. I was in the second group to be critiqued so I had to wait longer [several days] to be critiqued and in that time of waiting I really didn't have much confidence in my work. Then the dreaded day arrived and I sat nervously listening to people actually relating to and accepting this personal experience of mine that I turned into writing. I'm not so sure that my writing changed so much in style; I just had more confidence in it and wasn't scared to try new techniques. So what if I was shot down? At least I was taking a risk. To most people my writing probably doesn't sound very risky, but it is a big step for me to reveal personal pasts to a classroom of not-too-long-ago strangers.

Writing Student B

In a way I felt sort of robbed. The students in class took another student's poem and looked at it as though it were a classic piece of Melville or Cummings. They graded it with the utmost urgency. I felt as though my vital organs were being yanked from my gut and strewn across the Student Union Center.

Some people just don't realize that they aren't critiquing Walt Whitman—they are critiquing poems that ordinary, young students have written. Most, if not all of us, are not ready to publish any of our works. If we were that good, we wouldn't be a student in the class—we'd be teaching it.

3. As a class, practice responding by doing so, using any of the student works from this textbook or a sample provided by your teacher. After the ten-minute response session, talk together

about the roles each of you took: who was quiet, who talked, how peers and teacher responded. Before starting your first workshop using class members' work, take a few minutes to remember this practice session and to review your workshop "rules."

4. Your teacher will want to model and direct activities during the first several workshops. After that, try substituting student facilitators. Anywhere from one to three individuals can be "today's facilitator."

5. On days when the class is primarily responding to readings, students can ably provide successful leadership.

To Become a Productive Full Workshop Member

- Be prepared. Always read the workshop manuscripts ahead of time and write notes for the author.

- Don't waste time. Volunteer your responses quickly. Share your ideas in detail and then allow others to share their ideas.

- Give each writer your attention. Don't try to read a different manuscript from the one currently under discussion. Don't do work for another class during workshop.

- Connect ideas. When a classmate clarifies an issue, try to connect to that point and move the discussion on.

- Be patient with class members whose personal habits bother you. Try to listen to what they are *really* saying and respond to those ideas, not to their personalities.

- Treat other writers the way you hope to be treated yourself.

- Keep track of your participation. It's worth asking yourself if you're talking enough *and* if you're talking too much.

- Share your feelings. If workshop practices are bothering you, try to bring up issues individually with your teacher or during class discussion.

- Help keep the class on task. It's easy to slip into small talk with your neighbors. Volunteer your specific remarks about writing to help get the discussion back where it should be: on the subject of writing.

In Chapter 6, you'll learn a lot about methods for responding to writing in partner, small-group, or full-class situations. It's up to you, however, to make the best use of the workshop. John's journal, for instance, shows that it's useful to write down your feelings about each workshop. In addition, hang on to the peer remarks written on your workshop submissions. Keep them in mind as you revise your work throughout the unit or semester. Finally, if something goes awry in a particular workshop, always contact your teacher to discuss ways to keep that problem from recurring.

Since the workshop is for you, as a writer in a writing community, it is up to you to try to change anything in the workshop format that you believe is worth changing. Apply all the rules and guidelines I've gathered in this chapter as flexibly as possible. And finally, enjoy the rare opportunity to sit in a room full of sensitive writers who are eager to pay attention to your work and who, in turn, are waiting for your response to theirs.

Notes

1. These categories are taken from Ira Progoff and Tristine Rainer.
2. Stock 15, 95. See his book for serious (and off-beat) questions of this sort.
3. John's journal entries are reprinted from Bishop, *Released*.

Sources and Readings

Berthoff, Anne. "Dialectical Notebooks and the Audit of Meaning." *The Journal Book*, ed. Toby Fulwiler. Portsmouth, NH: Boynton/Cook, 1987. 11–18.

Bishop, Wendy. "Evaluating the Peer Group Process: The Group Folder." *Kentucky English Bulletin* 37 (1987): 81–88.

———. "Helping Peer Writing Groups Succeed." *Teaching English in the Two-Year College* 15 (1988): 120–25.

———. *Released into Language*. Urbana, IL: National Council of Teachers of English, 1990.

Fulwiler, Toby, ed. *The Journal Book*. Portsmouth, NH: Boynton/Cook, 1987.

Gere, Ann Ruggles. *Writing Groups: History, Theory, and Implications*. Carbondale: Southern Illinois UP, 1987.

Harris, Muriel. *Teaching One-to-One: The Writing Conference*. Urbana, IL: National Council of Teachers of English, 1986.

Lowenstein, Sharyn. "A Brief History of Journal Keeping." *The Journal Book*, ed. Toby Fulwiler. Portsmouth, NH: Boynton/Cook, 1987. 87–98.

Mallon, Thomas. *A Book of One's Own: People and Their Diaries*. New York: Ticknor & Fields, 1984.

Murray, Donald. *Learning by Teaching: Selected Articles on Writing and Teaching*. Upper Montclair, NJ: Boynton/Cook, 1982.

———. *A Writer Teaches Writing*. Boston: Houghton Mifflin, 1968.

Packard, William, ed. *The Poet's Craft*. New York: Paragon House, 1987.

Progoff, Ira. *At a Journal Workshop: The Basic Text and Guide for Using the Intensive Journal*. New York: Dialogue House, 1975.

Rainer, Tristine. *The New Diary*. Los Angeles: Jeremy P. Tarcher, 1978.

Stock, Gregory. *The Book of Questions*. New York: Workman Publishing, 1985.

Woolf, Virginia. *A Writer's Diary*. Ed. Leonard Woolf. New York: Harcourt, 1954.

Chapter 5

The Art of Exploration

Breaking the rules seems easy enough. Who hasn't ever wanted to be able to break a rule now and then, right? Actually, I found that breaking the rules was a little difficult. The only way I could convince myself that breaking the rules is allowable was to make breaking the rules a rule.

—JEAN

Most writers feel an obligation to read a lot and to *read as writers*, deriving "rules" from the texts they encounter. Writers imitate, borrow from, and adapt the texts they have read each time they compose, for writers want to be—and always have been—*influenced* by other authors and other works.

In this chapter, I encourage you to experiment, exploring the limits of what you can and cannot do with words. Look forward to Chapter 9 if you want a brief review of genres, and look backward to Chapter 2, where you explored those rules and genre constraints that you already knew well. Remember that, because you have been reading poems, stories, plays, and essays since grade school, you already have access to many of the rules or conventions for basic forms. You should find that the invention activities in this chapter help you to generate and improve a draft *and* offer you ways to chart the limits of your writing by providing you with some complex writing challenges.

Since exploration takes place not when you abandon restraints or rules completely but when you push against them, thoughtfully, this chapter highlights *exploration joined to self-analysis*. I encourage you to say, "Sure most writers compose alone, but what do I learn about writing when I create with another individual?" Or, you might decide to imitate your favorite author, to get under the writer's skin to feel and then analyze her techniques. Later, you may want to incorporate those techniques, topics, or themes into your own writer's bag of tricks where, slowly, they merge into the composite structures of your own polished work.

Writing Art About Art

The fine and popular arts have often provided writers with inspiration. Sometimes writers memorialize the lives of famous writers, painters, or singers. Other writers use the artist as a vehicle for exploring their feelings about art, as a way to make a statement about art, or, even more simply, as an imagistic prompt—a way to pay ghostly homage to works that have moved them and which they value.

One of the best ways to explore the other arts is to go to public performances such as operas, art exhibits, plays, and poetry and prose readings. Time spent in a museum with your journal and enough free time to sketch, scribble, and daydream is also worthwhile. During these excursions, you might try some of the basic invention techniques provided in Chapter 3. What happens when you use cubing or the reporter's formula to contemplate an ancient Roman coin? What do you discover as you feel the lines of a modern sculpture, then sit down and freewrite for ten minutes?

Wide reading can also prompt writing. For instance, I have written poems based on my college textbooks. In a history of photography by Beaumont Newhall, I found one of the earliest photographs by Charles Daguerre and this quote: "In only one of Daguerre's pictures does a man appear: by chance, a pedestrian on the boulevard held still during most of the image." This seemed so provocative that I explored that tiny slice of photographic history in a poem titled "The First Man." That poem was a self-assignment, a way of using poetry to explore the world. Another time, as a writing student, I was given a term-long assignment to write about a famous individual. Since I was working in a music library at the time, I wrote about the composer J. S. Bach.

Particularly during our college years, then, many of us have the opportunity to become more involved in the arts—working as ushers, typing for the music library, or hanging photographs for the arts festival. College is a rich environment for exploring arts you're not familiar with. You may find yourself attending a tuba concert, interviewing an artist who tie-dyes shirts, or constructing stage sets for the world premier of a newly written play. Here are a few student works that represent the broad category of art composed about art. They are followed by a variety of exercises you might undertake yourself.

In this poem draft, Tiffany reacts to a surrealist film by Luis Buñuel.

Un Chien Andalou

Tiffany Fussell

Listen!
A woman's eyeball is slit by a sharp scalp.
Once
Upon a time
Streaked clouds passed sallow moons.
It is
A nightmare of logic.
Sinister images from the subconscious,
Both from
Spain.
Soldier ants scurry from a hole in the palm
Of hands.
Gasp!
Cosmos bursting through their threaded sutures
Into chaotic breathless stratosphere.
It is
Peace at its best.
Prisoners paw a woman's white breasts
Her clothes vanish in the miserly minds.
Stink!
Slaughtered mules sling
Themselves across grand pianos.
Sanity takes them
For a ride past a red rosary.
Stall!
A dead bike boy is delayed by a killer cliff.
He is a fine pilgrim fellow in fetus position.
It is the Mayflower man
Once upon a time where sickness is rare and
Insanity is rational.
Scandal!
Fat earth bleeds from its binding chains and
The dish runs away with the spoon.
It is
The surreal.

In another piece, Tiffany chose to take famous characters from the movies, TV, sports, music, and art and place them all together in heaven. In that poem, she began to move from writing art about art to cultural criticism, as you might choose to do yourself. Where is the artistry in graffiti or flame throwing? Is a circus aerialist an artist? Is a skywriter?

This kind of questioning about artistic and pop culture may eventually send you on a pilgrimage to the actual landscape of an artist: You may look at Hemingway's writing stand or Dickens's house or writers' diaries in the British Museum, or you may take a tour of the homes of the stars in Hollywood. Here Kelly writes about the New Orleans Mardi Gras.

The Day After Mardi Gras

Kelly English

The old brick streets are empty now.
Nothing but beer foam and dried mud caked in the crevices.
A greasy stench of gumbo and crawfish lingers in the air
Enough to make a mouth water.
Faded gold, purple, and green papier-maché
Are left in the street to disintegrate.
Dangling from a light post a glimpse of lollipop
Lime-green beads can be seen.
Through a grate, a shiny gold coin gleams
Making no one rich.
No topless women yelling, "Throw me something."
No dancing men selling roses for a kiss.
No floats carrying black painted men
Calling themselves the Krewe of Zulu.

Self-Assignments, Challenges, and Explorations

1. Go to the most unusual museum you can get to. In Homer, Alaska, for instance, there is a comb museum kept in a private home. In your area, there may be a museum commemorating a famous citizen or event. There may be a small natural history museum. Art collections are often displayed in banks, malls, or private homes.
   a. Write a series of poems about objects in that museum.
   b. Write a story in which the museum and its caretaker figure in an important way.
   c. Do some historical research on an artifact from that museum and write about it. Or, relocate the object in its original time or place and write about that.
   d. Most museums prepare photographs, slides, or postcards illustrating the works in their collections. Find some of these and exchange yours with those collected by a classmate. Write about the images you receive, forgetting about the museum connection. You may also combine both sets of images and each of you write your own piece about them.

2. Go to an art performance or event that you've never before experienced—a live circus, a flower-arranging exhibit, dog trials, a supper theater, a one-performer play, a street festival, a frog-jumping contest, a celebration of local history in a small town, and so on. Write about any aspect of the event. You may want to interview the artist(s) and weave that knowledge into a piece of your own fiction or nonfiction.

3. Go to the library and check out all the available books on a painter you've always enjoyed. Absorb those books. Look through them for several days. Read bits and pieces of the text. If you can, get copies of the painter's diary or sketchbooks. Think about the artist as a "composer"—write a piece that captures *both* the artist's products and his or her composing style.

4. Pull out every album by your favorite popular or classical or jazz musician. Take an evening and listen to them straight through in chronological order from the earliest works to the latest. Sleep on those sounds. The next morning, rise early and write—about the musician or about whatever the music prompts you to write. The day after, rise early, read what you wrote, and write some more.

5. Your teacher will bring a set of postcards, photographs, or art reproductions to class. You will choose one, write about it, then exchange with a class member and write about the image he or she had been using. When you're done, you'll have responses to two images, images that were also used by a class partner. Look at the responses you each wrote for each image and, together, examine the different approaches you took when writing.

6. Your teacher will bring a set of postcards, photographs, or art reproductions to class. She will lend one image to you for a week. Write a piece for workshop. During workshop, when the class has finished discussing your piece, pass around the originating image and explain how it prompted your writing. During revision, the image may "disappear" from your work.

7. Read another writer's art about art piece; your teacher may provide some of these pieces, or you may find your own by looking through anthologies or literary magazines. Imitate that writer's approach. If the writer composes a poem in contemplation of a painting in a way that intrigues you, try to do the same. If he attends a play and then connects that work to a moment in his life, try to do the same. After completing the project, write a page about your success and how your work compares to the work you were imitating.

8. Write a story or a play in which historical artists, living or dead, become characters.

9. Write a poem, play, or story that turns the "scene" of a piece of artwork into a narrative with plot.

Writing With/Through Influences

All of us learn from the experiences of others, receiving instructions from friends or parents who are willing to teach us one of their own skills. You may have learned to make a quilt or a peach pie, pour a patio foundation or adjust a carburetor, research a family tree or prepare for a real estate license exam. You've also experienced some of the drawbacks of learning from others; although it's useful to have the example and advice of someone more skilled than you, it's also frustrating to be held back, to be told or shown how to do something without having a chance to get your hands in the mess and try it yourself. If you want to throw a pot on a potter's wheel, for instance, you may first watch a master potter, carefully examining her movements—the way she touches, holds, talks to the clay. But you also can't wait to place your hands on that clammy lump, slop on some water, kick the wheel, and feel the uncentered mass of material buck and flutter in your hands.

Writers imitate extensively, and they do so consciously and unconsciously. As writers, we're formed by the images we have of the writers we have observed—often siblings, parents, and teachers. Here's Toby Fulwiler remembering his mother's influence: "When I was quite young, my mother used to write stories and send them to the *New Yorker*. They always came back, but sometimes they wouldn't come back for a long time. Watching my mother made me a writer" (qtd. in Waldrep 88). We can see Toby absorbing the hard lessons of a writing life: First you need to write, then you need to submit, often the submission doesn't succeed, then you need to write again.

Writers are also influenced by all their previous reading, from comic strips to high school literature to the forgotten novel that was the only thing on the shelf at the beach house that summer. David Bartholomae explains: "As I think about how I write, I know that my work will always begin with other people. I work with other people's words, even as I do my own work. Other writers make my work possible, even as I begin to shape projects of my own" (qtd. in Waldrep 28).

For most writers, imitation is a two-edged tool—sharp, useful, but also dangerous. You want to read, to learn what you can from other writers, and then you want to break away, to explore, to incorporate what you learned into your vision, and to extend that vision. Poet Thom Gunn explains the inevitability of imitation:

> Students of literature speak misleadingly about being
> influenced. "Are you influenced by so and so?" they ask, or "Who are
> you influenced by?" It's as if one were willingly or consciously
> influenced. Most of the time when I'm writing I don't think, "Well,
> I'm sounding like John Donne here, or Yvor Winters, or Robert
> Lowell." Rather, I think that I'm sounding like nobody who has ever
> written on my subject before. It's only afterwards that you realize with
> a feeling of chagrin, if you realize it at all, that you got the intonation,
> the tone, the music, even the vocabulary from someone else. Of course
> there may be occasions where you deliberately set out to write in a tra-
> dition of some sort, or with deliberate reference to some writer, but
> those are special cases. (qtd. in Bartlett 89)

As much as we want to break away from influences—any rules
or rulers of writing—we also need to know our influences. We need
to study those we hope to imitate or whose work we hope to better.
And we need to explore the "special case" of direct imitation and
what can be learned from that activity.

For most writers, a serious "apprenticeship" to excellent writers of the past is a lifelong occupation. They read and read again;
they are influenced by good writing and transform that influence
into better writing of their own. Through an analogy to other arts,
Annie Dillard explains this continuous, lifelong adaptation:

> Only after the writer lets literature shape her can she perhaps
> shape literature. In working-class France, when an apprentice got
> hurt, or when he got tired, the experienced workers said, "It is the
> trade entering his body." The art must enter the body, too. . . .
>
> You adapt yourself, Paul Klee said, to the contents of the paint-
> box. . . . The painter, in other words, does not fit the paints to the
> world. He most certainly does not fit the world to himself. He fits him-
> self to the paint. (69)

How does the novice writer use imitation? I think by seeing it as
necessary, logical, and useful experimentation, not as the only option
or the final word on the best way to do things. You can learn by imitating a writer you love and by working in forms. If you learn the prose
moves of John Updike or the poetic contours of Adrienne Rich's "territory," you add to your writing strategies. If you learn a sonnet by writing sonnets, you may not want to rely on that form lifelong—and you
shouldn't overvalue it as a form, for after all it's only one among
many—but you'll gain facility with rhyme, meter, fitting large thoughts
into small spaces, and so on. Again, the facility is *for you* to use as you
will; it's not to turn you into a lockstep sonneteer.

We begin our look at imitation by examining parody. When
you imitate, think of it as an attempt to *impersonate*. As you work

toward the end product, the imitation, try to understand the process the writer went through, the decisions the writer made. You do this not only by writing the parody but also by writing a narrative of the imitation.

You parody best when you have strong feelings about a piece of writing, so you yourself should choose the author you wish to parody. Strong *negative* feelings, however, sometimes lead to heavy-handed or simplistic satire. Making fun of an author instead of understanding him or her does not lead you to greater understanding of a writer's concerns and techniques; choose an author you admire. To develop an understanding of the work you will imitate, read more than a single work by that author. Through reading and then analysis, you'll gain an implicit and then an explicit understanding of the writer's work.

Parody and Imitation Exercise

Directions

1. Choose an author and find an entire anthology section of her or his work or find a book of the author's works.[1]

2. Read the work carefully, some of it aloud. Make notes on the writer's technique, subject, vocabulary, and so on.

3. Decide if you will do a focused parody or a more general imitation.

    Writers create a focused parody by choosing one piece of writing (a poem or story or novel) in particular for imitation. Focused parody requires close technical analysis.

    Writers can also write an overall imitation of the writer—a general parody. General parody captures the original writer's representative tone and themes, possibly in a form the writer used often.

    First-time writers of parody often choose focused parody; advanced parodists often choose general parody, and in doing so, often move from humorous to more serious imitation.

4. Prose writers can follow an author's plot and modernize the writing (as *West Side Story* updated *Romeo and Juliet*). You can also do the reverse: Provide a plot but imitate the style of Margaret Atwood or Toby Olson, or others.

    Here is an anonymous draft, based on the poetry of William Carlos Williams.

So Sweet

Your velvety skin, I touch
I just want to hold you
My lips touch you in the ritual of the past
My mouth opens, I need to taste you
My tongue explores your inner sweetness
I can't
I stop there
I must taste you all over
The more I taste, the stickier you get
I work my way down to your hardness
Peaches are so sweet
What did you think I meant?

"So Sweet" teases the reader into imagining a sexy poem. Reread Linda Douglass's poem "Cape Breton" in Chapter 4 to remind yourself that imitations can also develop into more than simply a humorous takeoff on an author. Here is an imitation of poet Maxine Kumin's work in general and her poem "Appetite" in particular. Kumin's types of moves are imported into another cultural context.

Culture Transplant

Jose Marichal

Grandma's notorious
mango fetish enacted for
an unwilling spectator
suffering from Atari withdrawal,

she scurries outside to the
quarried patio table with gaudy
Woolworth's landscapes depicted
on placemats faded by the
swooning Miami sun.
I half-watch

the vibrating juice
stain her wrinkled chin.
She giggles giddily as
orange shreds reflect light
off of her denture work.

Someday I'll develop a taste for them.

Through imitation, you can accumulate an invaluable understanding of professional writers' techniques and themes. You may find that the first time you try a parody, you are likely to stick very closely to the original or create a repetitive or uninspired approximation. But careful attention to other writers' work will eventually help you to improve and extend your own repertoire.

Self-Assignments, Challenges, and Explorations

1. Take a story and write a new ending for it, or extend the story beyond the original ending by a few minutes, hours, days, or years.

2. Take a section from a well-known story, novel, or poem and rewrite it in a different person—second person singular or third person singular instead of first person singular, for example. Or rewrite the section you've chosen from a different character's viewpoint.

3. Choose the opening to a famous novel or first line of a well-known poem—"Call me Ishmael . . . ," for example, or "I heard a Fly buzz—when I died—." Reinvent it by writing a modernized version or parody.

4. Take the dialog from a story and create a one-act play from that dialog.[2]

5. Take the "plot" from a narrative poem and expand it into a short story using the same plot.

Many of these ideas ask you not just to imitate the work of art, the writing, but to extend writers' ideas, themes, and conceits, through original writing responses of your own.

Exploring Forms

Writing in forms has long been the most widely used imitation activity for poetry writers. If *content* is the "what" of a writer's craft, then *form* is the "how." How a writer shapes, sculpts, forms, and presents words on a page has to do with the effect of form. All of us are attuned to naturally occurring forms, from the symmetry of the human body—two eyes, ears, hands, feet that nevertheless result each time in a unique human being—to the geometrically precise repeated patterns of nature—crystals, flowers, atoms, and galaxies.

In the case of poetry, forms like the sonnet and sestina and villanelle have all been popular at times for the regularized challenges they present. Each writer plays her inventiveness, style, voice, and vision off of predictable, expected, and measurable patterns. Currently, we distinguish between free verse and formal verse, the latter having more regularized and identifiable patterns—numbers of syllables, accents, and recurring rhymes. But even free verse has form. At a minimum, it has the form of poetry as distinct from prose; poetry generally has an irregular right-hand margin, words grouped in lines and sometimes in stanzas, compressed language, and so on.

Most craft textbooks ask students to write sonnets, sometimes by first providing end rhymes.[3] Any formal verse structure, particularly those such as sonnets and villanelles, which require set rhyme patterns, can be started together in class. Do this by reading through several samples and then developing or borrowing sets of end rhymes. For instance, here are the end rhymes for Theodore Roethke's villanelle "The Waking": slow, fear, go; know, ear, slow; you, there, go; how, stair, slow; do, air, go; know, near, slow, go. Metaphorical webs can be useful for metered or syllabic verse and for sestinas. Such webs ensure that the poem's end words chime the same concept. For example, before writing about the ocean, you brainstorm connected webs of words like kelp, shell, sandpiper, foam, storm-gray. Clustering can provide webs, also.

Sestinas for Experimenting with Form

Even though the sestina constraints are awesome, when writing sestinas you have the opportunity to explore repetition, stanza, and line—even syllabics.[4] Sestinas require you to write using the following patterns of sixes:

Stanza 1:	Stanza 2:	Stanza 3:	Stanza 4:	Stanza 5:	Stanza 6:
A	F	C	E	D	B
B	A	F	C	E	D
C	E	D	B	A	F
D	B	A	F	C	E
E	D	B	A	F	C
F	C	E	D	B	A

followed by a tercet (3 lines):

AB
CD
EF

Directions

1. Pick six end words—it's useful if you choose some that have the possibility of multiple meanings, like sun/son. Here are the six words I picked for a sestina of my own: gray, office, empty, secretary, paper, Kaduna. I chose these because I already had a theme

and plot: I wanted to write about trying to get housing on a college campus in Africa since the poem was being written in Africa. So the words I chose had to do with the event that I was about to fictionalize. You might also choose words that evoke a mood, season, or place—for instance, fall harvest: tomatoes, sun, gleaning, vines, dirt, bursting.

2. I find it useful to make myself a prompt sheet. I fill out the required repetition pattern of words, keeping it near my paper so I can draft for meaning while also keeping an eye on the word I'll need to use to "turn the corner" into the next line. Here is what this looked like for the first two stanzas of my sestina:

Stanza 1: gray
Office
empty
secretary
paper
Kaduna

Stanza 2: Kaduna
gray
papers
Office
secretary
empty

3. You can decide before you start if you want the lines to have the same length or not. You can aim for a similar number of accented syllables in regular patterns, as in iambic pentameter verse, or for simply the same number of syllables per line, as in syllabic verse, or you can choose not to limit yourself. For a first sestina, simply getting in the repeating word before you move to the next line may be challenge enough. I found it was in this, the completed sestina.

Futility Sestina:
Getting Housing in Kano, Nigeria

Wendy Bishop

In the morning when the sky is gray,
you return to the Housing Office
hoping it won't be empty
again. A secretary
waves a piece of paper
and tells you Mr. Ojo has gone to Kaduna.

Everyone has gone to Kaduna.
You stride past the gray
doves that nest in papers
and torn grasses along the ditches. Office
after office and secretary
after secretary, you search the empty

buildings for Mr. Ojo or Shayshay. Empty
gesture, for the word *Kaduna*
comes too easily to the secretaries
who ignore your gray
and weary face. In their offices
you are no more than a piece of paper

and no less: an illegible paper
on a desk they prefer to keep empty
or a report sent to the wrong office.
Even for a rich man in robes of fine Kaduna
cloth these endless rounds would cause a gray
sadness. Everyone is as sorry as a secretary,

everyone has the eyes of a secretary:
secretive as the flat surface of paper.
Where ever you walk, gray
doves rustle in the greenery, echo to your empty
questions. Ojo and Shayshay you imagine in Kaduna
(although you know they are not) laughing about office

matters. Each day in their offices
the secretaries
wait for you. "In Kaduna?"
you ask wisely and hand them some papers
wishing you could be as empty
as they are, sleepy, sorry, feeling gray.

Kaduna only exists on the map's rough paper.
In your office you curse the God of secretaries
emptily. You have no home, you are aging, gray.[5]

I like sestinas because they allow for more narrative development than a villanelle, for example, and do all this without involving the writer in intricate rhyme schemes—although the repetition schemes certainly are complex. After trying the sestina, you'll probably want to explore the sonnet and villanelle and less well known forms that can be found in the writers' handbooks listed at the end of the chapter. Fiction writers, too, devote themselves to formal exploration, often by changing the size of their lens—from prose poem to short short fiction, to short story, to novella, to novel.

To examine what you learn when you write in forms, you may find it useful to complete a journal entry that talks about your satisfactions and dissatisfactions with your draft in progress. Here is Tammy discussing her sestina, which appears in Chapter 9:

> I had some trouble writing my sestina, and feel it can still improve. I feel good about it because I didn't get totally frustrated, and was able to include some vivid images. I worked on it late last night and finished it this morning. It was so great. I did the writing on the computer and feel bad about some of the images I lost when they wouldn't fit into sestina form. What I'm really pleased with is that I didn't fall into humorous things.

Borrowing, Adapting, and Creating Forms

Although many of us like the challenge of working in well-known forms, others enjoy forms most when they themselves are involved in setting the rules. Here is Kelly, in a journal entry, talking about creating her own forms:

> As a general rule, I do not like fixed forms. . . . I feel restricted by them. I *do* however, like the idea of us being able to make up our *own* form—I hope to write a poem with my own form. I was also interested in some of the more uncommon forms we discussed in class, and that were in our reading such as the sestina (still haven't tried one, but I want to).
>
> Although *forms* may tend to be restrictive, I am recently able to enjoy the *challenge* they pose for me as a writer—to withstand the "abuse" of a form and still retain *meaning*.

Here is the shaped, free verse poem that Kelly later wrote for class:

The Apple and the Orange

Kelly Sheets

Hunger.
Fruit beckons . . .
Indecision.
Never a choice
so hard to make
As the apple

And the orange
Crunchy tartness of apple
Juicy sweetness of orange.
I can not have both.

Apple?   Orange?
?Orange   ?Apple
Apple.   Orange.
?   ?

Imperative decision
Can no longer wait
And off I walk with apple in hand.
I am happy with my apple
But continue finding myself
Looking back at the orange
Wondering
Would I as well been satiated
Had I walked off with the orange
Wondering
If maybe I would have been happier
Had I walked off
empty   handed
balanced.
?

The challenges you can create for yourself are endless. At the same time, form challenges aren't for everyone and aren't the right exploration to undertake at all times, as you can see by these three journal entries:

Journal 1: Lance

Form poems are quite tricky. I tried to write a sestina, then a rhyming poem, both failed before the second line, so I just tried to pick three words, wrote three lines that were sort of coherent, then wrote two more stanzas that seemed to tie together. A problem arose, a person can get so tied up in perfecting the form, that the subject matter goes out the window.

Journal 2: John

I like form poems, but they also drive me crazy. It's fun to establish guidelines and work in them; it's sort of a mental exercise, because I have to work out how to relate the idea for a given line in those guidelines. Does it rhyme with the previous line? Does the line have ten syllables? This is the fun part.

The crazy part is *also* following the guidelines, though.

Journal 3: Paul

Well, I've tried a little form before this assignment. I understand form's purpose. The way I've come to understand it is, form can be interesting if it doesn't choke content. It should be that the content naturally gives form, the way a flower grows.

Lance, John, and Paul all had varying success with their first form poems. They were frustrated, but they came to respect the lessons and limitations of forms. Instead of simply looking at sonnets and analyzing them, they learned about forms by trying some.

Self-Assignments, Challenges, and Explorations

1. Choose a traditional form like the sonnet, villanelle, or sestina. Read several poems in that form. Imitate a poem you like by writing your own version, using the author's end words.

2. With a partner, compile end words for a form and then each write a poem from the same set. Share the pieces together in a group in workshop or share them privately for fun. Talk about the different directions you took from the same word set.

3. Find a piece of experimental fiction that you like, one that doesn't match your expectations for a "traditional" short story. It may be written in the continuous present tense, in second person singular voice with shifting points of view, in sections, very lyrically like a poem, and in many other ways. Imitate that form, using your own subject matter.

4. In a group of four, each member creates a form, writes a piece, and shares it. Then, each group member writes a second piece, trying to imitate the form created by another member of the group. For instance, if Kelly was in a group, other members might decide to imitate her symmetrically shaped poem.

Writing with Others: Collaborative Composing

There is a place for language experiments in the creative writing workshop. In such experiments, the owner of the final product may not be clear because the work is composed by a group (collaborative composing), or the experiment may not lead to a form or a revision or even a final product. The following two exercises are language experiments.

Chain Poems

Directions

1. Your teacher will place a line of poetry on a blank sheet of paper, either a line she has made up or one from an author that she admires.

2. The teacher passes the paper to the student on the left, who adds a line and then folds back the first line so it doesn't show. Only the new line shows. The student passes the paper to the student on his left, and that student writes a new line that connects to the line that is visible. Then, line two is folded back so that only line three is visible. This process continues until each student has added a line to the poem but has seen only the line that precedes her line.

3. The teacher or last student to add a line reads the complete poem. Someone may write the poem on the board. The class can create an appropriate title before discussing the ways poets link lines together—by plot, sound, rhythm, and other methods.

4. Is your chain poem successful? This activity can be undertaken with prose if you use a pad of paper, placing one sentence per page, and turning a page after each new sentence is composed.

Collaborative Prose

Directions

1. Your teacher will provide you with a list of twenty or thirty opening lines—either lines taken from well-known pieces of literature or lines he has made up.

2. Each class member chooses a different opening line.

3. Write your line at the top of a blank sheet of paper and start to develop a narrative, writing for two or three minutes.

4. After three minutes, your teacher will stop you and ask you to pass your sheet to the writer on your left. Read the story you've been given and keep writing, trying to continue the piece your neighbor began. Your teacher will ask you to pass your developing stories around the class at three- or four-minute intervals.

5. At the end of thirty minutes—or when every writer has added to every story—the last writer is asked to provide some sort of closure, a sense of ending to the story.

6. Your teacher may choose to play background music as you write.

7. Read as many of these collaborative stories aloud as time allows. What happened? What techniques did writers use to support a story line? How did they rebel? How did they end pieces?

8. If you like any part of the story you ended up with, revise it as a piece of your own.

Challenge Writing

Challenge writing fits loosely into the category of occasional writing. Traditionally, writers have been asked to write in memory of important events, persons, or places. You might challenge yourself to write occasional verse or prose, or you and a class partner might agree to attack the same theme from your own particular angles of vision. The "Same Images" exercise, which follows, can help you do this also.

When composing as a group, you need to be aware that many writers are extremely possessive about their drafts. They worry that others will steal their ideas, lines, plots. In a way, English teachers have contributed to this idea of spontaneous, pure, and original generation with lectures on great writers, creative geniuses, and seemingly inviolate genre distinctions—even by talks on research paper plagiarism.

You need to learn how few absolutely original new ideas there are in the world and how productive borrowing and imitation can be. Writers must capitalize on the fact that they exist in a world full of texts:

> Writers are always borrowing. . . . This is a basic element of textuality. Texts are produced through a combination of the writer's experiences as a human being and the writer's knowledge of earlier texts. Sometimes, however, the intertextual relationship is very much in the foreground: this is true in translation, interpretation, adaptation, and parody. (Scholes, Comley, and Ulmer 129)

Of course, you also need to understand what plagiarism is and what writers can do to become aware of and acknowledge their own influences. Imitating another writer's work is a compliment to that writer, but you would be wise to keep track of your own learning and borrowing in a journal or in notes to your work. In-class group writing practice sessions are particularly useful for bringing up these issues. They allow you to explore your own feelings about originality and borrowing.

In an effort to show the many directions a piece of writing can take, even when generated by the same image, Scott Herzer and Jill Robinson have devised an exercise that allows you and your fellow class members to compose poems or prose pieces from the same basic images in order to compare the results.[6]

Same Images Exercise

Directions

1. Divide into groups of three or four.

2. Each member of a group is given a 3″-by-5″ notecard and asked to write down four "original" images. Here are the images contributed by one student:
   - I shake hands with a handless man
   - A filmstrip on cell division
   - Green, glowing sheets of ice
   - The child cheers the snow shoveler with sharp barks

3. Next, group members read their images aloud, and the group lists the best image from each member on another 3″-by-5″ card. Here are the images compiled by one group (one image per group member):
   - Cassette tape of Albert King . . . "I been lookin' you over, but I see that your bread ain't done."
   - The blood had hardened like pavement
   - The lawn sprawled out like a dog
   - A filmstrip on cell division

4. Groups then exchange their best images' cards and, from the card they receive, choose the single most interesting image. Group members each freewrite about that image for ten minutes; in essence, they accept the challenge of writing from the same image.

5. Last, each writer takes his or her freewrite home and writes a piece, in any genre, that in some manner retains the reference to the image used in the freewrite.

When these pieces are compared during the next workshop, you will see that vastly different pieces of writing have developed from the same image prompt.

Experimentation: Writing Against the Rules

Clearly, experimentation is a matter of playing with control *and* with freedom. You need to know the rules in order to loosen them and to learn from breaking them. The following activities do just that— give you some rules and then ask you to play against those rules.

Reversals

In *Writing Poetry,* David Kirby describes reversals as writing pieces "in which a stereotype or received truth is simply turned on its head.''[7] Most of us can write reversals fairly naturally, as in the "Confessions of a Male Muse" found in Chapter 2. Here is another reversal, started during an in-class freewriting.

Another Silly Love Poem

Lance Nutter

Holding the flowers stem up,
I forcefully cram them down the
sink's garbage grinding unit.
I flip the switch and the room
is instantly filled with a cupboard
shaking incessant roaring
which slowly oscillates toward
a high pitched squeal
as the blades begin moving freely.
Still feeling less than vindicated,
I leave the grinder running,
slowly walk out of the kitchen,
and snap off the light.
After all, it is her house. . . .

Lance's vision predicts that love is a topic ripe for reversal. For an entirely different type of reversal, as a class, "rewrite" a famous poem by reversing the meanings of words. That is, *hot* becomes *cold* and *mothers* become *fathers* and *night* becomes *day* and *moons* become *suns.* Word-for-word reversals involving antonym swapping result in surreal, exotic collaborative parodies. Of course, the reversal soon breaks down but reversal word play helps you discover the effect of oxymorons—two words of opposite meanings that are presented together—and intentionally strained juxtaposition.

Multimedia Cross-Cultural Exercise

This activity is based on an exercise designed by Carolyn Kremers and relies on multiple sensory stimuli to give you access to other cultures and the world views of others.[8]

Directions

1. The teacher or a student brings in slides that illustrate life in another culture. The writing sample that follows was based on slides of life in an Eskimo village presented by Carolyn.

2. Class members are asked to freewrite after each slide.

3. The presenter shares a tape of storytelling, poetry, or music in the culture's language.

4. Class members write after listening to the tape.

5. The presenter then passes around photo books. For the presentation of Eskimo life, Carolyn also shared Eskimo language ABC books and other artifacts.

6. Class members choose a photo or book and then an artifact to write about.

7. The presenter then asks class members to write dialogue from the point of view of a character from that culture.

8. Class members take these extensive freewrites home and draft a piece for a future workshop.

My own writing from this activity resulted in a prose poem that used many of Carolyn's prompts, so I'll include it here to illustrate.

Cross-Cultural Genres

Wendy Bishop

Here is an Eskimo ABC book. Here is Tununak graveyard, filled with snow, blown in shapes of animals moving just beneath the cold skin. Picket fence pierces like spearheads, herds life toward an orthodox cross.

Houses in a white on white landscape sit as square ships, antennae pointed toward outer space which doesn't exist in a land where "they deny planning." The universe exists, yet an elder's narrative seems, unfairly, a mouthful of glottal stops, remolding my conception of story—plot, tension, dramatic moment—I drift and slip into another meaning system with Adam Fisher, nasal laugh and nasal laugh and nasal laugh.

We have no real patience for stories. We who "always talk about what's going to happen later" never stop to examine what is. She's young—just started having periods. Shimmys skinny slim hips, squeezes them into comfortable straight Wranglers, walks different but like her older brother, calls electricity to the ends of crackling black hair that she smooths in hanks.

> Silence is built into the land, pale off-tan
> grass, gathered Sundays after the traveling
> priest moves out of the village on a snow
> machine. Machine sputters and shrives silence
> then engulfs the Bering Sea while Adam Fisher
> tells a story, nasal laugh and nasal laugh and
> nasal laugh.
>
> Things with hair stand out: musk ox, seal,
> men, women. Perspective is plotted by color of
> bronze skin and enlivened faces against muted
> palette of weathered buildings, steam of sweat
> houses, undergreen of tundra, far gray of
> airplane shadow. "They are too indirect, too
> inexplicit. They don't make sense. They just
> leave without saying anything." In the Tununak
> graveyard, snow shifts shapes, graves fill, grass
> bows down, As Bs Cs tussle with sea wind. They
> leave, they leave without saying anything.[9]

Bilingual Writing Exercise

Another way to explore a different culture is to include words in a different language in your poem. For some writers, this is not merely an exercise but a way of saving and savoring the multiple cultures that influence their lives. For instance, as someone new to composing in English, Van often used Vietnamese to great effect in her poems, as in this one.

Rain of Yesterday

Van Mong Trinh

Black clouds race across the sky
Thunder roars every five minutes
Rain falls hard and seems to never stop
Chills cover my shaken body
My eyes are fixed in the direction of a water hole
That seems larger and fuller as minutes pass

> *Mot, hai, ba*—I count and jump naked into a puddle
> to the openness and bathe under the pure
> water that feels tingly, refreshing even when it's cold
> You call for me and tell me to come inside
> You dry me and put the clothes on my back
> You brush my tangled and brittle hair

> You make me go to sleep on a warm bed
> How can I? While the music of the rain
> *Tieng khe khe* of hollow bamboo forest
> *Tieng ruc rich* of Cam Nam Stream
> Echoes heavily on my warm soft bed.
>
> *Am, Am!* The sound of thunder strikes
> Awakening me from the rains of yesterday
> Now I'm cold and need the warmth of your touch
> To chase this blue and lonely world away.

Even if you are not bilingual, and, as Van was, experiencing that extra impulse to make sense of two competing language systems, you still may enjoy exploring the complexities of sound and sense that occur when you insert a second language into another text. You'll have choices to make. Should you explain what the words mean or can you do that by context? As you can see, it's fairly clear in Van's poem that the words "Am, Am!" are the sound of thunder, but this won't always be the case. Should you use only a few words or a lot? Should you use the title of your work to help explain your decision to use two or more languages?

Directions

1. Every student brings a foreign language dictionary to class—French/English, Chinese/English, and so on.

2. Choose a dictionary for a language in which you have *no fluency at all.*

3. Find ten words in the foreign language that intrigue you.

4. Write a poem draft or prose sketch that uses those words.

5. Share your drafts aloud.

or

1. Complete the same exercise using a language with which you do have some familiarity by first listing some of your favorite words from that language.

2. In workshop, look at revised versions of these pieces and discuss the ways the second language words add to or detract from the effectiveness of the piece.

or

1. If you are fairly fluent in a second language, translate a poem or piece of prose from that language and share your efforts with

the class, providing both the original language version and the translation.

2. Talk about the choices you made in moving from one language to another.

With all these exercises, be sure to read drafts and translations aloud. Here's a poem, written from a postcard that was shared in class, that uses and plays with language(s) and cultural clichés in several ways.

La Lune-Luna-Moon

Sean Carswell

Sitting *dans la classe de francais*
Regarde a picture of an arched back blue mermaid fountain in a
    Mexican veranda
I look closer and it is me inside.
Sitting shirtless, khaki shorts, toasting *la luna* and the shadow
    she casts on the fish-tailed two-armed Venus de *Mexico*.
The moon—resting on Her power to raise oceans and bloat women—
    winks and the avocado-breasted Venus smiles to me
"*Como esta*," she says with the open sexuality only possible in
    the tongue native to Celia Cruz, "*Yo estoy Luna Luna*."
I can only toss my book of Lorca poems into the fountain water
    and say (in my beaten dog language), "Then run Luna, Luna,
    Luna, lest the academy turn you to logic."
Feliciano is in the hills singing, "And these memories lose
    their meaning, when I think of love as something new."
She flips her spider spun-chili powder hair onto her refried
    shoulder and says, "You thought I was a blond, eh gringo?"
"I was betting pure Scandinavian," I say, "but I'm only an
    American with American dreams."
"*Que lastima*." Luna Luna swings her guacamole tail onto the
    marble pedestal, and scales dissolve to feet. She flicks her
    eyes to faraway hills, "*Vamanos*, James Dean."
I start towards her when my professor forces my potato shoulder
    back into my straight jacket school desk without as much as
    an, "*Adonde vas*?"
And I slip slop back into another *jour ordinaire*.

Collage Writing

I take the idea of collage writing from painting and the plastic arts. You may have seen paintings by Picasso and his contemporaries. In their work, strips of newspaper articles were added to painted areas, and eventually even objects were included. You may yourself have created magazine collages to decorate a wall in your room. The effectiveness of collage results from the juxtaposition of unexpected textures, print type, colors, and images. In prose, you may fragment experience and change the normal chronological order of presentation, or present only scenes or snapshots, as in the sketch "Fragments of Paul," found in Chapter 10. The following exercise forces you to create one form of a collage, a composite portrait of an individual.

The Fifteen-Sentence Portrait

This exercise asks you to write a portrait, following specific directions, about a person you know.[10] The constraints of the directions may help you to discover new aspects of this individual since you are following sentence-level prompts even as you develop your content. Following these prompts keeps you from directing your observations in familiar, perhaps predictable, ways. Take the results of your guided writing and create a collage portrait of that person.

Directions

1. Picture in your mind a person you have strong feelings about. You may not like them but you should feel strongly about them. They can be living or dead but they should be someone you know or knew personally rather than a famous character.

2. For a title, choose an emotion or a color that represents this person to you. You will not mention the individual's name in the writing.

3. For a first line starter, choose one of the following:
   - You stand there . . .
   - No one is here . . .
   - In this (memory, photograph, dream, or whatever), you are . . .
   - I think sometimes . . .
   - The face is . . .
   - We had been . . .

   Complete this sentence.

4. After your first sentence, build a portrait of this individual, writing the sentences according to the following directions:

   Sentence 2: Write a sentence with a color in it.

   Sentence 3: Write a sentence with a part of the body in it.

   Sentence 4: Write a sentence with a simile (a comparison using *like* or *as*).

Sentence 5: Write a sentence of over twenty-five words.

Sentence 6: Write a sentence under eight words.

Sentence 7: Write a sentence with a piece of clothing in it.

Sentence 8: Write a sentence with a wish in it.

Sentence 9: Write a sentence with an animal in it.

Sentence 10: Write a sentence in which three or more words alliterate; that is, they begin with the same initial consonant: "She has been *l*eft, *l*ately with *l*ess and *l*ess time to think. . . . "

Sentence 11: Write a sentence with two commas.

Sentence 12: Write a sentence with a smell and a color in it.

Sentence 13: Write a sentence with a simile (a comparison using *like* or *as*).

Sentence 14: Write a sentence that could carry an exclamation point (but don't use the exclamation point).

Sentence 15: Write a sentence to end this portrait that uses the word or words you chose for a title.

5. Now, read this freewrite to yourself. Underline sentences in which you discovered new things about this individual or about your feelings and attitudes toward him or her.

6. Volunteers may read portraits aloud to help the class discover the variation possible within the guided sentence format.

7. Use this freewrite as a starting point for a poem or prose portrait or simply revise what you have. Do anything you need to make this a piece of writing that you like. Choose a new title, use the person's real name, and so on.

Here is a journal entry that explains the effects of this exercise:

I really enjoyed the "portrait in words" assignment that led me to my first prose poem. The way the guided assignment forced me to write sentences that don't necessarily go together left my piece with a nice stream of consciousness effect. When I revised it, I tried to preserve the spontaneous quality yet break up the long sentences somewhat. I eliminated a part in the end about kissing a grandmother goodnight because it was sentimental and made me sick to my stomach to read aloud. . . . I changed the Buick to a Dart. I added some sensual details that I thought of later, like making the Dart into a square white dart. . . . I moved the line about hot peaches from the second line to the first at the suggestion of someone in my workshop. After revising, I was glad I had kept the early draft because I ended up changing some things back. I'm going to have to sit on this one further.

These revision comments show that collage is artfully shaped juxtaposition. You can start out as if you are playing pick-up-sticks: images dropping where they will on the page. During subsequent revisions, though, you'll want to eliminate the dross or overly easy, sentimental phrase, and add and expand in order to improve the piece.

Variations

1. Use the prompts to write a self-portrait or a portrait of a famous person.

2. Use the prompts for a collaborative writing activity: Each writer starts a paragraph using a narrative (storytelling) first line such as: "Listen Jim . . . " or "During those years, Sheila . . . ." Or, use first lines from famous novels or stories. Each writer, obeying the sentence directions given by the teacher, writes a line and then passes the paper clockwise. Stories grow as each writer writes a line and passes it along.

3. All writers begin with the same prompt line in order to see the variations possible when you add personal context to a predictable beginning, under the constraints of similar format directions.

Self-Assignments, Challenges, and Explorations

1. Find an artist who works with collage and try to write a piece in prose or poetry that captures the essence of the artist's juxtapositions.

2. After reading "Fragments of Paul" in Chapter 10, write your own "Fragments of . . . " piece, describing an individual from your past. Try for a snapshot effect. In fact, you might look through old photo albums for ideas.

3. Try a physical collage: Take pieces from several of your poems or prose and weave them together into a new whole; a computer speeds this activity. Or, dip into your journal entries, find some lines you like, and use each line to start a new stanza or section in a piece you're writing.

4. Mix found piece techniques with your own commentary. That is, alternate environmental text—directions, a speech, another author's prose or poetry—with your own.

Multiple-Voice Writing

At its simplest, you might think of multiple-voice writing as speech collage—a monolog or braided dialog in which the narrator of the poem is inconsistent, shifting from speaker to speaker, or in which the narrator's voice is interwoven with exposition. Voices may recur (one speaker/several selves) or several voices may enter in and then fade out. It used to be recommended that a writer try very hard to find his or her singular and personal voice. Nowadays, we recognize that all individuals have different personas and developing personalities. For example, the way we present ourselves to friends may be very different from the way we present ourselves to parents or teachers. Although most of us don't feel we are split into different psychological selves, many of us can identify healthy multiple aspects of our "self." Sometimes, we may find it profitable to let these selves and voices become manifest in our writing.

Multiple-voiced writings, then, may intentionally include:

1. Other speakers, identified or not

2. Interruptions and digressions

3. Parallel texts

4. Texts within texts

5. Incomplete and fragmentary texts

6. Rule breaking: continuous present tense, multiple points of view, foregrounding of voices

7. Disconnection, dreaminess, inwardness, illumination

Some of the writings presented in this chapter dip into multiple-voice writing. Tiffany Fussell in "Un Chien Andalou" describes scenes from a movie while an imperative voice (signalled by directives and exclamation points) tells the reader what to notice. Kelly Sheets in "The Apple and the Orange" presents an interior monolog with almost-voiced teasings of the two fruits that tempt the narrator to eat. My own prose poem "Cross-Cultural Genres" weaves direct quotes from a handout on cultural stereotypes into the visual narrative.

Self-Assignments, Challenges, and Explorations

1. For a warm-up, try writing in or through the voice of another person; for a persona poem, choose a famous or notorious character. Or write about an object; undertake the voice of an heirloom cup or become a personified fruit or vegetable.

2. Write a dialog between two voices that are aspects of a single person, place, or thing.

3. Write a piece in which you and someone with your opposite attributes are both given voice.

4. Choose some of your own ways of presenting yourself, for instance to a lover, to a parent, to a census taker, or to a doctor. Freewrite on the same subject in each of those voices, then compile those voices into one piece.

5. Write a piece and then show it on a page with written commentary in the margin (somewhat as I did in my presentation of the writing workshop in Chapter 4). However, allow your commentary voice to interact with the text, analyze it, respond to it, and so on.

6. Look back through your previous writings. Find pieces that seem to have definite "voices." Identify two very different voices and see if you can use them both together in a new piece.

7. Write a circular piece in which you end at the same line, place, scene where you began.

8. Take a story that you've written in traditional form. Create a new voice—a narrator who will interrupt and comment on the events of the story. Insert these comments or narratives into the old text, creating a newly interrupted or digressing story.

I hope this chapter has encouraged you to experiment and that your experiments have illuminated the ways in which writing challenges and self-set writing rules can work for you. Before you set your own rules, of course, you need to learn what rules had been agreed upon before you came on the writing scene. Writing is play, but it is play that demands a lot of hard work and preparation. Experimentation is part of that work and play; it allows you to expand your writing knowledge and increase the size of your bag of tricks. The books listed at the end of this chapter should prove particularly useful as you continue your travels into language.

Notes

1. Koch and Farrell's anthology provides useful readings for poetry parodies and imitations.
2. This exercise was developed by Scholes, Comley, and Ulmer, and is found in *Textbook*.
3. See Minot, Nims, or Wallace for discussions of various forms and some exercises. See Padgett or Turco or Preminger for handbooks and encyclopedias dealing with forms.
4. See Wallace for definitions and humorous examples, and Dacy and Jauss's anthology *Strong Measures* for instances of contemporary poets writing in this and other forms.

5. Published in *Kansas Quarterly* 19 (1987).
6. See Herzer and Robinson. Sections of "Same Images Exercise" are reprinted from Bishop.
7. Kirby 14. For a sample of his own writing in this form, see David Kirby's "The Cows Are Going to Paris: A Pastoral," in *Saving the Young Men of Vienna*, 67–68 (Madison: U of Wisconsin P, 1987).
8. See Kremers.
9. Published in *Tonantzin* 6 (1990): 17.
10. "The Fifteen-Sentence Portrait" directions are reprinted from Bishop.

Sources and Readings

Bartlett, Lee, ed. *Talking Poetry: Conversations in the Workshop with Contemporary Poets.* Albuquerque: U of New Mexico P, 1987.

Bishop, Wendy. *Released into Language.* Urbana, IL: National Council of Teachers of English, 1990.

Dacy, Philip, and David Jauss, eds. *Strong Measures: Contemporary American Poetry in Traditional Forms.* New York: Harper, 1986.

Dillard, Annie. *The Writing Life.* New York: Harper, 1989.

Herzer, Scott, and Jill Robinson. "Your Ideas Are Unique." *Exercise Exchange* 35 (1989): 43–45.

Kirby, David. *Writing Poetry: Where Poems Come From and How to Write Them.* Boston: The Writer, Inc., 1989.

Koch, Kenneth, and Kate Farrell. *Sleeping on the Wing: An Anthology of Modern Poetry with Essays on Reading and Writing.* New York: Random House, 1981.

Kremers, Carolyn. "Through the Eyes and Ears of Another Culture: Invention Activities and a Writers' Workshop." *Exercise Exchange* 35 (1989): 3–11.

Minot, Stephen. *Three Genres: The Writing of Poetry, Fiction, and Drama.* 3d ed. Englewood Cliffs, NJ: Prentice-Hall, 1982.

Nims, John Frederick. *Western Wind: An Introduction to Poetry.* 2d ed. New York: Random, 1983.

Padgett, Ron, ed. *The Teachers & Writers Handbook of Poetic Forms.* New York: Teachers & Writers Collaborative, 1987.

Preminger, Alex, ed. *Princeton Encyclopedia of Poetry and Poetics.* Princeton: Princeton UP, 1965.

Scholes, Robert, Nancy R. Comley, and Gregory L. Ulmer. *Textbook: An Introduction to Literary Language.* New York: St. Martin's Press, 1988.

Stafford, William, and Marvin Bell. *Segues: A Correspondence in Poetry.* Boston: D. R. Godine, 1983.

Turco, Lewis. *The New Book of Forms: A Handbook of Poetics.* Hanover: UP of New England, 1986.

Waldrep, Tom, ed. *Writers on Writing.* New York: Random House, 1985.

Wallace, Robert. *Writing Poems.* 2d Ed. Boston: Little Brown, 1987.

Chapter 6

Listening to Others

I do get other people to read my work before I send it to a publisher. My husband reads everything and he's very helpful. I also meet every week with a group of five professional writers, and we read what we're working on aloud to one another and have it criticized. I also send it off to my agent, and she tells me what she thinks of it. So, five or six people read my work before it goes off to an editor.

—JANE YOLON

In previous chapters, we've seen that enrollment in a workshop offers an immediate opportunity for a writer to "go public" with writing. But many other moments in a writer's life also lend themselves to sharing. Students may share their writing during conferences with their teacher. They may share with friends and family. They may share with informal writing groups outside of the academic classroom, and a few may share, eventually, with editors and agents.

Sharing also includes your willingness to explore and learn about the writing of others. Professional writers don't simply *produce* and export writing; they are also seriously attentive to the writing of others, whether in the form of a manuscript, a performance, or a published book. Novelist Wallace Stegner claims: "If you're not a hungry reader, you're not likely to be a writer. Reading is one way you learn writing" (qtd. in Bunge 119). Although some of us have been lifelong readers, we may nevertheless need to cultivate the habit of reading *for writing*—switching from mystery novels to collections of poetry, for example, if we hope to excel in that genre, and paying attention to the moves writers incorporate into their texts that usually go unnoticed when we're reading only to pass the time. This chapter suggests ways you can enter the reading/writing and the writing/reading transaction more thoroughly.

The Student and Teacher Writing Conference

Writers have some natural hesitations about sharing their work with others. First, they may have set themselves high, perhaps impossible, standards, and they may feel that others will judge them as not having met those standards. Also, they may be intimidated by the power of those works of literature they read and love. Others may be too humble or underconfident to set any standards at all.

Some of us start writing due to an inner drive to explore our current feelings or our past, and we need to develop ways to distance ourselves from our, perhaps, overly personal texts. To accomplish this, we often need outside help. In the next chapter we discuss in detail the ways writers can use the detailed revision suggestions of classmates. In this chapter, however, we look at one of your primary resources—the writing teacher. Usually your creative writing teacher is a published writer, with broad experience in both academic and creative genres. As a teacher, though, he works with many students and reads many manuscripts. The classroom time the teacher can devote to your work is limited, but it can be enhanced if you meet with him in conference. Many teachers arrange conferences as a regular part of the workshop; many others who don't require conferences are glad to meet with you on an individual basis, as time allows.

The following excerpt is from a midsemester portfolio conference. Portfolios, in which you present your best work to that particular point, are considered more thoroughly in Chapter 8. In this conference transcript, Missy and her teacher, Heather, review Missy's poems and stories and Missy's own midsemester self-evaluation. This transcript represents only a few minutes of a twenty-minute consultation. As you read, remember that each teacher has her own conferencing style: Some are direct, telling the student just what to do; some reflect, telling the student what they see or feel in response to the work; some elicit, asking only a few questions and working as a sounding board for the writer's shared thoughts and feelings; and some move from one of these styles to another.

A Writing Conference

HEATHER: How did you feel about your portfolio after you went over the evaluation?

MISSY: I was pleased. I didn't think I did as well as you said I did.

HEATHER: What are the strengths that you perceive, aside from what I said?

MISSY:	Um, I think I'm getting better at detail.
HEATHER:	Okay, that's what you wrote down here. And your editing and revision skills. And that's the main thing I'm evaluating, as I said in class. Can you take something and improve it and make it better, change it by what we did? And your details in the story are really nice. Let's talk about your story and then we'll go to your poems and then we'll talk about where you're at right now. Right in here, did you want it to be pretty ambiguous whether it was really happening, when she's in that dreamlike state?
MISSY:	I don't know. When we had the two people edit our papers? Both of those girls thought that it was a dream. And when I wrote it, I didn't mean it to be like that, but they both took it that way. So I don't know if I should change it around and like make it like that if that's how everybody was taking it or what? I wasn't really sure.
HEATHER:	I like the way as a writer that you're manipulating the facts there, and she's kind of floating in and out. To me it makes the story scarier and more threatening if she doesn't know this is really happening. I think you might want to give us a few more pointers here, maybe, to let us know that there is something really happening, maybe she thinks it's another sound or something. . . . Do you know what I'm saying?
MISSY:	Yeah.
HEATHER:	But, the story works. The atmosphere in the bedroom is very well done—you were supposed to do setting and character this time. I think you did a wonderful job of both. Great details and memories attached to all of the objects that he's stealing. I was robbed once, and it's bad enough just to be robbed when you're not there, but to be robbed when you're there—I can see where it would be wrenching, and that comes through in your story. And the parents come in—um, are the parents home?
MISSY:	Not at the time.
HEATHER:	But then they do come home?
MISSY:	They come home. This is like the next day, I guess.
HEATHER:	Okay, is that clear? Is there a clear transition?
MISSY:	It says in the beginning that they're not home.
HEATHER:	Okay. And so, they come home in the night and in

	the morning . . . that's probably clear. Okay. I was wondering if you wanted to add on to this story? How do you feel about the ending?
MISSY:	I didn't really know how to end it.
HEATHER:	Okay [slight laugh]—it could have gone on and on?
MISSY:	Yeah, I'm not good at that kind of stuff.
HEATHER:	After you read my comments, did you consider the ending further?
MISSY:	I was thinking about either stopping here or just not talking about him getting caught. Making the reader go back and think about, like it happened in the future, or some . . .
HEATHER:	That was my impulse too, not to skip way ahead, but to leave her right there, just have her waking up, sitting in the room and reacting to what's happened. I think that would be stronger because it keeps her closer to the story. . . . What about your poetry? What do you see as the strengths right now, and then what weaknesses are you working on?
MISSY:	I have a problem with line lengths. I always want it to go exactly how it should go . . .
HEATHER:	You mean with the phrasing? How we naturally speak the lines?
MISSY:	I guess. I'm writing it in a poem and the second line has five phrases in it or whatever, you would think that the last one would have to have it too, and I have a hard time switching it around.
HEATHER:	So you're very balanced, formal when you approach poetry and you'd like to loosen that up a little and play around some more?
MISSY:	And I've always been taught that I have to rhyme everything and so . . .
HEATHER:	So you're breaking away from that and finding out, what do you do if you don't rhyme? What are the rules here? Have you been trying? What techniques have you been trying in your second portfolio now? With the poems that you've been working on?
MISSY:	Varying my line length.
HEATHER:	Okay. What rules have you been using, making for yourself? How have you been making those decisions? I'm interested because that's a problem everybody has.

MISSY:	Usually I write it how I think it should be and then, if it's too compact, I just go and change it. If I end a line, I use a word, so you'd have to go on to the next line to read, so it doesn't just stop and you keep on reading.
HEATHER:	Good, that's a good way to do it, looking at the meaning of the sentence and getting the reader kind of surprised and twisted through the poem . . . that's good. I like that.
MISSY:	I'm trying to do that. . . . I'm not really succeeding that well but I'm trying. . . .
HEATHER:	Okay, I'd like to see some of your new poems in a second. [Conference continues.]

Suggestions for Preparing for a Teacher Conference

Conferences can take place informally—before, right after, or even during a class—and they can also take place by appointment in your teacher's office or at a comfortable campus location. The least effective conferences are those where one or both of the members are poorly prepared, and writing hasn't been completed or read ahead of time or been brought along for discussion. A little preparation can make conferences more comfortable and productive. Here are some suggestions for setting up a successful one.

When Arranged by the Teacher

1. Be sure you know the time and place for the conference.

2. Ask if there are any special materials (portfolios, drafts, peer response sheets, and so on) that you should bring.

3. Ask if the teacher wants to see any materials ahead of time.

4. Ask about the general purpose of the conference.

5. Ask approximately how long the conference will last.

6. Be on time, but expect to wait if conferences preceding yours run slightly overtime.

7. Try to formulate some questions that you have about your class progress or participation, in case there is time to pose them.

When Arranged by the Writer

1. Be sure to remind the teacher of the conference time. If you arrange for a conference a week ahead, it can't hurt to remind her during the class preceding the conference. Plan for a reasonable amount of time (10–40 minutes).

2. Try to be clear about why you've set up a conference: to discuss your class progress in general, to review your last story in particular.

3. Be sure to provide your teacher with a copy of your work as far ahead of the conference as possible. If she had a draft earlier in the term, don't assume she still has or remembers the draft.

4. If you want to share a new draft, be sure to provide a copy of the earlier draft. Even if the teacher commented extensively on the earlier draft, keep in mind that that was many, many papers ago.

5. Try to have several questions in mind and work to make the most of your conference time by being focused and prepared.

6. Be on time, and call ahead if you have to change times or the conference focus.

7. Help end the conference on time unless the teacher invites you to continue.

Don't Forget the Writing Center

Most colleges and universities today offer students individualized tutoring through an English department or campus writing center. Check and see if any of the tutors are willing to tutor in creative writing. Writing center tutors can provide a valuable audience, as you'll see in the journal responses that follow. Tutors sometimes *feel* less threatening than a teacher, yet they are still well-trained responders and editors whose interest is helping you develop as a writer. The suggestions for conferences that I listed above are applicable to writing center conferences as well, particularly since the tutor has not seen your work previously in the class workshop. Keep in mind that you can accomplish only so much in a thirty- to sixty-minute tutoring session. You'll probably want to return several times during the semester.

Writing tutors can help you generate ideas and draft and/or polish your writing. Here is John, who had "poem fright," explaining how tutors helped him get started with invention techniques: "What we ended up doing was to make a list of fifteen words pertaining to the ocean (my topic), each of us contributing five; this was the 'Safety List.' We started to write our own poems, and whenever we got stuck, we'd pick a word from the list, which usually helped." In this instance, the writing center tutors provided both an audience and help that the teacher couldn't have provided, for the teacher wasn't around the evening John started to draft.

Tutors can also discuss your already completed work in some detail:

Today I met with Marcia at the Writing Center. I brought four poems with me, two of which were to be evaluated portfolio pieces and two of which were to be extras. I had already decided which of the four I felt the strongest about but I wanted to see if she agreed with me. After reading the four, she *did* pick the two I had ("Grey" and "Escape," which has now undergone a title change to "Calligraphy"). We mostly worked on those two, but she also gave me some suggestions for my extras ("Night" and "An Old Man and a Tree").

We both felt that "Calligraphy" was good but needed some work—certain words taken out or changed. She liked the form of it. She really liked "Grey" and only had a problem with two lines of it. I agreed with her partially, and re-worded one of the two lines. The one line that I *didn't* change: "The grey passion" ("returns and I . . . ") bothered her a bit because I am recalling a childhood memory, and she couldn't associate "passion" with a "child." To me, this was an important part of the poem, however, because I *was* a very passionate (as in *emotional*) child, and if I had not been so, the memory of my feelings to the windy, grey sky on the island would not be as vivid as they still are today.

Being tutored on your work, as you can see, does not mean you lose control of your writing decisions. Instead, the tutor can offer you an expert but friendly response, helping you revise.

Sharing with Friends and Family

> Don't be afraid to ask for others' advice too. Your best friends and family can often be your very best critics and are only interested in improving your work, so don't be afraid! They may actually have good ideas, but you never have to take their suggestions.
>
> —Beth

> We can better understand, then, the effects of other people on our writing if we distinguish between a dangerous audience and a safe audience. Whether an audience is one or the other is partly an objective matter: are your readers a bunch of hostile critics just itching for you to make a mistake, or are they a crowd of friends or fans who look forward to enjoying what you have to say and won't hold anything against you even if you have difficulties?
>
> But safety and danger are partly subjective matters, too. Some people are terrified no matter how friendly the audience is, while others are not intimidated even by sharks.
>
> —Peter Elbow (*Writing with Power* 184)

Although many writers find it useful—perhaps even comforting—to share writing with family and friends, they also have reasons to feel reluctant about sharing writing in this way. In the quote above, Beth assumes you want to have the advice of others concerning your work. She assumes that friends and family are *primarily* concerned with supporting your work. She knows you may be afraid to share but lets you know you might get some "good ideas" if you do. She reminds you that you are always in control—you don't have to do anything to your work against your will.

In the second quote, author Peter Elbow lets you know that there are two types of audience for your work: safe ones and dangerous ones. Safe audiences support you; sometimes they just want to hear what you have to say. Safe audiences are forgiving. In a way, safe audiences don't see mistakes as any big deal, for mistakes are a necessary step in your development. Safe audiences are *in favor* of your development. Dangerous audiences have overly high standards. They compare your work with previous images of successful writing and expect to find your work lacking. Dangerous audiences are all too willing to show you the flaws in your work—each and every one. Dangerous audiences are unable to temper a plain reading with any appreciation of the potential of your work-in-progress.

Finally, Peter Elbow reminds you that those you view as safe or as dangerous for you as audiences may shift over time and be subject to your own (mis)perceptions. That is, if you're not careful, you can "read" an audience wrong, based on other criteria. For instance, your life experiences may allow you to define family and friends as people who generally say positive things about you. If you offer them a chance to respond to your writing and they note a flaw, however, you may perceive them as failing on two fronts: as family or friends and as audience.

Should you listen to these other audiences, other voices? Should you share your work with family and friends? In general, my answer is yes—if you value their opinion, clearly want to allow them into your writing world, and learn where to place them as safe audiences. Before giving you some guidelines for such sharing, I suggest you explore your own feelings about sharing writing with family and friends by completing the following journal entries and then sharing "stories" based on those entries with classmates in a small group.

Self-Analysis Exercise: Sharing with Friends and Family

1. In one column, list all the types of writing you do (letters, memos, stories, poems, academic writing—research papers, essay tests, and so on). In a second column, list all the people with whom you've shared your writing in the last several years (friends, family members, teachers, boss and/or employees, and so on). Be as specific as possible. Then, link up the types of writing with the person. Do you share each type of writing with one special person

or is any person the recipient of more than one type of writing? What does your list tell you about the audiences for your writing? Here's a partial example from my own list:

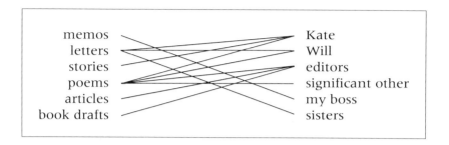

Is there anyone on your list whose audience role has shifted? For instance, you started out sharing only letters with this person but now you also like to share your stories.

2. From each of your audiences, decide how "critical" a response you prefer. Let 1 stand for "Just let me know you read it." Let 5 stand for "Tell me what works and mention a *few* revision directions." And let 10 stand for "Tear it apart and tell me how to write it better." Rate each of these audiences for your work on this 1–10 scale. For example:
   Kate 7
   Will 7
   editors 8
   my boss 1
   reviewers 1
   sisters 1
   significant other 4

3. Were there any surprises in the strength of response you expect from each audience? That is, did you suggest that you'd like some of your readers to be more receptive? Did you learn that you expect all your audiences, no matter who, to give you really detailed criticism?

4. Do your audiences respond like this? How do you feel when your significant other responds at the 10 level and your teacher responds at the 1 level?

5. Tell the story of the best response you ever received to a piece of your writing (from family or friends) and the worst response.

6. How do you indicate to a reader what type of response you'd like? In the case of those on your list, would you like to change anyone's response level? Explore some strategies for doing this.

Taking Control of Response Situations

When sharing with family and friends, it is usually up to you to set the rules of the exchange. Here are some suggestions.

Start by deciding if you are more committed, at that moment, to *sharing* or *learning*. If your object is simply to share a piece with someone you care about, don't expect more than you can hope to get. That is, people have different response styles. A quiet "that's nice" from a friend should be appreciated for the honest communication that it is. Generally, an individual won't change his general style just because you're venturing to share an important (to you) piece of writing. If your friend never jumps up and down in excitement over events in his own life, he's not going to do so simply because you shared a story. Conversely, with an outgoing, enthusiastic friend, don't underestimate an enthusiastic reception of your poem; don't say to yourself, "She says that about everything." You've just heard your friend's honest reaction to your sharing. Keep in mind as well that sharing isn't a one-way street. Reciprocate your audience's attention to your writing with your attention to her concerns.

Unless your friends and family have experience in responding to creative writing, most will have difficulty in expressing more than this heartfelt emotional support for you—support based, of course, on their affection for you. Don't underestimate that affection and wish that these people were more critical.

When you do exchange with more informed friends and family in order to learn from them, be sure to clarify your expectations. Tell your readers what type of response you're looking for—checking the ending, responding to the whole, helping you proofread or pick a title—and what degree of response you hope for—"Tell me honestly what you see" or "I know it needs revision. . . . " If they help you in a specified area, don't then turn on them and ask them *different* tough questions and make them feel as if suddenly they're taking a reading test. If you do want a more detailed response, give your reader enough time and space to respond responsibly. That means you should be sure to arrange a clear time for your discussion. Asking for an opinion when the responder is diapering a child, cooking dinner, studying for a big exam, or filling out tax forms is asking for an explosion or an opinion you don't want to hear.

A few last suggestions: Don't share "family stories" turned into art with your family unless you're pretty sure of members' feelings about this material. Don't share a play with your friend Betty in which the protagonist really looks, and acts, and seems like Betty— with all of Betty's infuriating mannerisms—unless you're pretty sure she can stand to see this reflection of herself. Even when you think you've drawn a flattering portrait, your friends and family are liable not to agree with you. Here is a story of the problems of such sharing, told by novelist Gail Godwin:

> [M]y mother, my sister, and I sat in my sister's girlhood bedroom, talking about a novel I had written. "I don't care," Franchelle was saying. "She'd better never put me in a novel again. I don't like being frozen in print for the rest of my life, forever wearing those silly panties and short skirts; and I'm *not* big like that, she's made me into some sort of amazon-freak."
>
> "Darling," our mother said, "the sister in *The Odd Woman* wasn't you. Gail just took part of you, the parts she needed. Writers work that way."
>
> "Well, I wouldn't know. I'm a lawyer and they don't work that way. Besides, it *hurts.*"
>
> Tears filled her eyes and she ran from the room.
>
> "It's unfair," I said, "She's being unfair by not trying to understand."
>
> "It's difficult when you haven't written," agreed my mother. "Now I understood why you had to make Kitty a more passive mother than I am, also a little stupid; that was necessary to your overall plan . . . "
>
> "Passive! Stupid! Kitty? Kitty was a beautiful character. I worked hard on Kitty."
>
> "She was a lovely character," my mother said. "I thought she was awfully well done. But what I mean is, I knew she wasn't supposed to be me."
>
> "But she was!"
>
> "Well, there was something left out, then." (qtd. in Sternburg 241–42)

Neither Godwin's story nor my suggestions are intended, though, to make you avoid sharing work with those you care about; friends and family often provide a writer with an important audience and a nurturing environment. Just be sensitive to the limitations of the situation.

Informal Writing Groups

Many writers continue to "go to school" with an informal writing group long after they leave the formal classroom. A writing group may have three members to thirty members and may convene in different ways and in odd locations. If you are thinking of setting up a group, you should read Peter Elbow's *Writing Without Teachers* and *Writing with Power* for discussions of group processes. You might even dip into Ann Gere's *Writing Groups,* which details the long and impressive history these informal "organizations" have had.

When you start a group, the information in Chapter 7 on responding and revising will prove useful. The few general guidelines provided here may help you avoid some of the ups and downs that all groups experience.

1. Be sure that all the invited members have *roughly* similar experiences and expectations. You may start with a group of three friends. As each invites another friend to join, be sure he or she lets that friend know the groups' ground rules, procedures, and general goals. You don't all have to think alike, but you should all be willing to communicate as your group grows, evolves, and changes.

2. Define your ground rules, procedures, and general goals.
   a. Is there anything your group does not want to be involved with—for example, sharing fiction in a poetry group? Harsh criticism? Drinking and gossiping?
   b. How will each meeting proceed? Is one person in particular in charge? Or no one? Who takes responsibility for making copies, convening meetings, providing a meeting place, providing refreshments, calling to order, calling an end to meetings, and so on? How can you make the group work smoothly and equitably? What will be your methods for response? Will you share revisions? How do you decrease or increase your membership? What if you gain a member no one wants to work with or who is proving unsatisfactory?
   c. Are you set up to help each member equally? How will this be ensured? Are you going to work for a set period on one genre and then change to another? Do you foresee an end to the need for a group? Do you hope to affect the literary scene outside your group (start a magazine, organize readings, and so on)?

Starting a writing group may sound a little like gathering together your childhood friends to build a fort and form a secret club. To avoid interpersonal explosions (you stole my shovel) and confusion (how big are we going to make it?) and quick disbanding (Ms. Arrowsmith suggests we don't build in the arroyo due to summer flash floods), it does help to plan, at least this much, before you commence.

Reading Writers and Writing Readings

> *I know a book is good for me when I cannot read a few pages without getting up to write.*
>
> —Tilly Warnock (70)

> *Who would call a day spent reading a good day? But a life spent reading—that is a good life.*
>
> —Annie Dillard (33)

Go to any local readings at bars, etc., sponsored by professionals (a book store, your English dept., etc.). Write down any ideas from the readers. Start to learn how to listen. You're already beginning to learn how to "tell" or write a story or poem, but try to learn to listen as well. Read! Go to a bookstore or library and if you don't want to get a book, at least thumb through it and look at titles, key sentences, characters, etc. But try to read, not only what you do like, but other things, kinds of styles and see if you like any of them.

—Tiffany

We write because we have read texts, and we read texts to learn how to write—to gain inspiration, directions, and influences—as well as to discover what to avoid. Reading theorists and researchers have shown us that just as we compose texts, we are composed *of* texts: "One develops as a writer by playing with material already in existence. The 'new' emerges as a function of this play" (Scholes, Comley, and Ulmer 132). Other theorists move beyond writing in their definitions and describe how our entire lives are formed in this "intertextual" way.

As humans, we are part of our own cultural conversations. We enter our families and interweave our family life with our own. We enter the world of school and adapt our life to the expectations of that community. Situated in our community, state, and nation, we partake of ever-enlarging spheres of "discussion." The discussion started long before we were born: For some in our culture it began with the landing at Plymouth; for others in our culture, with the overland migration across the Bering Strait. And the conversation, we hope, will continue when we are gone, with our children and our children's children representing us.

Philosopher and rhetorician Kenneth Burke describes this conversational community with a parlor metaphor:

> Imagine that you enter a parlor. You come late. When you arrive, others have long preceded you, and they are engaged in a heated discussion, a discussion too heated for them to pause and tell you exactly what it is about. In fact, the discussion had already begun long before any of them got there, so that no one present is qualified to retrace for you all the steps that had gone before. You listen for a while, until you decide that you have caught the tenor of the argument; then you put in your oar. Someone answers; you answer him; another comes to your defense; another aligns himself against you, to either the embarrassment or gratification of your opponent, depending upon the quality of your ally's assistance. However, the discussion is interminable. The hour grows late, you must depart. And you do depart, with the discussion still vigorously in progress. (110–11)

Our entrance, as writers, into the historical stream of previously written texts works much the way our entrance into the Burkean parlor might. We start reading, something, anything, as children. In school we acquire a developing awareness of "literature." We are sometimes mystified as well as interested in this category of writings, but we are not yet conversant with it. We go on to read more, study more. We write responses, imitations, parodies, include our own thoughts, our new, half-borrowed, half-created inventions. We share our work with others in a workshop. We all say a little—not enough, for there is never enough time—we walk out the door, still talking, to write some more.

Because we are so influenced by texts, writers consciously go out of their way to use other work to inform and inspire their own. Often writers will brag about borrowing, stealing, and amplifying the work of someone else, and often writing students will be confused by these brave forays into intertextuality, fearing that they will be caught plagiarizing. Professional writers reassure us that listening to others provides needed context for a writer's life without threatening to overwhelm the writer. Donald Barthelme claims:

> I keep reading while I write and I don't think it hurts me. My writing is sufficiently various that someone else's style doesn't take over. I don't suddenly turn into John Updike if I'm reading Updike. . . . Everybody is influenced by the people they read, but the pleasure in the situation is that usually there are so many influences—so many fathers [and mothers]—that they all get blended together. In the best case, no single influence dominates. (qtd. in Brewer, "Do Fiction" 118)

And Shirley Hazzard claims:

> Yes, I read all the time. I couldn't imagine my life without its current of reading. One doesn't read in connection with one's work, but in connection with life. . . . Reading is a private, intimate act for which we are accountable to no one. (qtd. in Brewer, "Do Fiction" 119)

What saves us, as creative writers, from charges of plagiarism is our ability to identify our sources through close attention to the works we read and share. Sometimes we know as we start to write that we plan to imitate. At other times, we reread a piece later and hear the echo of a favored author or a certain writing style. As long as we don't fool ourselves and imagine that we have created ourselves completely as writers—bright, clean, shining, rife with "original" ideas—we are safe to build from the supporting base of our community, to walk in and out of our parlor, to use the knowledge of writers from the past to aid our own writing development.

Exercises to Explore Intertextuality

1. Choose a piece of your own writing that is completed. Reread your own text looking for "influences." Highlight literary allu-

sions and mark any point where a family (or borrowed, or traditional) story comes into play. Examine your prose for stylistic influences from authors you have read previously.

2. Write up these notes as an informal essay on "Other Texts in My Texts," where you analyze your borrowing habits. You might want to set the scene with a discussion of how you read as a writer and why.

3. Complete an informal research project involving one of the following:
   a. Famous literary influences—talk to several English professors at your school and ask them to give you examples of literary influences on their work.
   b. Professional writers—talk to professional writers that you know or can contact and ask them about intertextuality and ways they borrow from and are influenced by other writers.

Setting Your Own Reading Agenda

Everyone will tell you to read a lot, but only you can decide on a plan for making the most of your reading time. You can turn your general habits into strengths. For instance, once I find an author I like, I enjoy reading all of that writer's works. With novelists, this may be six to twenty novels. I've taken to reading these novels in order—earliest to latest—to get the benefit of (re)experiencing the writer's growth. I can talk about her growing skills, recurrent obsessions, experiments, bombs, successes. What started as laziness, of sorts (I didn't want to find another author when I had such a pleasing one to "consume"), becomes a writing aid.

To set up your own reading agenda, take a good look at your current reading habits. Imagine you want to write poetry but seem to always read novels. Should you force yourself to read poems? Can you tempt yourself into reading a book of poetry every third time you sit down? Can you plan to read the poems in several literary journals on a regular basis? Can you promise to go to the set of ten live readings offered on campus this fall?

Once you outline your habits, make a list of changes, such as those I've suggested above, that would benefit you as a writer. Then, try just a few. You don't want reading to become penance for becoming a better writer; you just want to expand your reading world more, then more and more.

Use your teacher as a resource for suggested readings. Often teachers spontaneously offer you ideas for reading directions. Some writers don't enjoy this type of directing; I remember feeling aggrieved when a writing teacher responded to one of my stories by suggesting I read a particular novel—I already had read the novel and had not liked it. Short circuit this negative response to being "told" what to read by actively seeking out suggestions from readers you respect. Your teacher, generally, will have excellent ideas.

Collect reading lists if you like to read "the best" work in various historical periods. You can start with literature anthologies or exam reading lists for English M.A. candidates. Realize, though, that currently there is a great deal of discussion about what constitutes "best" writing. Many traditional lists excluded writers of varied backgrounds who lived marginalized lifestyles or held non-mainstream beliefs. By all means read the canonized work, but also look for teachers of cultural or feminist studies who can direct your reading in ways that help you to fill in missing gaps. To do this, you can read special series like Virago Modern Classics, a series that republishes important books by women authors who were ignored by traditional literary critics.[1]

Once you find publishers you like, you can also request and receive their annual catalogs. Again, most writing teachers receive many of these catalogs and will be happy to browse through them with you. Also, you hear of new work by reading book reviews in the local paper, literary journals, or national reviews such as *The Times Literary Supplement* and *The New York Review of Books*.

Your reading can and should work for you as a developing writer. Challenge yourself to undertake a reading task, and then use journal writing to explore the experience or write in imitation of that author. Read all of Proust and then write a Proustian short story. Reread all the fairy tales you loved as a child and write persona poems, examining those characters once again. Read in other fields—popular science (Stephen Jay Gould) or creative nonfiction (John McPhee, Joan Didion)—and transmute these readings into the types of writing you love best. If nothing else, keep a reading diary, including a short summary of each piece you read. Whether you do this for a short or long period of time, you'll be surprised to see the reading patterns you have developed. Above all, remember there are no rights or wrongs to setting up your own reading agenda—just the need to do so. If you don't read others, who will read you?

Public Performances

> *Poets [and fiction writers] now read everywhere, not just in colleges, bookstores, and poetry centers, but in lofts, cafes, prisons, on the Staten Island Ferry. . . . They may come dressed in masks, or chant and wear costumes.*
> *Younger poets read in pairs, or with a well-established poet. They may read their own work, the work of other poets, or poetry in translation. Well-known poets attract so many listeners that in some places reservations have to be made in advance; young poets have been known to read to an audience of one—someone who showed up just to get out of the rain.*
> —Daryln Brewer ("Poetry Readings" 231)

Writers read their works for as many reasons as audiences form to hear them. For many writers, the proof of their work with words is the response they receive from audiences, the pleasure of the music of the word sounding out loud. Readings, as Daryln Brewer explains, can be large or small, wild or quiet, and performers may be surprising or disappointing, quiet or exuberant. In a study of writers performing, Katharyn Machan Aal found that the readings tended to split into two types. Those writers she called "pagers" preferred to simply read their texts, and those she called "stagers" developed performances that were as important as the work being shared.[2]

Clearly, writers and audience both benefit from these performance events:

> [Audre] Lorde feels that "listening to poetry is like the high you get from going to the symphony versus listening to an excellent stereo. The contact has a liquid quality to it. A particular life and a breath illuminate a poem at a reading," she says. "People often make contact with a poet at a reading the way they don't on the page, and that makes a poetry reading a circular thing: not just a performance for the poet, but a dynamic that goes back and forth.
> "Readings bring you closer to the people you want to reach."
> (Brewer, "Poetry Readings" 234)

Here's a student response to her first live reading:

> When I was first going, I was kinda scared because I didn't know what to expect from a poetry reading. I didn't know if there was like a special thing I needed to wear, or if I would have to act differently. I somewhat imagined it to be a dark smoky room with all these people with long, greasy hair who wore off-the-wall blended colors, chanting quietly as a person read their poem. Boy was I wrong!! I finally found the place and held my breath as I walked in. I looked around, these people were no different than myself. No off-the-wall clothes, nor long greasy hair. There was a group of people on stage. Two were playing the guitar, one the violin, and another I believe a piccolo. They weren't playing satanistic music, but instead happy music. People were quietly chatting amongst each other. It was a very cute, different atmosphere. The first reader was introduced. You could tell he was nervous for he almost drank his cigarette. I honestly can say that I don't remember much of the story, I was more wrapped up in the atmosphere of the place and the reader's actions. For he was just as nervous as I had been going into the reading. I enjoyed the reading and plan to attend more of them in the future.

Recall that some of the writing activities in Chapter 5 suggested that you should attend readings in order to write about those performances. Readings broaden your experiences *and* give you ideas. If no readings happen to take place where you live, you can re-create the "feel" of live performances by ordering tape recordings of writers reading their works.[3] Also, think of organizing readings yourself or with the help of your informal writing group. Libraries, schools, cafes, and town halls are all possible locations. Remember, no writer writes alone. As you enter the parlor or join in the conversation, you'll meet people as eager as you to share creative writing.

Notes

1. Look for texts that introduce genres [James Pickering, ed., *Fiction 100: An Anthology of Short Stories*, 4th ed. (New York: Macmillan, 1985); or R. V. Cassill, ed., *The Norton Anthology of Short Fiction*, 4th ed. (London: Norton, 1990)]; that showcase genres by theme [Michael Nagler and William Swanson, eds., *Wives & Husbands: 20 Short Stories About Marriage* (New York: Mentor, 1989)]; that showcase writing by special author categories [Susan Cahill, ed., *Among Sisters: Short Stories by Women Writers* (New York: Mentor, 1989)]; that showcase new or emerging talents [Stephen Berg, ed., *Singular Voices: American Poetry Today* (New York: Avon, 1985)—these poems include commentary by the poets]. Useful series by publishers include Contemporary American Fiction (Penguin); Virago Modern Classics (Penguin), Poets on Poetry (Michigan University Press), and many others that you can find by browsing your local bookstores. Many presses, including University of Iowa Press, Yale University Press, University of Georgia Press, Word Works Books, and University of Pittsburgh Press, publish annual winners of poetry and fiction contests; these can be discovered by subscribing to and reading *Poets and Writers* magazine or *The AWP Chronicle* (see Appendix A for more information on writers' newsletters).
2. See Aal.
3. Start with The American Audio Prose Library, Inc. (P.O. Box 842, Columbia, MO 65205) or Poets on Tape; consult with your local reference librarian to learn about other catalogs.

Sources and Readings

Aal, Katharyn Machan. "The Writer as Performer: A Study of Contemporary Poetry and Fiction Readings, Based in Ithaca, New York." Diss. Northwestern U, 1984.

Bartlett, Lee, ed. *Talking Poetry: Conversations in the Workshop with Contemporary Poets*. Albuquerque: U of New Mexico P, 1987.

Brewer, Daryln. "Do Fiction Writers Read Fiction While They Write?" *The Writing Business: A Poets & Writers Handbook*. New York: W. W. Norton, Pushcart Press, 1985. A Poets & Writers Book dist.

_____. "Poetry Readings: Why Go to Them, Why Give Them?" *The Writing Business: A Poets & Writers Handbook*. New York: W. W. Norton, Pushcart Press, 1985. A Poets & Writers Book dist.

Bunge, Nancy, ed. *Finding the Words: Conversations with Writers Who Teach*. Athens: Ohio UP, 1985.

Burke, Kenneth. *The Philosophy of Literary Form: Studies in Symbolic Action*. 3d ed. Berkeley: U of California P, 1967.

Didion, Joan. *Slouching Towards Bethlehem*. New York: Dell, 1968.

Dillard, Annie. *The Writing Life*. New York: Harper, 1989.

Elbow, Peter. *Writing with Power*. New York: Oxford UP, 1981.

_____. *Writing Without Teachers*. New York: Oxford UP, 1977.

Gere, Ann Ruggles. *Writing Groups: History, Theory, and Implications*. Carbondale: Southern Illinois UP, 1987.

Gould, Stephen Jay. *Ever Since Darwin*. New York: W. W. Norton, 1977.

Lloyd, Pamela, ed. *How Writers Write*. Portsmouth, NH: Heinemann, 1987.

McPhee, John. *Coming into the Country*. New York: Bantam, 1979.

Scholes, Robert. *Textual Power: Literary Theory and the Teaching of English*. New Haven, CT: Yale UP, 1985.

Scholes, Robert, Nancy R. Comley, and Gregory L. Ulmer. *Textbook: An Introduction to Literary Language*. New York: St. Martin's Press, 1988.

Sternburg, Janet, ed. *The Writer on Her Work*. New York: W. W. Norton, 1981.

Warnock, Tilly. "An Analysis of Response: Dream, Prayer, and Chart." *Encountering Student Texts: Interpretive Issues in Reading Student Writing*. Eds. Bruce Lawson, Susan Sterr Ryan, and W. Ross Winterowd. Urbana, IL: National Council of Teachers of English, 1989.

Chapter 7

Revision and Your Writing

*Revision. According to Webster's Dictionary, revision refers to "an alteration."
To a writer, however, revision refers to loosened hairs, rubbed down erasers, and filled
wastepaper baskets. Never is a writer satisfied with the first thing that runs from his
pen to the paper, nor is he happy with the second or perhaps even the third. It isn't
until he's filled dozens of journals and started numerous new pens that he is able to
look at a finished piece and breathe a sigh of relief. For some, revisions are a way of
life; they write so that they may revise. For others, the opposite is true; they revise so
that they may write.*

—JIM

Jim's definition of revision encompasses the beliefs and actions
of professional writers as different as Annie Dillard and Donald Murray. Dillard says:

> You must demolish the work and start over. You can save some of
> the sentences, like bricks. It will be a miracle if you can save some of
> the paragraphs, no matter how excellent in themselves or hard-won.
> You can waste a year worrying about it, or you can get it over with
> now. (Are you a woman, or a mouse?)
>
> The part you must jettison is not only the best-written part; it is
> also, oddly, that part which was to have been the very point. It is the
> original key passage, the passage on which the rest was to hang, and
> from which you yourself drew the courage to begin. (4)

She appears to revise so that the act of writing may continue. Murray, on the other hand, makes it clear that initial drafting is a necessary first step that allows him to get to the work he prefers—
rewriting, revising, reshaping, rethinking, and re-forming a piece.
Murray claims, "There's something marvelously satisfying with

finishing a draft, no matter how bad it is. Now I can go to work. Before the piece of writing was all idea and vision, hope and possibility, a mist. Now it is ink on paper, and I can work it" (49).

Dillard's view explains why the process of revision may be uncomfortable, for when revising we often have to learn to give up portions of our original writing. Sometimes our first idea was ill formed. Sometimes it no longer fits, calling too much attention to itself. Sometimes the impulse to begin a piece—a title, first sentence, whole chapter—leads to the discovery of an entirely different piece of writing. When this happens, a poem turns into a story, a story turns into a novel on an entirely new theme, an original opening paragraph gets buried halfway inside a story or must be abandoned, or a character that helped generate a play is eventually cut and replaced with two new characters. Murray's view explains why having a chance to revise can also be an exhilarating experience, a time to roll up your shirt-sleeves and dig in, a chance to improve a draft again and again.

For most of us, then, revision is a necessary—but not necessarily easy—undertaking. We need to learn when to make major changes, minor changes, or no changes. We need to learn the difference between revision and editing. We need to learn to "see" our texts clearly and to evaluate and use the responses of other readers of our texts. Although I have separated revision from evaluation by making each the subject of its own chapter, truly, these are interrelated processes. In order to know what you should revise, you have to judge the quality of the current text. This chapter and the next should be read together, one and then the other, and then both, perhaps, again.

Revision Is a Recursive Process

Many of us begin to revise before we put words to paper—as we take a walk we raise and then reject or accept various "openings" or "developments"—but most of us start revision work in earnest once we have a draft. In this chapter, I draw a somewhat artificial distinction between early and late revision, and I separate both those ways of looking at your writing from the process of editing—that is, preparing a *final draft* for submission to a teacher or editor—which is covered more extensively in Chapter 8. Following is what a writer's fullest possible revision process might look like. Although I've described a sequence here, revision is actually always recursive; at any time, you may stop and redraft, add, delete, rethink a piece, and so on. To get to the finished product you want, however, it is useful to focus on certain aspects of revision at particular times.

Early Revision

- Concerned with developing your ideas

- Concerned with making initial decisions about what form will best convey those ideas

- Concerned with trying out options

- Concerned with the "big picture"

- *Not* too concerned with fine details, mechanics, spelling, punctuation, final word choice, and so on

- *Not* concerned with perfection

In early revision, you explore your first conceptualization of your work. Early revision may take place across several drafts.

Late Revision

- Concerned with finalizing your ideas

- Concerned with fitting those ideas to the form you have chosen

- Concerned with smaller options, particularly at the paragraph, sentence, or word level

- Concerned with the "smaller picture"

- Concerned with the final effect on the intended reader; will he or she understand/enjoy this?

- *Not* overly concerned with the finest of details, mechanics, spelling, punctuation, and so on

- *Not* yet concerned with perfection

In late revision, you finalize your original conception for a piece. Late revision, depending on the circumstances of drafting (particularly, what is your deadline?), may take place during drafts two through fifty, or more.

Editing

- Concerned with perfection, with surface-level clarity, with "getting the last draft right"

- Concerned with detail and mechanics—getting dark type from the typewriter ribbon or printer, setting standard margins, having a title, including your name, proofreading for spelling errors, checking for *unintentional* punctuation, and/or grammar errors

- Concerned with not alienating a reader or making a reader do the writer's work

- Concerned with near perfection
- *Not* a time to decide to remove paragraphs four to seven and rewrite them
- *Not* a time to change a text from a prose poem to a poem in stanzas
- *Not* a time to add a new character to a play

You edit whenever your writing is to be presented to other individuals in an evaluative situation (from publishing a family Christmas card that includes your poem, to sharing a "public" draft in a full-class workshop, to submitting your final class work to your teacher, to sending off your poems to a publisher).

Editing is part of a normal writing cycle. If you decide to rewrite an already edited piece after a period of time, you'll expect to edit your *new version* before presenting it publicly once more.

Some writers combine parts of this sequence, depending on their writing processes, writing products, and audiences. However, it is useful to go through a full sequence several times with several pieces of writing *in order to understand* the value of looking and looking again at your writing.

It is important to remember that *all* writers revise; *all* writers— novice and experienced writers and published and unpublished writers alike—work to improve a draft. For instance, authors Louise Erdrich and Michael Dorris share drafts extensively and even coauthor their work, sometimes writing separately and combining texts, sometimes writing together, but *always* revising extensively. When completing the revision shown in Figure 7.1, Erdrich and Dorris "wrote the first draft of specific scenes alone. They then passed the revisions back and forth, many times over" (qtd. in Passaro 36)

Using Computers for Revision

While some writers prefer to write and draft and redraft by hand, most writers' lives have been dramatically changed, usually improved, by the advent of easily accessible word processing. A word processor offers a particularly useful way to revise large pieces of texts, texts most of us would not want to type over and over or copy out by pen again and again. Here is Lynn Bloom talking about computer revision:

> Until two years ago, I always composed prose on the typewriter (and poetry in longhand on yellow lined tablets). Because I write as I think and think as I write, the faster I can get the thoughts down the

Figure 7.1 *Michael Dorris and Louise Erdrich—Collaborative Revision*

I shifted Violet to my other arm, impatient. She was frantic with hunger, hard to appease.

A tall Caucasian male poked his head from the airport building, pulled it back again. I caught just the flash of his profile, his beaklike nose. He was the only prospect. I approached him, identified myself, put out my hand. He was indeed Henry Cobb, crisply spoken man. His long face was broad and flat-cheeked, a bit horsey, and wore a contained expression of annoyance. He touched the tip of his chin like a talisman, and stared into my features, he got to the point. As he spoke, I recognized

"Did you bring it? Everything?"

I nodded. the handshake was crushing. He pressed my rings into my palm. I winced. Cobb was dressed in a brisk white polo shirt, navy blue tennis shorts, crew socks and hi-tech Pumas. Creases ran alongside his mouth — not laugh or frown lines, but perfect parallels. He had straight white thick hair and the lean muscles of a vigorous 60 year old.

His voice was low, rough, electric

Revisionists

I shifted Violet to my other arm, impatient. She was frantic with hunger, hard to appease.

A tall Caucasian male poked his head from the airport building, pulled it back again. I caught just the flash of his profile, the beaklike nose, familiar from Roger's clipping. Henry Cobb was dressed in a brisk white polo shirt, navy blue tennis shorts, crew socks, and hi-tech Pumas. Creases ran alongside his mouth — not laugh or frown lines but perfect parallels. He had straight, white, thick hair and the lean muscles of a vigorous sixty-year-old. I identified myself, put out my hand. As he spoke, the Buckley-esque whining frown at the end of each word. In person, his voice was even more commanding — low, modulated, and electric. Cobb's long face — broad and flat-cheeked, a bit horsey — wore a contained expression of annoyance. He touched the tip of his chin like a talisman, and stared into my features.

After the briefest of greetings he got to the point.

"Did you bring it? Everything?"

I nodded. Cobb's handshake was crushing. He pressed my rings into my palm so hard that I winced.

Dorris and Erdrich say they are each other's best editors, constantly revising and re-revising. On a manuscript page of "The Crown of Columbus," the 15th of 17 drafts, Dorris's comments are in the larger handwriting and Erdrich's in the smaller. The published version is at right.

easier the writing is. Hence the switch to personal computer. The computer also allows unlimited revisions as I write and rewrite. Sometimes I edit each sentence several times before I go on to the next; after I have enough text to work with I move sentences and paragraphs around to see (which one can do literally with a computer) which way looks best. The boundaries of the computer's screen have made me aware of the great extent to which I rely on the text I've just written as a guide to what is yet to come, and the enormous amount of rescanning I do in the process. As a nervous computer novice—and a realist . . . I print out the text every ten pages or so to have a working draft in hard copy; that makes the rescanning easier too. What a pleasure to have a clean copy to mess up instead of having to cut and paste a scribbled-over typed text already too cluttered to work on without retyping. (35–36)

On your word processor, you can easily make copies as well. This freedom allows you to cut and paste, to delete and add words to your new copy, trying out a variety of large and small changes, paragraph orders, line breaks, and so on. It is essential, though, when using a computer to regularly make and clearly label your back-up copies. Also, many computer revisers still rely on the printed word. They like to print out hard copy and then make on-text corrections by hand. The revision sample from Michael Dorris and Louise Erdrich shows this kind of annotation and hand editing.

If you've been using your word processor only as a type of elegant typewriter, for typing up final drafts, try entering your text earlier in the process and, through the use of multiple copies, see if revising on the screen helps your thinking as well as your visualization of your written product. Many of the exercises later in this chapter can be completed effectively on a word processor.

Early Revision

When you share your writing with classmates to get general, early revision suggestions, you should not expect your responders to correct your spelling and help you decide on a final title. In fact, during early revision, you may simply want them as listeners. In this case, every writer can bring an early draft, read it, and receive oral responses ("I liked it," "I followed it," "I got lost here," "I think it's dynamite, but you might add . . . " are typical oral response suggestions). As a writer, you should note these comments and return to your piece a few days later, renewed and ready to work on it again.

Here is Scott responding in his journal to an early revision workshop. Students had been sharing pieces they thought they might submit eventually to the English Department undergraduate literary magazine—*Kudzu*.

Revision. I've always despised it, so I always try to get it [the draft] perfect the first time. Well, not perfect, but good enough where I can get by without revising. Anyway, I think I've come to learn that no matter how good you think it is, you can always revise.

I got some very nice comments about my paper, so I guess I'll submit it. There were already a few things I had noticed needed changing (I need a title, maybe I need to put a hyphen in fenced in, and I might use the word "pulpit," but I'm not sure). I also thought of a few other ideas and I was told that maybe I could come up with some better adjectives, but I don't want to. I like it the way it is because when I write, I like it to sound like me. I try to use as much description as I can get away with and still sound like me, but I don't want to go too far. [Note added later—I did submit, and naturally it got turned down. Story of my life. First women, now the *Kudzu*—Geez. Must be telling me something . . . Scott, the failed, celibate writer!].

Scott continued to maintain his usual humorous composure in the face of multiple and conflicting responses to his writing. First, like any writer in an early draft session, he had to decide how much of his piece to change. Scott has clear ideas on this. Compare his decisions to the suggestions of Peter Elbow:

You can get feedback from one person or several. If you really want to know how your words affect readers, you can't trust feedback from just one person, no matter how expert or experienced she is. Besides it is somehow empowering to realize how diverse and even contradictory the reactions are of different readers to your one set of words. It's confusing at first but it releases you from the tyranny of any single reader's or teacher's judgement. It drives home the fact that there's never a single or correct assessment of a piece of writing. When you get conflicting reactions, block your impulse to figure out which reactions are right. Eat like an owl: take in everything and trust your innards to digest what's useful and discard what's not. Try for readers with different tastes and temperaments—especially if you don't have many readers. (*Writing with Power* 264)

In what ways did Scott "eat like an owl"?

To some extent, your own revision decisions will be driven by your concern for audience. Are you writing only to please yourself or to please another, imagined or real, audience? Issues of "writing to an audience" become more important the closer you come to a final draft. Here is Caroline discussing audience:

Although many people believe that it's unfavorable to consider your audience when writing, I believe that it's a necessity. I write in a totally different style when I write a "to-do" list or when I write to my bizarre best friend back home than when I write an essay for Dr. B— or a project for Wendy Bishop. Writers also shape their writing (I firmly believe) for their audience. Einstein wrote differently to/for small children than he did for adults, and even though he is not a "writer" this is still valid. Writers must consider their audiences in order for it [their work] to be understood. Readers who read on a fifth-grade level cannot read an article written for a college graduate and if the writer wants his article to be understood by everyone, then he must write accordingly. Writers' writing *is* shaped by audiences.

Taking Control: Asking for Response

As a class, you can decide on the focus of your revision response questions ahead of time. Essentially, you agree upon the attributes of good writing for the particular genre you expect to critique, such as drama, poetry, or prose; Chapter 9 can help you with this. Or, you can agree on general attributes of excellent writing, such as clarity, organization, logical transitions, interesting language, and so on; Chapter 8 can help you with this. You decide which attributes to focus on during your response session for this draft. Then each reader tries to respond to the piece of writing according to those points. These criteria are sometimes typed up by your teacher and may be called "Critique Sheets" or "Response Sheets." They are questions that can guide your discussion. Eventually, these criteria may be used by your teacher to evaluate your work. In Appendix B you'll find lists of response questions that can be adapted by your class for early or late response sessions. You might want to turn there now and look at the shift in focus that occurs between early and late response questions.

Getting revision response suggestions from classmates is the author's responsibility, too. The author should try to keep the group focused on those questions that really will be useful to her. She may want to add questions of her own. Sometimes, I ask writers to bring a readable copy of an early draft and a list of questions they have. We exchange these, and each class member reads the draft at home and responds to the author's questions. Authors can also provide their own specific questions for in-class response sessions. Figure 7.2 shows two completed response sheets for Nancy Shook's collage writing, "Fragments of Paul." A revised version of the work can be found in Chapter 10. The questions were drawn up by Nancy before she shared her work. Although this was an early draft, you'll see that Nancy asked for both general and specific suggestions and editing suggestions.

Figure 7.2 *Responses to "Fragments of Paul"*

CRITIQUE SHEET

Title: Fragments of Paul
Author: Nancy N. Shook
Audience: Something like <u>Kudzu</u>, or just anyone!
Critic (That's you): *Danny Keen*

1. To get the positive stuff out of the way, was there anything that you
   liked especially? *Yes, the images of your
   brother are very clear, I could see
   everything you did together and even had
   an idea of what Paul looked like,
   (I don't know why).*

2. How do you like my format? Is the piece clear? Confusing? What
   about the transitions? The beginning? The ending?

   *I was confused at first about the sudden
   shift to another time but when I saw
   the pattern you were establishing and
   it was completely clear.*

3. Did the tone strike you as formal? Informal? Inappropriate? What
   about word choice? Could have been better? How?

   *The tone struck me as informal and I
   loved it.*

4. What does this paper desperately need?

   *Nothing, except I want to know what
   happened to Paul. However, I see you're
   not telling us as part of the art of
   the story. NICE JOB!*

PLEASE NOTE WITHIN THE BODY OF THE PAPER ANY
PUNCTUATION, SPELLING, CAPITALIZATION, OR WORD USAGE
SUGGESTIONS!!!!

Figure 7.2 *(continued)*

CRITIQUE SHEET

Title: Fragments of Paul
Author: Nancy N. Shook
Audience: Something like <u>Kudzu,</u> or just anyone!
Critic (That's you): _____ *Bud Brown* _____

1. To get the positive stuff out of the way, was there anything that you
   liked especially?

   *I like the format – individual paragraphs
   like photos ... It keeps the readers interest.*

2. How do you like my format? Is the piece clear? Confusing? What
   about the transitions? The beginning? The ending?

   *As far as transitions go, you can even
   get along without them with this format.
   The overall focus of the paper is a bit
   unclear, however.*

3. Did the tone strike you as formal? Informal? Inappropriate? What
   about word choice? Could have been better? How?

   *Tone is good for "slice of life" paper. You
   could be just a bit more descriptive.*

4. What does this paper desperately need?
   *→ We need to know more about Paul. The purpose
   of the paper, I assume, is evident in the title,
   but what makes Paul so special that we should
   read about him – maybe the paper should be
   more personal (emotional?)
   – Give us more details on Paul's personality and
   why he is important to you.*

   PLEASE NOTE WITHIN THE BODY OF THE PAPER ANY
   PUNCTUATION, SPELLING, CAPITALIZATION, OR WORD USAGE
   SUGGESTIONS !!!!

The Interim Period: Between Early and Late Revision Workshops

Most of the revision you do takes place outside of class. Although I illustrate a few in-class exercises below, you'll learn your best revision skills by studying the revisions of others and, even more, by trying to improve your own work. Nothing ventured, nothing gained is the functional truism here. If you don't look at alternative versions, you'll be slow to identify the strengths of your own work. I suggest that you keep a large box in the corner of your closet and collect all the revisions you write during the semester. In essence, never empty your wastebasket and you won't have to fear that revision will "harm" your work. If you revise a piece out of existence or into a form you can no longer love, simply return to an earlier draft and move into final editing.

The next few examples show class writers revising their own work and/or talking about their revisions.

Example 1:
"Red Trees" by Don Lipps. An early version with comments by two of Don's classmates is shown in Figure 7.3. The same version of the poem with his teacher's comments is shown in Figure 7.4.

Questions

1. What did peer readers Aimie and Traci suggest for revision?

2. How did the teacher respond? How useful was that response?

3. What changes do you think Don should make at this point?

Figure 7.3 *Peer Responses to "Red Trees"*

Reader: Traci Landt

Don Lipps
Poem #4

RED TREES

I lay dreaming
of red trees
green skies — *Good because it goes with country*
and <u>blue grass</u>, Country music
is playing
and people are clogging
people are stomping, On bugs
as they crawl ——— *Kind of lost me*
and they fly, Like an airplane
through the green skies
to crash, And burn
in the trees
the fire is red.

Why are you dreaming of red trees? I think you need to expand this poem so we can understand. The descriptions you used were good but go further.

I lay dreaming
of red trees . . .

Don Lipps
Poem #4

Reader: Aimie Reinker

(RED TREES) — *Title fits well*

I lay dreaming
of red trees } *Surrealism*
green skies

and blue grass, Country music
is playing
good { and people are clogging
       people are stomping, On bugs
as they crawl
and they fly, Like an airplane — *simile*
through the green skies
to crash, And burn
in the trees
the fire is red.

— I like the use of surrealism in this poem. It is very descriptive and I can see it in my mind. Great poem!

I lay dreaming *nice*
of red trees . . . *ending*

Figure 7.4 *Teacher's Response to "Red Trees"*

Don Lipps
Poem #4

RED TREES

I lay dreaming
of red trees
green skies
and blue grass, |Country music |
is playing ⟍
and people are clogging
people are stomping, On bugs
as they crawl
and they fly, Like an airplane
through the green skies
to crash, And burn
in the trees
the fire is red.

lie
I lay dreaming
of red trees . . .

Example 2:
Ashley Bristow's poem "Equus" in two versions. The first, workshop version, is the sample she turned in to class workshop. Underlined sections are those parts that she eliminated after receiving class responses. In the next, revised version, underlined words are those she added to improve the poem.

Workshop Version

Equus

Sleek and bright like sunlight on amber sap from a tree.
You arch your veined neck and swish your violin string tail with
impatience.
Staring at me with eyes, deep as the darkest mahogany
What do you think of me? Am I your friend? <u>Can you understand me?</u>
Or am I just a shifting weight—<u>a</u> tiresome burden <u>to your sharply
defined</u> backbone?

<u>You</u> nip my outstretched fingers
Not deterred, <u>I shall stretch my body even further</u>
Just to touch—that's all, I swear

<u>You are such a beautiful creature</u>
<u>Never could I imagine a better specimen of perfection</u>
<u>You are certainly a creature of Gods, to be worshipped and adored</u>

<u>You nip my outstretched fingers</u>
Not deterred, <u>I shall stretch my body even further</u>
Just to touch—that's all, I swear

For to touch a creature like you
<u>Is enough to</u> keep my spirit dreaming,
Dancing on clover, pawing at the air with elegant forelegs
Like you do <u>as I try in vain to bridle you</u>

<u>I do not want to subdue you</u>
<u>Just to touch is fine</u>
<u>Yet to ride upon your back as you gallop through space—</u>
<u>My heart overflows with sheer joy.</u>

In the next, revised version, after cutting the underlined sections marked above, Ashley added words, phrases, and lines, and played with the order of the lines. By the time she finished the poem, it retained much of the original but was greatly changed. She eliminated a great deal of the sentimental exposition and allowed the visual image of horse and rider to tell the story.

Revised Version

Equus

Sleek and bright like sunlight on amber sap from a tree.
You arch your veined neck and swish your violin string tail with
      impatience.
Staring at me with eyes, deep as the darkest mahogany

What do you think of me? Am I your friend?
Or am I just a shifting weight—
<u>that</u> tiresome burden <u>on your</u> backbone?

<u>I extend my arm across the fence</u>
Just to touch <u>you</u>—that's all, I swear

Your velvety lips nip at my outstretched fingers,
Not deterred, I reach even further

For to touch a creature like you
keeps my spirit dreaming,
Dancing on clover,
pawing at the air with elegant forelegs

Like you do on this cold and bright winter morning.

Ashley was aware of her revision intentions and also of those places where she couldn't solve problems. When turning in the revised version of her poem, she noted:

> I like this version much better than the original poem. I worked very hard on direct imagery, cutting out some of the wordiness. I like the second stanza a lot—especially the part about "a shifting weight/That tiresome burden." I think that adds something, somehow. I also had a problem with the first line of the fourth stanza—I really didn't want to say "For to touch," but after a zillion different alternatives I came back to it. To say "because" just won't impart what I want the reader to feel.

Questions

1. What do you think about Ashley's self-analysis? Can you see a solution that she couldn't for "For to touch"?

2. Do you feel the poem is finished? If not, what further changes could she or should she make?

Revising Late Drafts

By the time you're working on late drafts, you may find yourself paying more attention to audiences for your writing. But, by that time, you have a strong idea of the shape and form of your piece. And these strong ideas may come into conflict with your audience's expectations in two ways. Those in your audience may have equally strong feelings about your subject, based on their past histories, and they may ask you to revise your piece to meet their expectations more closely. Also, they may have particular genre expectations—assuming, for example, that all poems rhyme (or don't rhyme), that all stories start with an evocative depiction of landscape and characters, or that all stories close with a thump, and so on. Your audience may like "realistic" comedies and dislike ironic, parodic, or humorous drama, or they may feel that tragedy is always preferable to comedy.

When you share late drafts in workshop, you are "negotiating" these issues. You'll be asked to justify your own decisions and feelings. A reader may wonder why you wrote a prose poem instead of a poem and, by implication, you may learn that that reader doesn't like prose poems. You may be told by an opinionated reader that your subject—a poem to your girlfriend—is too sentimental and not the material of "great art." Instead of feeling irritated or misunderstood when such questions arise, however, use them to help you clarify your sense of audience and to make decisions about the final revision of your poem. Chapter 9 will help you explore your understanding of, attention to, and belief in genre conventions. Lily describes her growing ability to revise, keeping such constraints in mind:

> I always used to think that poetry was something that just came naturally and that you really didn't have to work at it. I am amazed at how wrong I was. There is an awful lot of work and effort that goes into writing poetry and fiction. With the poetry you have to pay close attention to rhyme scheme, meter, similes, metaphors, and line length. Every word that you use must fit in perfectly, and so they must be chosen with care. This pretty much applies to fiction, also. Only you need not worry so much about line length and meter, because stories are in paragraph form.

Overall, by sharing your work with workshop readers, you learn about audience expectations for both form and content.

As you learn to revise, remind yourself that although most writers consider revision essential, few consider it easy or a surefire process. Due to space constraints, I've only been able so far to provide revision examples of poetry writing. For those working in prose, David Madden's book *Revising Fiction* is useful. Madden lists questions you can ask yourself throughout the drafting and revision of a piece of fiction. The answers you provide should give you insights that will help you with subsequent revisions. Madden also explains that writers' revision skills develop over time; he lists these levels of revision fluency.

> In his or her development, the writer goes through four stages in the matter of revision, and you may recognize where you are:
>
> 1. He makes a mistake but fails to see it.
>
> 2. He makes a mistake, he sees it, but doesn't know how to fix it—or reimagine it. He hasn't learned enough about the techniques of fiction.
>
> 3. He makes a mistake, he sees it, he has learned how to fix it, because he has learned some of the techniques of fiction, but he just can't do it.

4. He makes a mistake, he sees it, he knows how to fix it, he fixes it—and by now he has learned that solving technical problems in the creative process is just as exciting as writing the first draft. (11)

I think these stages hold true for any writer in any genre.

Since the response of peers helps you to see *where* to revise, the following revision exercises may help you to explore revision methods: *how* to revise. At this point, Madden's fourth step, learning to enjoy the problem-solving aspect of any revision session, becomes your reward for dedicated attention to this essential aspect of craft.

Group Revision

When you work with others to "improve" another writer's draft-in-progress, you illuminate the complexity of the revision activity. By working with someone else's piece—a piece in which you have no emotional or professional investment—you can more clearly name and understand the kinds of decisions involved in rewriting.

Directions

1. Your teacher provides your group with a number of copies (several more than the number of group members) of an anonymous work-in-progress. The piece will have been written by a student writer and should be used for this exercise only with that writer's permission. If you're in a computer classroom, you can do this exercise collaboratively on screen.

2. You and your group members provide scissors, tape or glue, marking pens, and plenty of ideas.

3. Read the piece aloud and ask yourself what should or could be done to improve the piece of writing.

4. Together, try to improve the piece. Change anything and everything but retain *at least a loose* connection to the original work. Add, subtract, rearrange, or substitute any words or formal structure in order to improve it. Produce a single improved text.

5. As a class, share versions and discuss the changes each group made.

Variation Each group member tries, individually, to improve the piece. You then share these versions within the group, discussing the changes each of you made. Choose the group's "best" revised version to read to the class.

Sample: Revising "Yukon Float"—Original Version

Yukon Float

The morning sunlight shines through the tent as I awaken. My breath, meeting the cool air, becomes mist. Outside the river still flows by. Only God knows how long it has followed this routine. Misty clouds cover one side of the valley, like a blanket rolled back. An occasional silver is heard breaking the water's surface as it works for a morning meal. The cold sand on my bare feet gives me a rush of sensations, assuring my existence.

A few feet away the small campfire struggles to keep aflame. The camp coffee from the charburned can begins to simmer, it is ready. The kayak, laying there on the beach, will take us down river to our next destination.

The maze of islands below, that separate the river's channels, have kept men of the past humble. This river has beaten many. Those that have floated here before: explorers, gold miners, and trappers, have learned to give this river respect. An old homestead still dots the shore, filled with the memories of the Glory days.

I stand on the shore, reflecting, like the bright sun on the water's surface. Today I am here, tomorrow I will be gone. But the river will keep flowing. For how long? Will it ever cease?

. . . Only God Knows.

Now look at the two group revisions in Figures 7.5 and 7.6.

Questions

1. Judging by the changes each group made, what problems in the original version were the groups attempting to resolve?

2. Did the groups seem to revise or edit? Did they make global and/or small-scale changes? Do you agree with any of their revision directions?

3. If the original author of "Yukon Float" looked at these revisions today, what might he learn about his writing? His readers?

This activity provides *insights* into revision. However, don't make a habit of appropriating another writer's work to this extent. Many writers don't feel comfortable with peers or teachers even writing on their texts, much less cutting and pasting them into new creations. The next exercise, in circle editing, protects writers from feeling coerced into changing their work by intentionally keeping your revision suggestions off the author's text and allowing the writer to decide entirely which changes should occur in a new version. Circle response focuses primarily on near-final and final draft changes.

Figure 7.5 *Sample: Group A Revision of "Yukon Float"*

Yukon Float

The morning sunlight shines through the tent as I awaken. My breath, meeting the cool air, becomes mist. Not twenty feet away the river flows by. Only God Knows how long it has carried the silt and sands to the ocean.

Misty clouds cover one side of the valley, like a blanket rolled back.

An occasional salmon is heard breaking the water's surface as the silver jumps for its morning ~~breakfast~~ meal. The cold sand beneath my bare feet gives me a rush of sensation. The tingling of my toes assures me of my existence.

A few feet away the small campfire struggles to keep aflame.

I stir the coals, add a branch or two, and sparks float overhead. Heat reddens my cheeks as I lean over to set the ~~char broil~~ charburned ~~camp~~ coffee can on the embers.

Figure 7.5 *(continued)*

Soon ~~it~~ the water begins to simmer and then it is ready.

Fresh brew in my cup warming my hands, ~~o~~
I look over to my kayak laying ~~on~~ there
on the beach, it will take ~~us~~ me down river
to ~~our~~ my next destination.

The maze of islands below, that ~~separates~~
                                    separates

The maze of islands below, that separates
the river's channels, have humbled men
out of the past.

Those that have floated here before: explorers,
gold miners, and trappers, have learned to
respect the Yukon.

Old homesteads dot the shore, each
summoning a picture in my mind of past
glory days.

I stand on the shore, reflecting, like the bright sun on the water's surface. Today I am here, tomorrow I will be gone. But the river will keep flowing. For how long? Will it ever cease?
                                    . . . Only God knows.

Figure 7.6 *Sample: Group B Revision of "Yukon Float"*

I awaken as ~~The~~ morning sunlight ~~shines~~ *filters* through the tent.
meeting the cool air, My breath becomes *a* mist.
~~Misty~~ clouds, *like a* blanket roll~~ed~~ *ing* back. cover*s* one side of the valley,
Outside *the canvas walls* the river flows by, *as a hungry*
~~Only the slap of~~
← ~~A hungry~~ Silver salmon, ~~broke~~ *breaksing* the surface of the
river, *when* ~~as~~ it lunge*s* ~~d~~ after a hap*p*less mosquito.
interrupting the stillness

A few feet away the ~~small~~ campfire struggles to keep aflame. The ~~camp~~
coffee from the charburned can ~~begins to~~ *barely* simmer, ~~it~~ *s* *but* is ready. The kayak,
laying there on the beach, will ~~take us~~ *carry us* down river to our next destination.

↗ *Explorers, gold miners and trappers have
learned to give this river respect.*

An ~~o~~ *O* ld homestead *s* still dot*s* the shore, filled with the memories of the Glory
days.

I stand on the shore reflecting, like the bright sun on the water's surface.
Today I am here, tomorrow I will be gone. But the river will keep flowing.
~~For how long? Will it ever cease~~?
...~~Only God knows.~~

↘ Downstream lay a maze of islands that br~~oke~~ *eak*
the river apart, interrupting its race to the delta.
The Yukon resent~~ed~~ *s* their intrusion and boil~~ed~~ *s* in
anger around them.

Circle Editing

Joseph Tsujimoto has developed a revision activity called "circle revision." Writers tape a separate piece of paper to the side of their poem after numbering each line. One reader then suggests line by line changes and passes the poem to the next reader, who agrees or disagrees with the suggested changes and then makes her or his own suggestions. I found that the circle response activity, which I have explored with sections of prose also, leads more directly to *editing* concerns—punctuation, word choice, line breaks, paragraphing—than it does to whole text response, so I've renamed it. Here are several variations of circle editing that you might want to try.

Directions

1. Prepare your poem *or short* piece of fiction for class by taping a piece of lined paper to the side of your original. Number the lines of your poem or the paragraphs of your piece of prose. Number the blank sheet of paper the same way. Allow some space between the paragraph numbers for written response.

2. During class, hand your papers to the writer to your left. You'll have a few minutes to read the work and to suggest *specific* changes on the blank sheet of paper. Do not write on the original copy but do feel free to change or offer suggestions at the word, phrase, or sentence level by writing in a new version at the appropriate number on the blank sheet of paper.

3. Your teacher will ask you to pass the papers on again. Follow the same process, but this time, feel free to comment also on the previous reviewer's suggested changes (written on the blank sheet of paper). If you run out of room, use an arrow and continue your remark on the back of the paper.

4. Your teacher will ask you to pass the papers several times. Continue to remark on the original piece and on the other reviewers' remarks.

Variation To complete circle editing on longer pieces of work, you will have to take the work home and respond, returning it during the next class period. Over the course of a week or two, authors will receive detailed editing advice, and response to advice, from four to six responders. Choose a paper that you are particularly interested in submitting for end-of-term evaluation; this time, double- or triple-space your text, allowing for responses to be written directly on the text, between the lines.

Figures 7.7, 7.8, and 7.9 comprise a sample of in-class circle editing—the original prose sketch, the class editing sheet, and the author's revised version, respectively. On the original version of "Minuet," the editing marks on the text were made by Carolyn as she considered the circle editing response and began to plan her revision.

Figure 7.7   *Original workshop version of "Minuet"*
with Carolyn's editing marks

Minuet

traipse
trudge
shuffled   — trudged

1   She ~~groped her way~~ into the Pearl-Dak Washomat, balancing a bottle

of liquid Tide between two unmatched pillowcases stuffed with dirty

lost

laundry. Her right brain was still ~~engrossed~~ in Gluck's "Minuet and

Dance of the Blessed Spirits," a deceptively simple flute piece that

required a full range of tonal expression and huge amounts of air, and

was often requested in orchestral auditions. She'd been practicing it for

three hours, so her left brain was temporarily out of service. She felt

spaced— the way she usually did when she walked into the Pearl-Dak

Washomat. But while she was measuring out Tide and fumbling for

quarters, she felt somebody looking at her. She glanced across the bank

of dingy yellow machines.

His

2   ~~The~~ brown eyes of a working man ✗ jeans and generic blue shirt

hung   the   of ⌃

~~hanging~~ on ~~a~~ lanky body⌃—met hers, turning her serious mouth up into

half a smile.

3   "I can tell you're smart," he said. "Doing your laundry on Friday

night. I always do mine on Fridays—beat the crowds. Done by seven

and I got the whole night free. I hate coming in on Saturdays.

Everybody's using five dryers apiece and sorting enough socks 'n' shirts

to dress a kinneygarden. This way all I got left to do is the groceries,

clothes in the

and I can do those anytime." He finished loading his ⌃ washing machines

left

and ~~took off.~~

4   She settled into an orange plastic chair with her new <u>National</u>

<u>Geographic</u> and had become deeply engrossed in the Kalash tribe of the

ed

Hindu Kush when he walked back in and ~~made her jump~~, yell~~ing~~,

"HEY! You're doing this all wrong! You're s'posed to put in your

laundry, then come on over to the bar next door and have a drink or two!

They got great Mexican food, too. I mean it. And real cheap. Why

Figure 7.7 *(continued)*

don't you come over and have some?"

5 She laughed. "Gotta read my National Geographic, you know. I've been looking forward to this all week."

6 He looked at her through his steady brown eyes. "Sorry. I don't usually talk to people in laundromats." Pause. "I just like your smile, that's all. Gotta get back to my pool game." He turned and was gone.

7 She folded her laundry, and was whistling and humming an old Beatles tune. clean clothes always made her feel rich, when he came back in to fold his. "Have fun," she called, groping her way behind a pile of warm sheets and towels toward the door, carefully balancing the bottle of Tide on top.

8 "Next time I see you here, I'll buy you a drink," he said, earnest as a child. "I promise."

9 She felt a breath of fresh air, even before he reached over to open the door for her and she walked through. It wasn't his compliment or his invitation. It was his style.

Figure 7.8   *Circle editing comments for "Minuet"*

Minuet

p.1   She ~~stumbled~~ ... [into ...] ok ✓   yes

p.1   She entered the Pearl-Dak ...

#2   ~~The brown eyes of a working man met hers, turning her ... smile. [I don't know where to put the jeans & blue shirt but not in the middle here.]~~   nope

Paragraph 2:   His working-man brown eyes -- jeans and generic blue shirt hanging on a lanky body -- met hers, turning her serious mouth into a half smile.   double nope

p.3   ... He finished loading his clothes in the washer and left.   yes

p.4   She had settled ... and was deeply engrossed

walked back in and yelled "HEY etc. ...   ok

#7 — change groping (repetitive)   ok

p.7   Clean clothes always made her feel rich. She ∧ folded the laundry ...   was

Figure 7.9 *Revised Version of "Minuet"*

Minuet

She trudged into the Pearl-Dak Washomat, balancing a bottle of liquid Tide between two unmatched pillowcases stuffed with dirty laundry. Her right brain was still lost in Gluck's "Minuet and Dance of the Blessed Spirits," a deceptively simple flute piece that required a full range of tonal expression and huge amounts of air, and was often requested in orchestral auditions. She'd been practicing it for three hours, so her left brain was temporarily out of service. She felt spaced— the way she usually did when she went to the Pearl-Dak Washomat. But while she was measuring out Tide and fumbling for quarters, she felt somebody looking at her. She glanced across the bank of dingy yellow machines.

Jeans and generic blue shirt hung on the lanky body of a working man. His brown eyes met hers, surprising her mouth into a smile. Quickly, she looked back down at her quarters.

"I can tell you're smart," he said. "Doing your laundry on Friday night. I always do mine on Fridays—beat the crowds. Done by seven and I got the whole night free. I hate coming in on Saturdays. Everybody's using five dryers apiece and sorting enough socks and shirts to dress a kinneygarden. This way all I got left to do is the groceries, and I can do those anytime." He finished loading his clothes in the

Figure 7.9 *(continued)*

machines and left.

She settled into an orange plastic chair with her new <u>National Geographic</u> and had become deeply engrossed in the Kalash tribe of the Hindu Kush when he walked back in and yelled, "HEY! You're doing this all wrong! You're s'posed to put in your laundry, then come on over to the bar next door and have a drink or two! They got great Mexican food, too. I mean it. And real cheap. Why don't you come over and have some?"

She laughed. "Gotta read my <u>National Geographic</u>, you know. I've been looking forward to this all week."

He looked at her through his steady brown eyes. "Sorry. I don't usually talk to people in laundromats." Pause. "I just like your smile, that's all. Gotta get back to my pool game." He turned and was gone.

Clean clothes always made her feel rich. She was folding her laundry, whistling and humming an old Bèatles tune, when he came back in to fold his. "Have fun," she called, groping her way behind a pile of warm sheets and towels toward the door, carefully balancing the bottle of Tide on top.

"Next time I see you here, I'll buy you a drink," he said, earnest as a child. "I promise."

She felt a breath of fresh air, even before he reached over to open the door for her. It wasn't his compliment or his invitation. It was his style.

Revision as Productive Risk Taking

Creative writers especially revise to learn about words and language, and about forms and the effects of experiments. Writers talk about the urge to get the words right as well as the urge to discover through trying alternative, sometimes riskier, versions. Here is a student writer talking about how she learned to work words. She is responding to a quote from Ernest Hemingway, where he mentions that he revised the ending to *A Farewell to Arms* thirty-nine times in order to get the words right.

Student Response

I never realized I had it in me to take the time and make my writing good. Usually, I was satisfied with one draft with a change of only a few words. Now, however, "getting the words right" is important. I also like group response. This is an easy way of looking at your paper as a reader.

I have now incorporated into my writing process this extra step of getting the words right. Revision *is* essential. After reading this quote (from Hemingway), I realized that writing isn't only a talent but it is work too. I always thought that all the greats just sat down and wrote with the thoughts easily flowing from their heads to the paper. Fortunately, they are just like us—planning, revising, suffering through a writer's block.

Knowing that I have a writing process and knowing what it is can only help my writing. Already, I have improved my process by practicing true revision and by not procrastinating until the very last minute! I have become much more interested in what I write and care more about the way it sounds to the audience. I don't dread writing assignments anymore and actually look forward to writing my best.

Exploring Voice

When a writer achieves some of the insights this author did, he may be ready to turn his hard work into fun again by experimenting with voice and style, through intentional revision challenges.

Voice is used variously in creative writing classrooms ("Have you found your poetic voice?" "I don't like the voice you chose in this story." "The voice of your lead character seems off to me." "Your text lacks a strong voice"). One of my colleagues, Rick Straub, has suggested that the various assumptions about "voice" can be charted this way:

READER	TEXT		WRITER
Voice as Tone	Voice as Sound	Voice as Persona	Voice as Writer's Own Voice

I'll attempt to illustrate these distinctions using one of my own paragraphs. After reading my variations, you might want to draft a similar sequence, using your own writing. Finally, I'll suggest some additional ways you can experiment with voice revisions.

Voice as Tone   Tone concerns the relationship I have taken to my imagined audience. Am I objective or subjective? Am I personal or impersonal? Is my tone appropriate to my subject? Look at these initial paragraphs from three different stories and try to identify the tone I have taken.

Paragraph 1

Here is the scene: while picking up my mail at my ex-husband's house, I check his mail, as usual. At noon, all the houses on the street appear empty and the hot sun of a late fall day warms my shirt. I hold up one of Steven's letters to the sky. *She* has written to him again. I know it is her, Mary, the Other Woman. She has used stationary more fragile than I would choose and I am able to see her signature by pressing the thin envelope tightly against the letter inside.

Paragraph 2

My subject might seem not worth remarking on, but I find that it sticks in my mind. For some time now, someone has been placing a large rock on the roof of my car while I am inside the General Classroom Building teaching a class. I come out of the class to the parking lot, carrying all my folders and notes and books and a thermos empty of coffee, and there I find a large, jagged rock placed directly above the driver's door on the car roof. I remove it carefully so as not to scratch the paint while thinking, momentarily, of how I might approach the class saying: "Tell me now, which one of you is putting a rock on my roof?" but I give up the idea. Twenty-three students would stare back at me, pretending to know nothing about what I'm saying.

Paragraph 3

I am sitting on my bed listening to a marimba program dedicated to the best piccolo player in the district of San Marcos. It is good marimba. The wooden sticks tangle high and low into a cat's cradle of clear notes. The cheap transistor brings it in scratchily but the tunes themselves have the flavor of old masterpieces: not ugly, modern marimba, made to order for generals with dark glasses, full of irritating brass and flattery, but the brown-seamed marimba of the old players, the late night Indian marimba that goes on now to fill my room beautifully.

For me, paragraph 1 is abrupt, asking the reader to believe this information. Facts are presented rapidly and bluntly. This paragraph seems to want to persuade the reader to accept *this* version of the facts.

For me, paragraph 2 makes its argument by piling on the detail, by filling in one complete scene, including the narrator's thoughts and imagined actions. Paragraph 2 is both apologetic and insistent; it tries to engulf the reader in the story.

For me, paragraph 3 works for both these effects, and does so through a mixture of short and long sentences, declarative statements ("It is good marimba"), and detailed defense of a viewpoint (only corrupt generals like modern military marimba). This paragraph attempts to evoke immediacy and hide the argument, which is stronger than those in the previous two paragraphs (generals are bad; Indians are good; the issues are art, taste, beauty).

Voice as Sound   To understand voice as sound, look at the ways these paragraphs make you hear the narrator's voice. For me, paragraph 1 doesn't have much sound, relying as it does instead on cinematic and visual images. "Here is the scene" asks you to *watch* the paragraph. Paragraph 3 is also visual (telling me something about myself as a writer), yet, since the subject is music, the image of a cat's cradle of clear notes helps me "hear" the piece. Also, the syntax in this paragraph moves from a long opening sentence, to a short sentence, to a third sentence that balances with the opening sentence, while the final sentence unrolls almost like the music it tries to describe: statement, qualifying statement, addition, addition, addition. Paragraph 2 includes the only oral statement "Tell me now . . . ," but the narrator in this piece seems to run along in a "voiced" internal monologue.

Voice as Persona   Another way to think about voice is to think about the person that is being created by that text voice. A persona can be a clearly assumed character. In Chapter 5, recall, I talk about writing intentionally with/for/through the voice of a historical character. At the same time, a writer's narrator is always a fictional approximation; even—some people think—when we write nonfiction, we may assume a persona: me, the time I saved the family. . . .

For me, the persona of paragraph 1 is modern and cagey. She apparently tells stories on herself we wouldn't expect most people to tell (she reads mail), but we imagine she must be doing it for an effect if she is willing to "tell all."

For me, the persona of paragraph 2 is nervous, picky, high strung, perhaps a little paranoid. She has the need to tell it all but in nutty, meticulous order.

For me, the persona of paragraph 3 is romantic and isolated, speaking from a slight distance, trying to communicate something in a difficult medium, language.

Voice as a Writer's Own Voice   Although we might consider whether a piece of writing "sounds" like a real, actual, live writer talking, speaking, moving through the world, our understanding that voices can be "assumed" makes that a difficult question. When considering whether a voice is a writer's own voice, we're more often looking for something like a voice fingerprint. Would we guess that all these pieces were by the same author? Does he or she use the same strategies, look at the world from a predictable viewpoint, build characters or scenes or sentences and paragraphs in a signature way? In one sense, only a writer with his or her own voice is open to imitation. If he or she didn't do some of these things regularly, intentionally or not, we wouldn't be able to imitate them. Yet some of these "individual" strategies must also be generic and open to imitation. For instance, I think my sentence in paragraph 3, "It was good marimba," has distinct echoes of Hemingway's terse "voice." In Chapter 5, I pointed out that we now know we may be many-voiced and that we may adopt or abandon "voices." Many writers and readers believe, though, that a writer's "voiceprint" can be found and described.

In looking at paragraphs 1 to 3 and other paragraphs that open my stories, I was surprised by my voice. I used similar gambits to open and set scenes, to put my character in the here and now of the story, and to get the action going, as in these six first sentences from six of my stories:

The nights at Haute Dog go on forever and tonight is no exception.

It was January. He would neglect his friends to stay home with his love.

At the bakery, I smell the yeast.

We are flying over a small California town, emerald green in the early spring, pressed into a setting of low foothills, veined in the draws by stands of oak trees.

It is Pierce's house. Judith will never really live here.

Eve sat on the left-hand side of the bus looking at her hands.

Although I varied person (I, we, she) and tense (continuous present, past), and gender (she, he), I seem to have similar ways of letting narration open.

Voice Revision Exercises

You can intentionally change the tone of a piece in several ways.

Experiment with formality and informality by:

1. Changing register. Decrease the number of multisyllabic words. In fact, write with words of only one syllable. Write using dialect or

slang. Choose simple, clear words over elaborate words ("It was a gray rain" instead of "It was a debilitating time of wren's wing-gray precipitation"). You may want to chart these registers:

SLANG	INFORMAL	FORMAL	PRETENTIOUSLY OVERBLOWN
raining cats and dogs	raining		wing-gray precipitation

It's possible to mix registers for a purpose. A writer simply needs to see register as part of a palette for creating a particular voice for that text and as part of the overall stylistic effect of the final product.

2. Changing point of view. Certain characters will require a more informal voice than others. Conversely, moving from a first person narrator to an omniscient third person narrator changes the formality of your piece. Often, changes in point of view require changes in register.

Experiment with the sound of voice by:

Including more dialogue, thoughts, or words that might be spoken. Take a piece of writing that has no voices and give it voice(s).

Experiment with persona by:

1. Exploring that character more fully. Sometimes your character lacks voice because you don't know what he or she is really like or would really do. Write a family history for your character. Include all of his or her relatives, childhood stories, dreams, moments of success and/or tragedy. Use some of the invention activities in Chapter 5 to "invent" your character's full life by treating him or her as a real person about whom you are writing.

2. Assuming a persona now, especially if you rarely normally do so. Take one of your favorite stars, heroes, historical characters, or book characters, and tell a story in his or her voice. The story doesn't have to be historically based or true—you're working for an accurate rendition of voice, not of fact.

Experiment with your own voice by:

1. Completing any of the multivoice writing exercises in Chapter 5.

2. Analyzing your voice. Do you have one? What is it? How does it become manifest? Can you accentuate it? Can you write without it?

3. Collaborating on a piece of writing with someone else. Did you lose your voice? Does the resulting piece of writing have a voice?

Yours or your partner's or both? As you negotiated changes, were those changes in voice?

The Pleasures of Style

Any stylistic revisions you make will of necessity affect the tone and sound of your writing, and in so doing affect the voice of the piece. The following exercises will help you look more closely at the effect of word and sentence and genre transformations, or revisions. These involve risk taking, to some extent. But remember, since you will be saving your drafts, you have the opportunity to make extensive changes, examine them, and then return, if you wish, to an earlier version if it is more effective. For these exercises, as well as for the voice revisions above, plan on talking with classmates and/or your teacher or making a journal entry about the changes you made. Putting your changes into words—verbally or in writing—is always helpful.

Descriptive Word Exercises

To understand how writer's particular word choices affect the final success of a piece, you can take any work of prose or poetry and test your word choices against the writer's original choices. You and a partner should each choose a favorite piece of writing. Type up the piece with all the adjectives and adverbs missing. Those are the words that "color" the piece. Here is a sample:

Cache Creek

Wendy Bishop

Late on a _____ day, all views were deceptive. The creek was

as _____ as the air upon it and the _____ water's

roar like waves on a _____ shore. The pool we swam

in _____ seemed limitless: the diving could never end or

the arching and treading, the _____ play. On one bank we

slid, naked, across the _____ rock and _____ clay.

A _____ time, the death of _____ summer, each minute

was full of _____ sweetness and _____ heat. When

you put your fist through the _____ plate of the pool,

water _____ around us, lapping with _____ and

_____ tongues.

The mystery of _____ moments is how they end. At the edge of an

ocean we would have _____ and taken stock. On the banks

of Cache Creek, we _____ off, then went _____ .[1]

For comparison, the complete version of "Cache Creek" appears in the notes to this chapter. This exercise works well with prose, too.

Sentence Revision Exercises

Winston Weathers calls the labyrinthine sentence and certain other experimental forms an alternative grammar, or grammar B; traditional grammar he labels grammar A.[2] He finds that certain literary writers regularly exercise their abilities in the realm of grammar B, intentionally using discontinuity and ambiguity, for instance. In essence, Weathers examines the ways writers highlight their language—working words to their own ends—by writing against the "rules." For example, although writers generally work to vary their sentence length, some writers follow their own rules and have signature sentence styles—William Faulkner is renowned for his long, intricate sentences and Ernest Hemingway for his simple, often monosyllabic- or bisyllabic-word sentences. Weathers also finds that some writers use the long, labyrinthine sentence, often in conjunction with the sentence fragment of one or two words; Gertrude Stein was famous for her fragmented writing style. The following exercises ask you to explore the labyrinthine sentence and the single-syllable-word sentence before moving on to several other sentence-level experiments: drafting cumulative sentences, free-sentence combining, and experimenting with sentence symmetry.

Labyrinthine Sentences

1. Write a sentence of fifty words or more. You may do this by starting with a paragraph you already have and combining and connecting your sentences. Then, learn to draft with a long breath, intentionally working for a longer unit of meaning.

2. Write a paragraph that has three sentences: a labyrinthine sentence followed by a fragment followed by another labyrinthine sentence.

3. Find a writer (other than any of those I've mentioned already) who uses long sentences. Try to rewrite a paragraph of your

current writing into that sentence style. What did you have to alter? How do you like the new version? To decide, read both versions aloud.

Here is an example of exercise 1 using one of my own story paragraphs:

> I am sitting on my bed listening to a marimba program dedicated to the best piccolo player in the district of San Marcos, and it is good marimba for the wooden sticks tangle high and low into a cat's cradle of clear notes, and the cheap transistor brings it in scratchily but the tunes themselves have the flavor of old masterpieces: not ugly, modern marimba, made to order for generals with dark glasses, full of irritating brass and flattery, but the brown-seamed marimba of the old players, the late night Indian marimba that goes on now to fill my room beautifully.

Notice that I connect all this material mainly by adding on sentences using *and, but, for.* Here is another version, where I try to pack the information together more elegantly.

> I am sitting on my bed listening to a cheap transistor radio, bringing in a scratchy marimba program dedicated to the best piccolo player in the district of San Marcos, a good marimba with wooden sticks tangling high and low into a cat's cradle of clear notes, a marimba where the tunes themselves have the flavor of old masterpieces—not ugly, modern marimba, made to order for generals with dark glasses, full of irritating brass and flattery—but a brown-seamed marimba of the old players, a late night Indian marimba that goes on now to fill my room beautifully.

Remember that these sentence exercises can be useful for poetry as well as prose. Often, poets will use similar sentence patterns; an entire sonnet, for instance, can be constructed from a single, deftly punctuated sentence.

Syllable and Word Experiments While labyrinthine sentences allow you to connect many ideas, single-syllable-word writing asks you to weigh the effect of each word, to stay close to regularized, simple speech patterns.

1. Write a paragraph of seventy words or more. At first, try to use only words of one syllable. You may do this by starting with a paragraph you already have and simplifying your language while trying to maintain your meaning. Later, try to draft with a simple breath, intentionally working for a plain style.

2. Write a paragraph that has regular multisyllabic-word sentences, punctuated by several single-syllable-word sentences. Try starting

with plain sentences, then get more complicated, and then return to single-syllable-word sentences. Try alternating sentence styles fairly regularly.

3. Find a writer (other than any of those I've mentioned already) who writes with a general leaning toward monosyllabic- or bisyllabic-word sentences. Rewrite a paragraph of your current writing into that sentence style. What did you have to alter? How do you like the new version? To decide, read both versions aloud.

Here is an illustration of exercise 1, again using one of my own paragraphs:

> Here is the scene: I get mail at my ex's house. I check his mail, too. At noon, all the homes on the street are dark and the hot sun of a late fall day warms my shirt. I hold up a piece of Steve's mail to the sky. It is from her, again. I know it is her, Mary. She has used paper more frail than I would choose and I can see her name. I press the thin skin to the note inside.

I managed to stay with single-syllable words until I got to the word *paper*. I also found I needed to stay in the present tense to avoid -ing and -ed endings. Again, this experiment can prove interesting for poetry, too.

Cumulative Sentences   As you drafted your labyrinthine sentences, you may have done so in three ways: by creating periodic sentences —ones with lots of modification before the main clause—or cumulative sentences—ones where most modification is added after the main clause—or, of course, you could have added modifications equally, before and after the main clause, but most of us don't balance sentences so intentionally. My first sentence in this section would be periodic if I stopped after the first main clause:

> As you drafted your labyrinthine sentences, you may have done so in three ways.

I can turn this into a cumulative sentence in this way:

> You may have drafted your labyrinthine sentences in three ways, by creating periodic sentences, or by creating cumulative sentences, or by creating a balanced sentence, although most of us don't balance sentences so intentionally.

Francis Christensen is best known for his work on generating sentences and his advocacy of the cumulative sentence—where information is added after the main clause. He studied the work of professional literary writers and found that many of those writers best noted for an effective style used cumulative sentences flexibly. His most famous example is taken from author Ernest Hemingway:

"George was coming down in the telemark position, kneeling, one leg forward and bent, the other trailing, his sticks hanging like some insect's thin legs, kicking up puffs of snow, and finally the whole kneeling, trailing figure coming around in a beautiful right curve, crouching, the legs shot forward and back, the body leaning out against the swing, the sticks accenting the curve like points of light, all in a wild cloud of snow" (112).

Exploring the Cumulative Sentence   You can work to develop your skill at making cumulative sentences by attempting and then improving on some of the following patterns:

1. Main clause,

-ing _____ ,

-ing _____ ,

and -ing _____ .

2. Main clause,

his (her, their) _____ ,

the (object) _____ .

3. Main clause,

a person _____ ,

his (her) _____ ,

-ing _____ ,

-ing _____ ,

a person _____ ,

his (her) _____ ,

-ing _____ .

4. Main clause,

with _____ ,

and _____ ,

like _____ .

5. Main clause,

the _____ ,

its _____ ,

the _____ ,

a _____ ,

a _____ ,

and a _____ .

Here's some play with two of these forms.

Sentence after pattern 1:

The patrons at Haute Dog stay all evening,
    laying paper bags on formica counters,
    savoring noisy portions of over-brewed burnt coffee,
    and telling the same story, the same story, telling it to the sleepy fry
      cook.

Sentence after pattern 4:

Haute Dog lights up a small corner of the city's sky, with a foolish glow—a three-Musketeer dog in neon—and rude sound from the corner TV spilling into the street, a place like home and not like home.

    Remember, these forms are taken from real sentences. You might easily construct your own sentence forms by studying an author you admire. You might also, in pairs, examine your own and a partner's writing for the sentence patterns each of you seems to rely on regularly.

Free-Sentence Combining   Through these sentence manipulation exercises, you will quickly realize that there are many ways to put clauses together to form longer sentences, from simple primer prose—where clauses are connected by *ands*—to more complicated subordinated and coordinated sentences like those you've explored above. To experiment with free-sentence combining, you will take apart a passage of professional prose or a passage from your own writing. Give those passages to group members, who will combine the sentences to form the most expressive and elegant passage each member can, trying to stay fairly close to the meaning signaled by those sentences. After this combining, compare the paragraphs to see what stylistic choices each member made as she reconnected the sentences. A sentence-combining exercise looks something like this:

    I am sitting.

    I am sitting on my bed.

    I am listening.

    I am listening to a marimba program.

The program is dedicated.

The dedication is to the best piccolo player in the district.

The district is San Marcos.

The marimba is good.

The wooden sticks tangle high and low.

The wooden sticks make a cat's cradle of notes.

The notes are clear.

The transistor is cheap.

The transistor brings the marimba in.

It brings it in scratchily.

The tunes have flavor.

The flavor is of old masterpieces. The flavor is not ugly.

The flavor is not modern marimba.

Modern marimba is made to order for generals.

The generals have dark glasses.

The generals are full of irritating brass and flattery.

The flavor is the brown-seamed marimba.

The brown-seamed marimba is that of the old players.

The marimba goes on.

It is late-night marimba.

It is Indian marimba.

It fills my room.

It is beautiful.

You can easily see that no two writers will combine these core (sometimes called kernel) sentences in the same ways. If you want to learn more about combining sentences in a way that will teach you about sentence structures and clauses, textbooks by Donald Daiker, Andrew Kerek, and Max Morenberg, who researched and popularized this method, will interest you.[3]

Synchrony and Genre Collage   Traditional writing in grammar A relies on diachronic—past, present, future—time order. However, writers will want to experiment with synchronic time order: past, present, and future coexisting and/or writing shifting unexpectedly in tense. Winston Weathers suggests that scrambling can help you experiment with synchrony.

1. Arbitrarily change the order of the paragraphs of a piece of diachronic writing—try adding white space between the paragraphs, perhaps numbers, to indicate change should be expected.

You may want to try adding transitions that make at least minimal sense of the intentional discontinuity.

2. Scramble a single paragraph and then try to pinpoint what is gained and what is lost from such mixing:

> *She* has written to him again. Here is the scene. She has used stationary more fragile than I would choose and I am able to see her signature by pressing the thin envelope tightly against the letter inside. While picking up my mail at my ex-husband's house, I check his mail, as usual. I hold up one of Steven's letters to the sky. I know it is her, Mary, the Other Woman. At noon, all the houses on the street appear empty and the hot sun of a late fall day warms my shirt.

3. Try arbitrary scrambling—cut and paste sections of poems and/or prose together. Or, use this method: Pick every second or third or fifth sentence throughout a story and then repeat, starting with the second sentence and following with the fifth from that one, and so on. Cut and paste work always goes more easily on a computer.

4. For a genre collage, you may pick and choose between pieces from different genres—a few lines from a poem followed by a journal entry followed by the conclusion to an essay, followed by. . . . You may choose to organize these "pieces" thematically; that is, use pieces that all have to do with loss or love. Or you may take fragments and weave a narrative around them, using the fragments to prompt the developing story.

While I want to encourage you to take risks and to extend your revision beyond simply fixing up spelling problems or tacking on a better ending, I also want to remind you that exercises like the ones I've shared here are not useful unless you explore them within the context of your own writing. Also, I have offered only a brief indication of the possibilities of grammar B and the pleasures of revision for style. If you feel that you don't have a firm grasp of the conventions of standard English, you'll want to study conventions while you continue to write. Usage rules can be found in any college-level handbook.

Fluent writers are always dipping into and out of style revision as they learn about the force and flexibility of their own language. My best advice in this area is that you take risks, but study what you risked and what you gained. Joy Harjo captures for me the essence of revision when she says:

> I begin with the seed of an emotion, a place, and then move from there. It means hours watching the space form in the place in front of the typewriter, speaking words, listening to them, watching them form, and be crossed out, on the paper, and so on, and yes,

revision. I no longer see the poem as an ending point, perhaps more the end of a journey, an often long journey that can begin years earlier, say with the blur of the memory of the sun on someone's cheek, a certain smell, an ache, and will culminate years later in a poem, sifted through a point, a lake in my heart through which language must come. . . . (qtd. in Coltelli 68)

Revision helps you discover the ongoing conversation that your writing has with itself. Revision helps you enjoy the long and necessary journey of writing. And revision helps you use language to plumb the depths of the lake in your heart.

Notes

1. "Cache Creek" is reprinted from *Prairie Schooner* 60, no. 2 (1985), by permission of University of Nebraska Press. Copyright 1985 University of Nebraska Press. Here is the complete version:

Cache Creek

Wendy Bishop

Late on a summer's day, all views were
    deceptive. The creek was as warm as the
    air upon it and the rock-tumbled water's
    roar like waves on a distant shore. The
    pool we swam in suddenly seemed limitless:
    the diving could never end or the arching
    and treading, the dolphin play. On one
    bank we slid, naked, across the crumbling
    rock and blue clay.
A sly time, the death of another summer,
    each minute was full of mineral sweetness
    and salty heat. When you put your fist
    through the clear plate of the pool,
    water foamed around us, lapping with
    smaller and smaller tongues.
The mystery of certain moments is how they
    end. At the edge of an ocean we would have
    paused and taken stock. On the banks of
    Cache Creek, we dried off, then went on.

2. See Weathers.
3. See Daiker, Kerek, and Morenberg's text, *The Writer's Options.*

Sources and Readings

Bloom, Lynn Z. "How I Write." *Writers on Writing*. Ed. Tom Waldrep. Vol. 1. New York: Random House, 1985. 33–37.

Christensen, Francis. "A Generative Rhetoric of the Sentence." *Rhetoric and Composition: A Sourcebook for Teachers and Writers*. Ed. Richard L. Graves. Portsmouth, NH: Boynton/Cook, 1984. 110–118.

Coltelli, Laura, ed. *Winged Words: American Indian Writers Speak*. Lincoln: U of Nebraska P, 1990.

Daiker, Donald, Andrew Kerek, and Max Morenberg. "Using 'Open' Sentence-Combining Exercises in the College Composition Classroom." *Rhetoric and Composition: A Sourcebook for Teachers and Writers*. Ed. Richard L. Graves. Portsmouth, NH: Boynton/Cook, 1984. 100–9.

_____. *The Writer's Options: College Sentence Combining*. New York: Harper and Row, 1979.

Dillard, Annie. *The Writing Life*. New York: Harper, 1989.

Elbow, Peter. *Embracing Contraries: Explorations in Learning and Teaching*. New York: Oxford UP, 1986.

_____. *Writing with Power: Techniques for Mastering the Writing Process*. New York: Oxford UP, 1981.

Madden, David. *Revising Fiction: A Handbook for Fiction Writers*. New York: New American Library, 1988.

Murray, Donald. "The Feel of Writing—and Teaching Writing." *Learning by Teaching*. Portsmouth, NH: Boynton/Cook Heinemann, 1982.

Passaro, Vince. "Tales from a Literary Marriage." *New York Times Magazine* 21 April 1991: 34–43, 76.

Straub, Richard. "What We Talk About When We Talk About Voice." Unpublished manuscript.

Tsujimoto, Joseph I. *Teaching Poetry Writing to Adolescents*. Urbana, IL: National Council of Teachers of English, 1988.

Weathers, Winston. "Grammars of Style: New Options in Composition." *Rhetoric and Composition: A Sourcebook for Teachers and Writers*. Ed. Richard L. Graves. Portsmouth, NH: Boynton/Cook, 1984. 133–47.

Chapter 8

Evaluating Your Writing

The word is reevaluated as the phrase is created and recorded. The phrase is reevaluated as the sentence is created and recorded. The paragraph is reevaluated as the page is created and recorded. The page is reevaluated as the entire piece of writing is created and recorded. And then the writer, having once finished the writing and put it away, picks it up and evaluates it again.

—DONALD MURRAY

It's natural. After you write, you want to know how well you succeeded. Did you scare the reader of your Gothic mystery? Did you write a poem about the moment your father first shared his feelings and his trust in you, and did your reader pause at the crucial line, rereading and savoring feelings it called forth? Did your classmates laugh at the right point in your comic drama when the first act was read aloud during workshop?

Because writing is an endlessly reiterative activity, evaluation is inevitable in a writing process; it occurs at each decision point along the way. This chapter will have succeeded if it extends your understanding and use of evaluation techniques. I ask you to be an active self-evaluator and to participate with your class and teacher to make evaluation a procedure that tells you both *what* is happening and *how well* it's happening. Essentially, you should continuously ask yourself: "What have I done?" *and* "What have I learned from what I have done?"

Before now, your experiences with evaluation may have been purely prescriptive; that is, an "expert" told you only what you had done—usually what you had done wrong. As a result, you now probably have a tendency to sit back and wait for the teacher to make claims about your writing: how it worked or didn't work, whether you produced A, B, or C grade work for the semester. However, you learn more, feel better, and act more like the writer you are and want to be when you actively ask for and participate in evaluation. Professional writers are always setting goals—often simple ones like "Just get it written today!"—working toward those goals, reevaluating work, and then continuing. Evaluation contributes to their growing skills just as it will contribute to yours.

The Writing Classroom and Evaluation

Because most of us learn about evaluation within the classroom, by relying on the insight and opinions of others, this chapter starts with a survey of the many ways evaluation can be organized as part of your workshop. However, because many of us do as much or more writing outside the workshop, the ultimate goal of this discussion is to have you learn to make evaluation a part of your personal writing process. Although this is *self*-evaluation, I hope you'll continue to rely on the response of other writer-friends and editors that you meet or seek out, for those individuals can help confirm your maturing insights into your own work.

Group Evaluation

Most of us set writing goals based on our own reading; that is, we read works that move us and we try to emulate those writers we admire. We also, however, need to negotiate writing criteria within our first writing community, the writing workshop. Criteria can be developed in several ways. For instance, your class can develop genre criteria by first reading samples of free verse or formal verse or classic short stories or science fiction or one-act plays. Next, you discuss the success and failure of several of these readings. Finally—drawing on all your previous reading experiences and your class discussions of new work—you make up charts that list attributes of an A, B, C, and D grade one-act play, story, or lyric poem. This can be done also by substituting categories like Great, Average, Boring.

In many classes, criteria development begins as you define elements of successful writing *in general*. That is, you and your classmates decide that an A, B, C, or D piece of writing has, in general, certain identifiable attributes. Later, these categories can be tailored to the genre of the piece under discussion. Below, I illustrate criteria setting with definitions negotiated by four three-member writing groups. Each group worked to define its own general categories. Next, the teacher compiled the four sets of group definitions into a handout of class criteria. This handout, which also, of course, reflected the teacher's knowledge and concerns, provided the class with a community-defined, preliminary grading rubric—that is, rules or criteria— for evaluation.

Group 1

Overall—meaning is clear, good choice of words, originality, fluency

1 = contains good stuff—meets/exceeds criteria

2 = good, enjoyable but could be improved

3 = off base, needs work BUT good effort?

+ or − = degree

Group 2

Way above average: A sense of purpose

Easy to read

Interesting

Good title

Originality

Flow

Above average: Clear

Good variation

Good word usage

Good intro and conclusion

Average: Title

Sense of organization

Needs variation

Unclear purpose

Group 3

A—Clear description and detail

Eye-catching title

Images, metaphors, similes

surprises

B—Clear description and detail

Title doesn't fit poem

Lacks images, metaphors, similes, or surprises

C—Vague

Average

Bland

D—Too general

Abstract

Too many questions

Not well defined

Poor title and ending

No flow

Group 4

A—Flows, clear purpose, interests the reader, good intro and conclusions, grammar, original and creative

B—A weaker intro or conclusion but good details and background, good ideas, knows what he's talking about, grammar could be improved

C—Clichés, have basic idea, needs more structure, better word choice, repetition, mechanical problems, weak intro or conclusion

Before I present the teacher's composite version, try writing down your own criteria or do this with a class group. Start by exploring the following issues.

Questions

1. What are the basic, essential criteria in each category?

2. What do you think these writers meant by "flow" and "cliché" and "original"? Equally important, what would you mean by those terms?

3. Many groups included "title" as an important element of a piece of writing. Do you? Why or why not?

Now, here is the composite version of these students' criteria.

Creative Writing Evaluation Criteria:
By the Class, for the Class

An A means: Meaning is clear. Excellent word choices. Work is original and reads smoothly. Fluency meets and exceeds criteria for assignment. It has a sense of purpose, is interesting; the title is good, and the reader does not have to stop reading because of distraction due to obscurity or error. Descriptions are clear and detail is eye-catching. Also, it has to have images and surprises. It probably has metaphors and similes. The grammar is right. It is creative. All this, in addition to all of the strengths listed below.

A B means: The piece is clear, has variety, good word usage, and starts and ends nicely. It is enjoyable but could be improved. Description is clear and there is a lot of detail. It is original and creative and the background is set up well. The writer seems to know what he is talking about. There may be a few mistakes, and one or two weak spots, like the ending or beginning, that could be improved in another draft.

A C means: Average, predictable, clichéd. The basic ideas are there, but the piece needs more structure and better word choices. There is a feeling of any of the following: vagueness, blandness, averageness. It has a title and a sense of organization, but needs variety. The overall purpose of the writing may not be clear to the reader. The writer has put forth a good effort, but is somehow straying off base. The piece has not been polished. The reader has questions after reading the piece, or feels confused. The writer needs to make more major changes between drafts or do more drafts.

A D means: Below average, abstract, confusing; things are not well defined. Poor title, poor ending, and a lack of flow. The piece is not a pleasure to read; the reader wonders why the person wrote it.

Questions

1. How important is it to understand these terms: *polished, straying off base, averageness, clear, weak spot, interesting?*

2. Do you, your group, or your class, agree with these criteria?

3. These criteria don't seem to have been listed in any particular order; take these lists (or lists your group or your class made up) and agree on an order of priority of criteria elements within each grade category. First, an A piece should . . . , second, an A piece should. . . . Does order of criteria make any difference to the writer and/or the evaluator?

4. Although your group or class can agree on criteria for each grade category, applying these criteria still requires a subjective judgment from the evaluator. What do you think about that? Is there any way to make the judgment less subjective? Should evaluation be objective or subjective?

Practicing Evaluation Evaluators improve through practice as they gain experience and articulate what they are doing as they develop and apply evaluation criteria to texts. In Chapter 7, on revision, I pointed out that revision and evaluation are so highly connected that Chapters 7 and 8 should be read nearly simultaneously. All the response skills you develop in your groups—the ability to read carefully, to identify the strengths and weaknesses and possible directions for a piece of writing, to discuss and undertake stylistic alternatives—help to construct you as an evaluator: someone able to define, set, and respond to community-sanctioned criteria.

Different kinds of evaluation can and should take place at different points in the composing process. For instance, as you work out an idea by doing a lot of unpolished freewriting, you need and crave nonevaluative response—an audience to read to, rather than an evaluator who might be pointedly critical at the wrong time. When the work being offered is clearly in the early draft stage, it is a mistake to apply detailed criticism. And when a draft is ready for final, detailed editing, it is of no help to the writer if you give only a supportive response.

Evaluation Exercise

As a class, it can be useful to take a practice piece of writing through several types of response and evaluation.[1]

1. Freewrite a beginning to a work in class together (use any of the exercises in Chapters 3 or 5). In groups or as a full class, listen as several freewrites are read aloud. No one comments.

2. Take your freewrite home and extend it into a sharable draft.

3. Next, circulate copies of your new—*second*—draft to the three to five members of your group. After reading this draft, each group member writes a "movie of the reader's mind," narrating everything each thought as she or he read this second draft. For each author, one or two group members reads her or his "movie" aloud.

4. During the next class, each author reads the same second draft and group members answer any or all of the following metaphorical response questions:

   What color is the piece?

   What adjective describes the piece?

If it were an animal, what animal would this piece be?

If it were a sound, what sound would this piece be?

What is the wish of this piece?

What is hidden in this piece?

What is almost—but still not—being said?

This piece is a puzzle with one piece missing; what is that missing piece?

What does this piece make you hope?

5. Take your draft home, and, using the movies or metaphorical statements you collected, write a *final draft*. Make enough copies for a group but don't put your name on the piece. In class, your group exchanges work with another group. Individually or as a group, evaluate the pieces of writing using the A, B, C, D criteria given above or the criteria developed by your class for your class. Write the grade on each of the papers you are evaluating and briefly list the reasons for those grades. Groups exchange the work again, returning to each member his or her own graded piece. Groups now decide if they agree or disagree with the evaluations given by the other group.

Self-Evaluation and the Portfolio Method

Self-evaluation takes many forms. Often, the journal is your best forum for setting writing goals, responding to class and critique sessions, and evaluating class progress. In many of my classes, I ask writers to complete a writing process cover sheet for each piece of writing. This cover sheet is a narrative, the story of the writing from conception to final revision. Each time the work is taken up again, the writer is encouraged to add to the process cover sheet narration. The writer's self-evaluation helps me, as the final class evaluator, to understand the context of the writing—what was learned along the way—as I respond to the final product. Here is a sample narrative (the writing under discussion appears in Chapter 10).

Sample Writing Process Cover Sheet
Writer: Sarah
Paper Title: "Attack of the Foibles"
Instructor: Wendy Bishop
Date: 9 October 1989
Audience: Instructor, Fellow Students, Humor Column Readers

Discussion:

This portfolio draft of my columns "Attack of the Foibles" went through several processes of creation. The idea was sparked by my instructor mentioning her problem with writing interesting letters to relatives. My own personal letters were filled with the foibles of daily life which regularly attack me, shared with my family for laughs.

When the instructor requested of us four paper ideas, a series of these letters or perhaps a column like them was one of the ideas I presented to her. She, in turn, expanded the idea to a challenge to write seven one-page columns of this type. I accepted with enthusiasm.

I had intended to work on a more serious paper, one of equal interest to me, prior to the columns challenge. But the very evening after that class, the columns started writing themselves in my head, intruding upon my other activities. Two ideas awoke me during the night, forcing me to scribble them on my bedside pad. A third came during my morning coffee out on the patio. Since I had just the weekend for a first draft and my previously planned paper topic required some digging, needing research, I gave in to my persistent column muse.

The first drafts seemingly wrote themselves. Before I sat down at the typewriter, I had worked out, then fixed a light breakfast, since writing is, for me, an all day process, not to be interrupted. Then I drafted. I took these first drafts to class Monday for critiquing. Although we only had time to critique two of the seven daily columns, I received a lot of solid, useful suggestions from a new group member. This is the first time I can remember feeling even more excitement about a project when facing revision; it made me appreciate the insight and constructive criticism of this new member.

Armed with his suggestions, I spent the next morning reviewing all seven of the columns, using his critique of the first two as a test of the others. I revised them all, some more extensively than the others, and two of the columns I revised a third time. All of this was done in pencil on the original drafts.

Between classes that same day, I returned to the typewriter, following the penciled revisions on the first draft revisions and typed out clean copies of the second and/or third draft revisions of each column.

I am fairly happy with the new revisions, with some worry in one area. Most of the columns start with a personal experience then relate it to a larger issue at the end. Two are strictly humorous with no ending moral or political connection. These are the first two I wrote; the more/political tie-ins at the ends of the others seemed to creep in on me unnoticed. Perhaps this isn't a problem since the humor columnists I read display this same inconsistency. And, I'd hate to have to make every piece a soapbox when there should be a time to laugh at something just for the sake of the thing.

Overall, I spent about eight to ten hours on the first draft (not counting the times ideas intruded upon other activities and had to be scribbled down). The second and third drafts took about four to five hours of thought, writing, and rewriting. The retyping for the final drafts took about four to five hours.

For most of us, evaluating writing is a demanding task. Evaluating a single piece of writing (especially if it isn't accompanied with the writer's self-evaluation or process narration) is even more difficult. Because of this, in many writing classes, teachers request that single pieces of writing be evaluated according to mutually negotiated goals; this is called individualized goal setting. That is, you and the teacher agree beforehand what you will concentrate on and what you hope to accomplish before the next (often final) draft. Also, many classes are now evaluated through some version of a portfolio method. Both are described next.

Individualized Goal Setting   In individualized goal setting, the following steps allow you and your teacher to tailor the process to your needs. Remember, you can substitute a tutor or writing group friend for the teacher and use this technique outside of the classroom.

1. In an early one-to-one conference on a sharable draft of a piece of writing you want to revise, you and your teacher share impressions of the strengths and weaknesses of the work at that point.

2. You and your teacher each take a moment to list goals for your next revision. She might list these: Explore a new opening paragraph (or stanza); eliminate clichés; retain that great metaphor about seagulls weaving seaweed shrouds, but make all the other metaphors extend and deepen the ocean imagery. You might write these: Get rid of trite (expected) ways of saying things, vary the way I start my sentences; think about adding another character to the opening scene (or stanza) who will be able to clarify what I want the reader to feel about this desolate beach.

3. You and your teacher look at both lists and agree that the final draft will be evaluated by the general class criteria as well as by the goals from both lists that the two of you have agreed on. For example, she will look specifically at how well you (a) open the piece, (b) use vivid, original language, and (c) use ocean imagery and set your beach scene.

4. When the teacher evaluates the next draft, she reviews the individualized goals you set together and makes sure to include thoughts about them on her final response to your piece. You may also comment on these goals at the end of your process cover sheet, if you write one.

5. If time doesn't allow for a conference with your teacher on each

piece of writing, you can set goals yourself or use your group to help you set goals that your teacher can comment on. Remember, you won't achieve all of your goals on each piece and you may continue to set the same goals for a while, adding new goals when you're ready to juggle new writing demands. Don't forget to add new goals that help push you to experiment with your writing.

Portfolio Evaluation   Writing portfolios are collections of your class work that are reviewed several times during the semester and/or at the end of the semester. Portfolios can contain all your work—sketches, drafts, and final versions—or only your best work—your three best pieces and your own self-evaluation, for example. Portfolios can be done in cycles: You draft, prepare, and share work up to midterm and then "retire" this work. Next you draft, prepare, and share your work from midterm to the end of term. Portfolios represent your development as a writer through this period.

Portfolios are interactive; they allow both writer and teacher to review classroom growth and agree on the worth of your semester's work. They also allow you to mobilize all of the evaluation possibilities reviewed so far. In addition, portfolio reviews present you with an opportunity to set goals and evaluate a certain number of writings *and drafts*. With portfolios, I call early drafts *rough drafts*; these are the pieces you share orally for nonevaluative feedback. I call late drafts *professional drafts*; these are works you have shaped fully enough to share in typed form with members of your group, and for which you usually request descriptive or criteria-based response and evaluation. *Portfolio drafts* are edited versions of your work, and, since those drafts are, essentially, being "published," they represent the best those pieces can be to that point.

Submitting the Portfolio   Sharing a portfolio with your teacher partway through the semester allows you to see where you have been and where you might go. For a mid- or end of the semester evaluation, your teacher usually asks you to place your writing in a two-pocket folder. In one pocket are *rough* and *professional* drafts for each piece of required writing and possibly your journal. In the other pocket are *portfolio* quality drafts of required work and, possibly, a *letter of self-evaluation*. Your teacher will read the portfolio drafts carefully, review other portfolio materials briefly, and respond both to the portfolio as a whole and to your letter of self-evaluation, if used.

Understanding Teacher Evaluation

There is an excitement in having an "authority" look at your writing. If everything goes well, she will like what you have done and validate you as a writer. When you receive a positive response, this encouragement and support spurs you on, making you eager to write. When you receive a negative response, however, you feel mistreated, misunderstood, depressed. There seems no reason to go further with your draft and no reason to have spent so much time already.

In the first scenario, you may be relying too much on the opinion of a single, fallible human; that is, experts are expert but each represents only one voice and one opinion, and another person with similar qualifications might respond to your work somewhat differently. In the second scenario, you're again relying too much on an opinion but in a different way; you're confusing a critique of a work with a critique of your self.

There is no doubt, however, that some teachers are more able than others and more sensitive in expressing their evaluations, reflecting what they see in our work. You can ensure that you receive the most information about your writing by actively participating in evaluation at all stages of your writing. Ask questions in class, share conferences and drafts with your teacher, listen to what he says to you and to others, and spend some time thinking about the evaluation issues presented in this chapter.

Evaluation Vocabulary

Having experienced peer response sessions, you already know that finding clear yet sensitive ways to talk about writing is difficult. You know that hearing that your work is "nice" or "interesting" or "flows well" isn't particularly informative. Equally though, you know that hearing that your work is "bad" or "superficial" or "seems to lack commitment" could be a devastating way to talk about a writing product that absorbed so much of your time and energy.

To understand your own response to evaluation you will benefit from looking back at writing you have done during any class in your past. You might want to make lists of words or phrases teachers have used to respond to your writing. You'll find that in some cases, you have little or no idea what they were talking about. Equally, you'll find that some teachers prefer to write notes to you at the end of your work rather than edit your work and that some prefer pencil rather than the English teacher's (in)famous red pen. Following are short student responses to teacher evaluation that show the strong reactions some of us develop when evaluated.

Response 1

For example, since childhood when all the paper had to say was "see me" in ink from the teacher, it just created fear. When I entered college, I was afraid of my professors—I looked at them as if they were academic Gods and tended to shy away. As my years progressed, I found they are (most of the time) willing to help and to share their knowledge in a way which will benefit the students. When a student receives a negative comment from a teacher, he or she should go to conference with the instructor immediately.

Response 2

Ms. C. is an avid responder. More importantly, Ms. C is a reader and lets me know what feelings my writing evoked. I do not feel Ms. C's responses are automatic or from a "menu" or canned sayings to be added to student papers. There seem to be a minimum of those subjective words like "Good," "Weak," etc. that cry for explanation.

Writer Alberta Turner analyzed the response language used by creative writing teachers and found some of the following vocabulary choices that she felt were less than effective. When you look back at your earlier writing, see if your teachers' comments match any of these observations. In class, discuss ways of speaking that she brings up that you find acceptable and ways the teachers' comments she explored could be improved or made more informative and exact.

> [T]hese poets seem almost deliberately to avoid using many of the standard critical terms. For *theme* they tend to say *center* or *impulse*. For *persona* or *point of view* or *tone* they tend to say *voice*. They use colloquial and slang terms, such as *gut, cute, quirky, schmaltz;* moral terms, such as *self-indulgent, earned, committed;* metaphors such as the poem that *disintegrates,* the *view that takes breath;* euphemisms, such as *this bothers me,* instead of *this is cacophonous* or *this is a mixed metaphor.* They use abstractions which have been worn smooth in lay language to perform some very important value judgments—for example, *interesting* to mean *significant* or even *profound; surprise* to mean the effect produced by the most skillful fusion of theme, image, rhythm, and diction. Only rarely do they speak of *tension* or *texture* or *irony.* (*Poets Teaching* 5)

Turner's observations show both writing students and writing teachers that attention to evaluation vocabulary can help the necessary communication between writing novice and writing coach.

Finally, here are two samples of creative writing teacher commentary. The first is a response sheet to a five-page short story. The teacher has filled out his evaluation sheet with comments intended to help the author revise "The Man in the Woods." The portfolio draft of this story can be found in Chapter 9.

After filling out a response sheet (see page 212), this teacher added responses to the student's text, saying "good" and "nice

WRITER'S NAME: Jackie

CONSTRUCTION—CONFLICT, CRISIS, RESOLUTION—SCENES

Great situation. c|c|R doesn't seem to
be present enough — he leaves because she
didn't come 1 day? Too extreme. If he is
that sensitive, we need more evidence.

SHOWING AND TELLING—SIGNIFICANT DETAIL—MECHANICS—ACTIVE VOICE

Good use of telling detail. Few mechanical
errors.

CHARACTER—PROTAGONIST—ROUND—SPEECH/ACTION/THOUGHT/GESTURE

Both are believable characters. Nice use of
the four methods of presentation, with the
exception of thought — more of this.

ATMOSPHERE—SETTING—ENVIRONMENT SYMBOLISM—DESCRIPTION

Nicely sad. He could leave with more
apparent regret, looking over the place
with more emotion.

POINT OF VIEW

Third is right — we need to look
from a distance.

THEME—IDEA AND EMOTION   We do feel sad, but
we might feel more if there was more of
a story, if we spent more time with
these two characters if they did more.

MISCELLANEOUS

Strong tonal control -- good work (85)

detail" in the margin, correcting mechanical errors, indicating the place where the writer had "nice tonal control," and so on.

The second teacher filled the text and margins of a four-page story, "The Bassoon Blues," which appears in Chapter 9, with similar comments, written in pencil, and ended with a summary—a short note to the author. On the text itself he wrote "deliberate clichés" and "nice cartoonish feel" and "irony clear without this rhetorical question," and he crossed out some words and asked for a few grammatical changes. The teacher's final comments to the portfolio draft of this story read as follows:

> Aimee:
> The ideosyncratic kinds of characters here are conveyed in a similarly quirky, almost cartoonish style. The fictional equivalent of Pee Wee Herman. Strangest of all, I think, is the relationship between Reg and Marie, which seems to hang on the bassoon playing. The more natural, human element of the piece cuts against the grain of the farcical surface. You could do more with this effect of making the humanity of these comic creations sneak up on the reader with a kind of unsettling depth. Reminds me a little of Confederacy of Dunces or Modern Baptists in this way.
>
> Points: 95

Without even reading the story each teacher refers to, we can begin to define their response styles. To me, the first teacher has some clear assignment goals and uses the response sheet rather like a checklist, telling the writer whether he or she has accomplished the task. The second teacher is concerned with giving the author an idea of his reading experience—what he thought as he read the story: that it was cartoonish—and what texts in his personal reading past the story reminded him of. In a way, this teacher is saying, "You might enjoy reading *Confederacy of Dunces* since you take on some of the challenges that the author of that book completed successfully." It's easy to see from these teacher comments that you can expect a range of response focus and intensity. Remember the advice given to you earlier by student writers: Always take advantage of conferences to learn more about what your teacher means with his or her written commentary. Always remember, too, that the remarks are discussions of your writing, not of you as a person.

Looking for Wider Evaluation: Publication

At some point, you will feel that a piece of your work is publishable. In order to find out if this is so, you'll want to submit your work to journal editors. Journals and editors, of course, vary, and so does the quality of the responses they are able to give you. Still, when you learn about and then participate in the world of small press publishing, you gain insights into writing and the world of writers.

Start Locally

In most communities, particularly university communities, you'll be able to find a number of fellow writers. These writers may have already helped to establish local publishing opportunities for workshop students—with your city newspaper, your college newspaper, your school's English department journal, and various city or regional small presses.

Newspapers If your newspaper doesn't already provide opportunities for literary publishing, you may want to contact the appropriate editors and suggest this possibility. For instance, the newspaper might accept creative writing pieces on a regular basis, have them reviewed by a local writer, and periodically publish the best of them in a special Sunday supplement. You might collect and prepare writing for holiday issues or for special issues on local and regional events, or offer to put together a collection of writings that represent what is going on in the college workshops. Through the responses of community readers, you may receive enough encouragement to turn the special issue into a weekly or monthly or seasonal publishing opportunity.

A college newspaper may be even more receptive to printing writing by workshop students on a regular or special issue basis. Talk to students who are already on the staff about how best to approach the editor.

The English Department Most English departments with developing or established writing programs support graduate and/or undergraduate creative writing journals. Usually, interested students work under the guidance of a student editor and department faculty member/advisor to review submissions and print work on a quarterly, biannual, or annual basis. Financial support comes from subscriptions and contributions by local advertisers or donors. Working as part of the editorial staff on one of these magazines is a fine way to learn about publishing from both a writer's and editor's viewpoint. Experience on one of these journals will also give you the credentials to contact local newspapers about special issues.

Local or Regional Journals   Local or regional journals may be run by graduates of your university writing programs or by devoted book enthusiasts who may own or run local bookstores. These individuals want to have a chance to share work they value, and they often put in long hours for little monetary return. Their presses may be staffed by volunteer editors and run on a shoestring—perhaps from an inheritance helped out by a national grant. These days their work is enhanced by desktop publishing. Small presses are committed, often idiosyncratic, odd, and enlightened.

Sometimes small presses rise to prominence: an example was the magazine *kayak*, published by George Hitchcock in the 1970s and 1980s, which became an archive-in-progress of American surrealistic writing. Published out of Hitchcock's Victorian house in Santa Cruz, California, the magazine was shaped by his taste and wide connection with underground and emerging writers.

Most often, though, small journals are not known nationally. Nevertheless, they contribute greatly to their local community by publishing work that might otherwise be overlooked; they also network with other small presses in the region. Regional journals as well as journals from all sections of the United States and Canada are listed in *The International Directory of Little Magazines and Small Presses,* published annually by Len Fulton of Dustbooks. If you could arrange the first twenty-five editions of this reference book together on a bookshelf, you would see, literally, that interest in small press publishing in these two countries has increased steadily over the years. The most recent directory has 900 pages and 4,800 listings.

Submitting Your Work

Every writing teacher and published author has a different opinion about whether and how to submit work for publication. Here's what I think: (1) If you've worked hard at your writing and have a pretty good idea of what you were trying to do in a piece; (2) if you've drafted, revised, shared, and undertaken improvements in a piece, considering the sound advice of trustworthy readers; and (3) if your readers or your own best sense tells you this is a piece to be proud of—then go ahead, share your work.

After that rousing send-off, however, remember that there is sharing and there is sharing. You don't have to share your work right off with *The New Yorker*, especially if you haven't seriously read work printed in that prestigious magazine. Plan to submit your work *appropriately*—to your local and regional audiences first, and then, if you receive positive responses in that arena, to the wider audiences of university publishers and national magazines. In either case, you have to have some understanding of the forum you wish to enter. Remember that public readings or readings on local radio stations should be considered a form of "publication" of your work. Also, you need to prepare a manuscript that is worthy of another busy person's attention.

Preparing the Manuscript

An exquisitely edited manuscript is essential. You want to be sure that any language exploration in your piece is intended—not an accidental typo. Preparing your work for public is much like doing the same for yourself. That is, when you dress up for a job interview, you put a lot of thought into grooming, into imagining the interview from the opening greeting to the closing comments, into being ready for alternatives, and into knowing about your prospective employer, colleagues, and company. Similar things hold true when you submit your work to the public.

First, prepare a clean copy of your poem, story, play, or sketch.[2] Your work should be typed; when using a computer printer, laser copy is preferable to dot-matrix copy. Use black ink on good quality 8½"-by-11" paper. Your name should be clearly shown, unless you are entering a competition that asks for anonymous entries and gives you directions for manuscript format. You always want to include the title of your work, and your address and, sometimes, phone number. At the editor's discretion, poetry can be single-spaced; most other manuscripts should be double-spaced. Consecutive pages should be clearly numbered, and tagged with the author's last name or a short form of the title.

For prose, fiction or nonfiction, usually your name and address (and sometimes a word count) appear in the upper left-hand corner, your title appears a quarter or a third of the way down the page in block capitals, and then your double-spaced prose begins.

For poetry, your submission begins the same way; word count is not necessary although line count may be substituted. Generally, a poem starts each line at the left-hand margin; sometimes poems have a wider than usual margin—up to 2 inches from the left edge of the page (1½ inches is standard for prose). If the poem continues to another page, you can type "Continued" at the bottom of the page. If you break at a stanza, you may want to type in "white space" to indicate this; in certain prose manuscripts you may need to do this also.

For plays, convention asks you to single-space lines but double-space between speeches. Center the character's name on the page and capitalize it for reading ease. Speeches run across the page; stage directions are indented halfway across the page and placed in parenthesis. The act, scene, and page are typed at the top right-hand side of every page.

Most writers, after submitting their pieces to workshop, have a sense of what shape manuscripts should be in. You follow manuscript conventions when preparing your work for workshop since these conventions tend to make your work clear and readable. Following manuscript conventions prepares your work for the best possible reading it can have, short of being published. A presentable manuscript is its own best argument for a careful reading from friends, workshop peers, and editors.

More mysterious to the first-time submitter may be the substance and form of a submission cover letter. Any time you send your work out, you'll want to include a letter telling who you are and why you are asking the editor to read your work. Since editors read a lot of submissions (and remember they usually do this for *no* money), you want to be brief and to the point. At a minimum, your cover letter explains that you have included a manuscript, of what sort, to what journal. Sometimes, you will want to note special circumstances: you are sending this in at the suggestion of a teacher or friend of the editor's, why you think the work particularly appropriate for the journal, and, when possible, previous publications in which your work has appeared. However, be careful about what you decide are special circumstances. Editors hate pretentiousness in the form of special stationery or extraordinary claims for your work based on nothing but your own opinion, and they dislike an author who seems to know nothing about their journal and its potential audience—at the least, you should have read an issue in the library. My own letters usually take some form of the following:

Return Address

Date
Editor's Address

Dear _____ :

Please consider the enclosed story (poem, play . . .) for publication in _____. Do not return the manuscript but use the enclosed SASE for your editorial decision. You may be interested in knowing that my work has appeared most recently in _____.

Thanks for your reading time; I look forward to hearing from you. Sincerely,

Note: Do not stuff reams of material into a microscopic envelope. Also, *always* send a self-addressed stamped envelope with postage sufficient for the return of the entire manuscript or, if you only wish notification, a stamped legal-size envelope. Do not use a post office metered tape for the return envelope since the post office will accept metered mail only on the date that postage is purchased.

Publication, as you can see, represents a considerable investment from all concerned. The author needs to invest time in composing, revising, and proofing before he can hope to submit a truly impressive text. He needs to have read the newspaper or journal to which he is submitting his writing. He needs to provide a return envelope and adequate postage and to write a brief but informative cover letter. He must keep track of where he submits and then be prepared to wait; answers from magazines and journals can take from one week (unusual) to over a year (disappointingly long—send a polite query after three or four months to find out the fate of your work). Publication, the work's appearance in print, can be wearisomely delayed—six months to two years is not unusual.

The editor invests also. She carefully reads innumerable legible and illegible manuscripts, keeps records, returns work, accepts work (often after providing editorial suggestions), and then spends untold hours publishing the work. The publishing side of little magazines is complicated, and I don't cover it here, but you may want to learn about it by working on a magazine staff someday. There you'll learn to estimate a manuscript by its quality and honest presentation, not by its fancy typescript and expensive stationery, and to sympathize with the long hours required to produce a slim journal of prose and poetry.

When you move on to wider publishing, or at least want to consider a wider audience, you can consult some of the books listed at the end of this chapter. Most writing texts like this provide you with insights into the world of publishing that you'll later augment with your own experiences. Beyond local publications, your next audience will be the literary magazines of other universities. Some of these have long histories and solid reputations: *The Georgia Review* (University of Georgia), *Western Humanities Review* (University of Utah), *The Massachusetts Review* (University of Massachusetts), and others.

There are also associations and national "trade" magazines for academic and professional creative writers; you'll find the most important listed in Appendix A. Join these for their newsletters, the books they print about writing as a business, and for information about contests, summer institutes, and writers' retreats.

One last warning: Don't expect to become a published author by working entirely on your own, sending out work to editor after editor without thinking carefully about the journals they represent. Editors are willing to give you encouragement only if they can see that your self-preparation has been adequate. That means you've taken workshops or otherwise worked with published writers; you've read widely; and you've prepared readable manuscripts in the appropriate formats that address the journal's intended audiences.

To show the clear but tenuous connection of publishing to evaluation, I close here with a taste of editorial comment, culled from a variety of submissions. Remember, editors are committed but busy people. Sometimes they answer with encouragement, sometimes with a form letter. Sometimes they teach a writer a lot; sometimes they provide nothing more than a reminder that the publishing world is very competitive. This competitiveness explains why I suggest that you start locally and participate in the world of writing-into-publishing in a responsible manner, through active commitment and careful work. When you do, you'll find it a rewarding enterprise. If you're not ready to consider publication beyond the workshop, that's fine, too. There's a lot to be learned about your craft and many years in which to do so.

A Bouquet of Editors on Submissions

Dear ——:

I'm in my mountain adobe near Taos without typewriter and proper paper. Please excuse the untidy — and perhaps unwelcome — letter. "Girlfriend" seems to fall a little short of publication.

By and large, the story lacks texture and resonance. We do get a glimpse of Pierce's "cowboy code," a boyish clod hiding between layers of sentimentality. Of Judy, we know almost nothing (the ex-life that "might respond to carbon 14 dating" seems a bit droll and exaggerated). The device of the photograph could be avoided. Mind you, I like your writing. For example, J's shoes as "floundering boats" is a good, telling detail.

I'd be glad to read other submissions should you hazard this editor's whims, again.

Sincerely,

Dear _____:

I'm happy to inform you that the editors have decided to accept "A Short History of Modern Art" for publication in an upcoming issue. We all felt it was a strong and gutsy story, and we look forward to seeing it in the magazine.

Would you please send me your social security number along with a brief contributor's note, and I will process your honorarium. Thank you.

> Dear ___,
>
> We're taking "Touching Liliana" from this group. Thanks for sending them and we'd be glad to look at others.
>
> Sincerely,

Dear _____:

[name] and I liked "O" a great deal, especially in how you end, but we feel the tense consistency and syntax/rhythm in the first ten lines makes the poem difficult to read. We'd love to see it again, if you're willing to re-work it. Also, we'd be happy to see other work any time.

[*Note*: Revision was resubmitted but not accepted for publication—not an unusual occurrence.]

Dear Ms. _____ :

Thanks for trying [journal name] again. "Shaved at Faggo" is the best of these as far as feeling and rhythm go. In the other poems, we have minor problems with vagueness and awkward linebreaks and sometimes, as in "The Immigration Office," with an unclear focus. The last stanza of "The Street" is marvelous, rich in feeling and imagery, but we're not convinced everyone feels alone, or that the speaker feels alone in the same way the others do.

Best wishes placing these elsewhere.

Form letter:

[journal name] 31/32 was the last issue. We are closed for good.

Form letter:

Thank you for submitting your manuscript to [journal]. We regret that we cannot accept it for publication. Unfortunately, we are able to use only a small percentage of the submissions we receive. We appreciate the opportunity to see your work.

Dear _____:

I am pleased to inform you that our poetry editor has selected your poem, "Journey," for publication in the [journal name]. We receive literally hundreds of poems and are able to publish only a few each year.

Please read the enclosed notes to authors carefully before you sign and return to us one copy of the consent to publish and the personal data sheet.

Thank you for your interest. We look forward to hearing from you soon.

Sincerely,

I hope that these letters show you that the publication-editing loop includes topics raised in earlier chapters. Writers invent, read, learn, draft, revise, refine, self-edit, submit, and enter and reenter the loop again and again. Self-evaluation and continuous effort produce your best writing and are the keys to eventual publication. The rewards? Readers *and* satisfaction—readers who care as much about your work as you do and the satisfaction of knowing that your work was well done.

Notes

1. This assignment is based on Peter Elbow and Pat Belanoff's four levels of response, outlined in *Sharing and Responding*: simple sharing, descriptive response, analytic and metaphoric description, and criterion-based response.
2. See DeMaria for a creative writer's editing handbook.

Sources and Readings

Burack, Sylvia K., ed. *The Writer's Handbook*. Boston: The Writer, Inc., 1986.

Burroway, Janet. *Writing Fiction*. 2d ed. Boston: Little Brown, 1987. [A third edition is in progress.]

DeMaria, Robert. *The College Handbook of Creative Writing*. New York: Harcourt Brace, 1991.

Drury, John. *Creating Poetry*. Cincinnati, OH: Writer's Digest Books, 1991.

Elbow, Peter, and Pat Belanoff. *Sharing and Responding*. New York: Random House, 1989.

Frey, James N. *How to Write a Damn Good Novel*. New York: St. Martin's Press, 1987.

Fulton, Len, ed. *The International Directory of Little Magazines and Small Presses*. Paradise, CA: Dustbooks, published annually. (Address: P.O. Box 100, Paradise, CA 95969).

Gardner, John. *The Art of Fiction: Notes on Craft for Young Writers*. New York: Alfred A. Knopf, 1984.

Goldberg, Natalie. *Writing Down the Bones*. Boston: Shambhala, 1986.

Grossman, Florence. *Getting From Here to There*. Upper Montclair, NJ: Boynton/Cook, 1982.

Hills, Rust. *Writing in General and the Short Story in Particular*. Boston: Houghton Mifflin, 1987.

Hugo, Richard. *The Triggering Town: Lectures and Essays on Poetry and Writing*. New York: W. W. Norton, 1979.

Jason, Philip K., and Allan B. Lefcowitz. *Creative Writer's Handbook*. Englewood Cliffs, NJ: Prentice-Hall, 1990.

Kirby, David. *Writing Poetry: Where Poems Come From and How to Write Them*. Boston: The Writer, Inc., 1989.

Koch, Kenneth. *Wishes, Lies and Dreams: Teaching Children to Write Poetry*. New York: Harper and Row, 1970.

Longman, Stanley Vincent. *Composing Drama for Stage and Screen*. Boston: Allyn and Bacon, 1987.

Minot, Stephen. *Three Genres: The Writing of Poetry, Fiction, and Drama*. 3d. ed. Englewood Cliffs, NJ: Prentice-Hall, 1982.

Murray, Donald. *Learning by Teaching: Selected Articles on Writing and Teaching*. Upper Montclair, NJ: Boynton/Cook, 1982.

Nims, John Frederick. *Western Wind: An Introduction to Poetry*. 2d ed. New York: Random House, 1983.

Packard, William. *The Art of the Playwright: Creating the Magic of Theatre*. New York: Paragon House, 1987.

————., ed. *The Poet's Craft*. New York: Paragon House, 1987.

Rico, Gabriele L. *Writing the Natural Way*. Los Angeles: J. P. Tarcher, 1983.

Shellnutt, Eve. *The Writing Room*. Marietta, GA: Longstreet, 1989.

Spreading the Word: Editors on Poetry. Columbia, SC: Bench Press, 1990.

Stern, Jerome. *Making Shapely Fiction*. New York: W. W. Norton, 1990.

Turner, Alberta. *Poets Teaching: The Creative Process*. New York: Longman, 1980.

————. *To Make a Poem*. New York: Longman, 1982.

Wallace, Robert. *Writing Poems*. 2d ed. Boston: Little Brown, 1987.

Willis, Meredith Sue. *Personal Fiction Writing*. New York: Teachers and Writers Collaborative, 1984.

The Writing Business: A Poets & Writers Handbook. New York: Poets & Writers, Inc., 1985.

Chapter 9

Genre and Writing

When we see a new game played a few times, we intuitively abstract its "rules"—the underlying structure of it, the thing that makes it one game, no matter how many times it is played.

—MARIE PONSOT AND ROSEMARY DEEN

Genre, when used in discussions of literary art and creative writing, refers to the form a piece of writing takes and the underlying structure and rules that appear to make it "one game" and not another. We expect certain forms to have certain general characteristics, and we categorize writing according to its textual forms. In English and writing departments, generally, we distinguish between three major literary genres: poetry, fiction, and drama. We also tend to distinguish nonliterature (writing primarily to communicate) from literature (language shaped artfully—work that is imagined rather than real), and to value literary works more highly than those we define as nonliterary.

Genres can be defined by looking at "classic" texts that clearly exhibit the agreed-upon basic characteristics of that category. Using those criteria and classic examples, we may write our own versions, trying to encode the required characteristics within our work. We expect a reader to use her knowledge of genre characteristics (gained through reading) and her ability to decode texts (gained through writing about writing) to come up with a "reading" of our work: Is it or isn't it an adequate representation of that genre?

Genres exist then in the *transaction* among expectation (conventions), encoding (writing), and decoding (reading) of a piece of writing. Nowadays, we don't really think that writers just write and readers just read what the writer wrote, either "getting it" or "not getting it." Writers can incorporate a lot of what they hope to share, but not all that they wish to share. Because readers bring themselves, their backgrounds, associations, experience with texts, and so on, to each reading occasion, writers cannot *fix* a text so that each reader will read it in exactly the same way. And, since a text can never be completely fixed, it is open to interpretation. Readers can offer several possible readings of a text without doing the work a disservice, although certainly some readings appear more "sophisticated" or may turn out to be closer to the author's original intention than others. At the same time, authors often fail in their intentions. They are unable to incorporate some of those characteristics they had hoped to use, thus leading to a less than successful text. Reading and writing are *both* interpretive acts, then, requiring intricate intellectual negotiations from all parties concerned.

Genre is also used to discuss subcategories of the main literary categories. Literary novels, mystery novels, romance novels, and science fiction novels are all part of the larger category of *novel*, just as novel is part of the larger category of *imaginative prose*, which also encompasses subcategories such as short stories and novellas.

Traditionally, an important part of an author's education has consisted of learning and articulating the characteristics of genre categories, shaping writing to those characteristics, and reading new works with insights gained from experience with these "learned" categories.

The key term here is *learned categories.* All category systems offer one lens, one way of looking at a set of texts, terms, or objects. Many hope that literary categories provide the best way to look at writing. However, when using any category system, we must remember that our discussions are tentative and open to interpretation and dissent from those using slightly different lenses or those seeking new ways of looking at traditional categories.

In the next several sections, I outline several ways of looking at text categories and genres, hoping to provide an overview of traditional genres in order to help writers understand that it is inevitable and even productive that disagreements will arise about what constitutes creative prose and poetry. As Marie Ponsot and Rosemary Deen explain, by observing "typical" examples of texts, we may easily abstract the underlying rules of poems, stories, and dramas. We can do this because our games and our rules are socially constructed, agreed upon by our community or by the communities we wish to join: the literary scholars or creative writers or storytellers, and so on. Understanding genre—categories, forms, rules, and conventions —helps you as a writer to have intentions, to understand how successfully your intentions have been realized, and to imagine how your work will be interpreted by readers. This chapter ends with samples of student writing in traditional creative writing categories —poetry, short story, and drama—while Chapter 10 offers samples of writing in less well defined or more popular categories, such as the sketch and prose poem, science fiction and children's stories, and journalists' columns and family stories. In both chapters, the student writing represents work-in-progress for you to review, respond to, and enjoy.

Looking at All Writing

Discourse theorists look at the way the universe of texts seems to fit together. I use the work of James Britton as a starting point here to diagram writing in general. Britton and his colleagues looked at thousands of pieces of writing and categorized them as expressive (writing to explore, often through journals, freewriting, sketching, and so on), instrumental (writing to convey information, such as lab reports, computer software directions, how-to essays, and so on), and imaginative (writing in which the language strategies are foregrounded; this category includes *all* creative writing).[1] Look at these categories, though, as just one lens for understanding texts. In Figure 9.1, you'll see that none of these large category areas can ever be fully fixed.

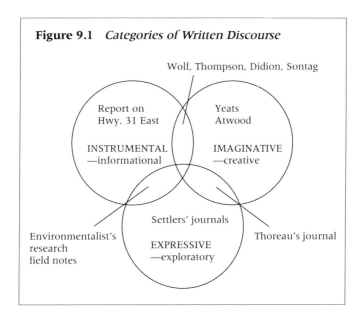

Figure 9.1 *Categories of Written Discourse*

Wolf, Thompson, Didion, Sontag

Report on Hwy. 31 East

INSTRUMENTAL —informational

Yeats Atwood

IMAGINATIVE —creative

Settlers' journals

EXPRESSIVE —exploratory

Environmentalist's research field notes

Thoreau's journal

Some works clearly belong to one or another of those three categories. A turn-of-the-century settler's journal, for example, may be clearly expressive, written by a woman in an attempt to explore and understand her feelings and deal with the loneliness of her life in a new western state. A report on the feasibility of a freeway bypass on Highway 31 East clearly exhibits instrumental characteristics. And a poem by William Butler Yeats or a short story by Margaret Atwood are firmly in the imaginative category. Each work uses specialized language that calls attention to the genre to which it declares allegiance.

When you move from the center of these categories to their edges, and particularly to those spots where the category circles overlap, the genre characteristics of work in each category become less clear, some works showing characteristics of more than one genre and others showing characteristics that are poorly defined. In the overlap between expressive writing and imaginative writing, for instance, we might place Thoreau's journals. In the overlap between expressive writing and instrumental writing, we might place a naturalist's field notes, later to be incorporated into his environmental impact report. And, in the overlap between instrumental and imaginative writing, we can easily place the work of the new journalists like Tom Wolfe and Hunter Thompson, essayists like Joan Didion and Susan Sontag, even the novel *Executioner's Song* by Norman Mailer, which declares itself to be both nonfiction and fiction. Instead of saying, "Mailer can't do that," we may instead say, "His work resides here, between the two genres." In their prose, these borderland writers offer readers information, but they deliver it in highly shaped language, both poetic and imaginative.

Explorations to Do as a Journal Entry or for Small Group or Class Discussion

1. List writers and their works that fall clearly within these major types of writing—expressive, instrumental, and imaginative— and then list writers and their works that seem to embrace two categories of writing. To do this, you might review anthologies of literature and essays that your teacher provides or that you have collected during English writing classes.

2. Examine how these particular texts "announce" their genres.

3. What do you think you, as reader, bring to the texts, that helps you to identify the authors' and/or texts' intentions? For instance, have you read a lot of instrumental reporting in your local newspaper that lets you know that the journalistic prose of Hunter Thompson or the travel writing of John McPhee is attempting to do more than simply share factual information?

Looking at Creative Writing

To understand creative genres, we can imagine, again, a series of overlapping circles, as in Figure 9.2. Traditional fiction relies on chronology, character development, consistent point of view, and so on, but fiction also relies on metaphor and images. Poetry is deeply concerned with metaphor and images, yet narrative verse relies on common fictional devices: character, chronology, point of view, and dialog. Drama depends on character and can be written in verse, but, also, during performance, drama is interpreted by actors and audiences.

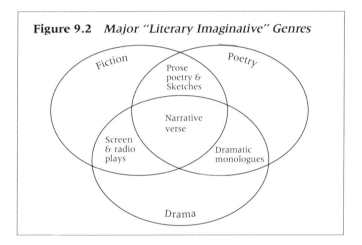

Figure 9.2 *Major "Literary Imaginative" Genres*

Although we can easily name examples of classic novelists, dramatists, and poets who work well within the rules of these major categories, many other writers ply the territories between genres—writing prose poetry, short short fiction, sketches, and so on. I call these intergenre forms, forms that capitalize on their mixed genealogies. Between the borders of fiction and drama we might place screen and radio plays. Between the borders of drama and poetry we might situate drama in verse and poetic monologs. Between the borders of poetry and fiction we might find prose poems and short short fiction.

Next, it is possible to view literature for a moment as nothing more than a development, an intentional shaping, of everyday language, represented in Figure 9.3 by two more circles. Most of us begin to write well within this overlap. Then, as we learn the conventions of our preferred forms, we move more and more into the territory of literature as intricately shaped written language.

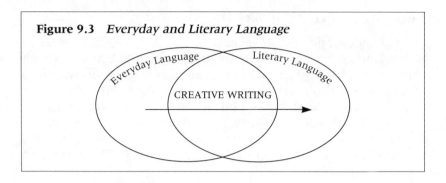

Figure 9.3 *Everyday and Literary Language*

Figure 9.4 diagrams the problems that exist in trying to claim strict separation between fact and fiction. Anyone who has ever been involved in a fight with another family member knows that his "true story" of the fight represents only one version of the event: his. And anyone who has tried to create a totally fictional world without any reference to her past and her life experiences finds that sort of world impossible to achieve, sterile and unimportant to her readers.

Certain literary questions have always been with us and are best answered by the nonanswer of these circle diagrams; that is, categories don't start and stop but shade into each other. Is literature fact shaped by the imagination? And, to what extent can nonfiction be unshaped, uncolored by the author's views and opinions, imaginings, and "real life" situations? Perhaps the best we can say is that although some fiction relies very little on real events and some fact may be presented with very little apparent personal coloring, most of the time our work declares its facticity or fictionality primarily through accepted literary devices like "Once upon a time" or "On June 2, 1989." And most writers know that they work the undefined territory between fact and fiction most of the time and that the overlap is greater than they sometimes like to admit.

Traditionally, creative writing instruction has focused on genre differences. To counteract that tendency, my aim with these diagrams has been to make more explicit the many shared features of all texts. In addition, this book has focused through the first eight chapters on similarities; for instance, all writers use metaphor and narrative because metaphor and narrative provide basic ways for us, as language users, to make sense of our worlds. Only now will I look at differences, since teasing out differences can be done fairly easily. Simply, poetry usually doesn't move, typographically, clear to the right-hand margin of the page while fiction almost always does. Concerning subjects, Grace Paley says, "Poetry is addressing the world and fiction is getting the world to talk to you" (qtd. in Shapiro and

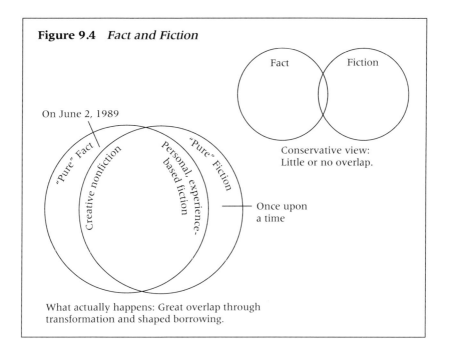

Figure 9.4 *Fact and Fiction*

Fact

Fiction

On June 2, 1989

"Pure" Fact

Creative nonfiction

Personal, experience-based fiction

"Pure" Fiction

Conservative view:
Little or no overlap.

Once upon
a time

What actually happens: Great overlap through
transformation and shaped borrowing.

Padgett 47). Intriguing and informative dichotomies and differences like these can always be set up, but the danger in adhering to them too firmly is the danger of category systems in general—that we believe the world exists in just this way rather than understanding that we use our categories to make sense of an otherwise chaotic world. Genres help us regularize our ways of talking about texts, even though they don't adequately explain—and may actually inhibit the development of—intergenre forms. Ideally, as a writer, you want to keep your developing adherence to genre conventions in productive tension with your explorations outside of and beyond convention; that way you learn the most you can about your language.

Poet and novelist Kelly Cherry, along with many writers, believes that you gain from exploring many genres, both the ones you are naturally more adept at and those whose rules and techniques seem more difficult:

> I not only see no contradictions among the various kinds of writing, but I believe they reflect and refract one another. I often find that working on a poem will, for example, help me to understand some problem that I'm facing with a novel. They may be different forms, but, after all, they're all part of literary art, and the more familiar you are with one facet, the more you are learning, in a backwards sort of

way, about another facet, and having learned all that, whether it's intuitive or conscious, it seems a shame not to walk around the diamond and explore that other facet. And so you keep going and there turn out to be more and more facets. I don't see any reason not to do it all and not to give oneself wholly to whatever it is one is doing. It's all words. It's all the same thing and what makes it the same thing is that it's all structurally so various and fascinating. (qtd. in Bunge 34–35)

At the same time, this argument for productive tension in no way assumes that you shouldn't participate in the community of genres. If your writing goal is, ultimately, to become a mystery novelist, you can't ignore the limits and limitations of that type of writing. Agatha Christie claims:

> If you were a carpenter, it would be no good making a chair, the seat of which was five feet up from the floor. It wouldn't be what anyone wanted to sit on. It is no good saying that you think the chair looks handsome that way. If you want to write a book, study what sizes books are, and write within the limits of that size. If you want to write a certain type of short story for a certain type of magazine you have to make it the length and it has to be the type of story that is printed in the magazine. If you like to write for yourself only, that is a different matter—you can make it any length, and write it in any way you wish; but then you will probably have to be content with the pleasure alone of having written it. (334–35)

Writing, then, is a social activity, an entry into the arena of texts, a movement from private exploration to public accommodation and sharing. Use the writing samples and charts that follow to help you to make explicit your already wide implicit knowledge of texts. Keep in mind, though, that these genres represent only some of the many ways of working words.

Explorations to Do as a Journal Entry
or for Small Group or Class Discussion

1. In the past you have probably tried writing in different genres. Share your attitudes toward, strengths and weaknesses with, and questions about each.

2. What types of writing would you like to try? Discuss why you haven't, what is stopping you, what you need to learn about writing in that genre, and so on.

3. Some authors who work in intergenre forms (multiple-voice writing, prose poetry, and so on) feel that these forms are harder to read and ask more of the reader. Do you think that is so? Do you think that is fair? What should writers in these forms do to ensure

careful readings from their audiences? What can readers do to increase their ability to read new or strange genres?

4. Do you think any writer can excel in more than one genre? Why or why not?

Writing Poetry

A loose definition: Poetry is language that is condensed, arranged, and shaped to express experiences and ideas; language that may rely on certain devices (images, metaphors, similes), on sound (assonance and alliteration and rhyme) and on rhythm (meter); language that focuses on the line and the arrangement of lines on the page.

Writers' Definitions

For me, all poems begin in some fragment of motivating language—the task of writing a poem is the search for context.
—Louise Gluck (qtd. in Berg 77)

It used to be that a poem did not *approach*. A poem arrived full-grown and unfinished, wearing a suit of chicken feathers and aluminum, jumping about, clawing the furniture and leaving green spots on the rug. Now, as befits the ponderosity of late-middle years, poems *approach*, on leaden feet.
—Donald Hall (qtd. in Berg 101)

But poetry is more than description, just as a living creature is more than the sum of its parts. Poetry is a drama in which objects are cut loose from their moorings and sent flying to make their own connections.
—Louis Simpson (qtd. in Berg 215)

Images haunt.
—Robert Hass (qtd. in Berg 115)

Basic Terms

Formal and Free Verse   Poetry is generally divided into formal and free verse. Formal verse relies on *meter* and regular line lengths, *stanzas, rhyme,* and other regularizing devices. Formal verse can range from "literary" writing like Shakespeare's sonnets to "bad verse," which ineffectively overapplies these techniques –advertising jingles, greeting card verse, poster verse; in fact, the term *verse* is sometimes used to denote "bad" poetry.

Free verse is poetry that loosens or avoids the demands of formal constraints. Some poets claim that no verse can be completely "free" since poetry always relies on at least some of the techniques mentioned here to attain its power and to stay within its genre category.

Many students explore free verse most comfortably and take on writing in forms as a later challenge that lets them understand the breadth of poetic technique.

Lines and Stanzas   Generally, you know you are reading poetry before you read it. The lines do not reach the right-hand margin of the page. The lines may be arranged in regular or irregular groups—stanzas; in formal verse, stanzas often rhyme in regular patterns.

Meter   In formal verse, lines of poetry have predetermined rhythms, and poets play with readers' expectation of rhythm and with variations on those rhythms. Metered verse in English relies on accent and syllable counts. All words in English receive particular syllabic stress, like par-TIC-u-lar. Poets can arrange stresses in patterns (poetic feet). There are four basic patterns for this:

> iamb   da-DUM
>
> trochee DUM-da
>
> anapest da-da-DUM
>
> dactyl   DUM-da-da

And feet can be counted off, so many per line:

> dimeter = two feet to the line
>
> trimeter = three feet to the line
>
> tetrameter = four feet to the line
>
> pentameter = five feet to the line

and so on. Iambic pentameter (iambs, five to the line) is the most famous English metering—da-DUM da-DUM da-DUM da-DUM da-DUM. Most modern writers, however, favor writing in free verse or syllabics (simply counting the number of syllables per line and making sure they're equal) although many also explore metered verse.

Rhyme, Assonance, Alliteration   Formal verse often rhymes, while free verse often chimes its sounds through the use of assonance (repeated vowel sounds—*look, pool*, airborn) and alliteration (repeated consonant sounds—the boy *that t*ripped and *t*ried to *det*ain us). Formal rhyme schemes can utilize full (moon-June) or partial (stone-gone) rhyme, and rhyme may be used at the end of the line or imbedded within it.

Images and Figures of Speech   Poems rely on the evocation of the senses through detailed description using taste, touch, sight, sound, and smell. These senses evoke images in the mind of the reader—not the deep sound of the ferry horn, for instance, but the "Ferry's bullfrog dirge." Images, of course, can be precise and evocative or strained and unsuccessful. The most used figures of speech are metaphors (two items joined in an inexplicit but powerful comparison—the Ferry takes on attributes of (is) a large bullfrog). Similes make such comparisons explicit by yoking items using *like* or *as*: "the ferry's horn like a bullfrog, gathering night into the marsh and the bay."

Comparisons and Contrasts

How is poetry different from everything else?

- It is language shaped for effect, relying on the conventions of precise words, images, and figures of speech at the sentence level. When printed, it looks condensed, packed, dense.

- Poets often see/feel in images, starting with a particular moment and then elaborating on it. Revision often takes place at the word level. Poetry allows for a great deal of drafting and revision due to its (generally) small size.

How much can poetry change and still be itself?

- Poetry becomes a prose poem when it loses compression, relies on full sentences rather than elliptical or fragmentary ones, reaches the right-hand margin, approaches speech, avoids careful language as its primary technique. Poetry becomes song when it repeats *and* relies on ritual (clichéd) phrases and seems dependent on the accompanying music.

- Poetry usually works by analogy more than by narrative. It doesn't have to be written every day. It doesn't require many voices or staging and auditory sculpting like drama. It takes a smaller breath than the story.

How does poetry fit into larger systems?

- Poetry is one of the three main genres favored as "literature" by English departments. It is shaped, "fictional," and limited, often, to a category of "special" and "valuable." It is often considered "difficult" or "esoteric."

- Poetry represents the microcosm of literature—the resonant instant.

Student Poems: A Sampler

Hometown

Mark Winford

The bus terminal has shut down—
the place where I sat excitedly
slapping my ticket to my knee
swearing never to come back.

Hometown Girl

Mark Winford

Shy green eyes looking at me, hair fluttered back; white
    shoulders sloping
from the strands of a cotton summer dress rippling.
I can feel the sawdust between my toes
as I leave the last night of the fair, and walk home.

The Scarecrow

Lisa Igneri

Sleeping on a park bench
Ignoring the damp night air
Newspapers stuffed in his coat.

My Grandfather's Season

Anji Marable

All Winter
he sat waiting
for the spring
to return.
He complained
of harsh weather
attacking his arthritis
and biting at his toes.

All spring
he sat waiting
for the summer to return.
He complained
of flying pollen
teasing his allergies
and giving him cause
to sneeze.

All summer
he sat waiting
for the fall
to return.
He complained
of constant rain
swallowing his crops
and flooding his mind
with inconsistencies
of the past.

My grandfather had
a favorite season
for every season
to come.

The Feline Professor

John Pelz

"What is reality?" the professor asks,
glasses dancing at the end of his nose,
"Is it light? Is it a book? Is it religion?
Is it possible even to know?"
He leans far back in his wooden chair,
wraps his legs around its rungs,
slowly adjusts his Lennon glasses,
then he waits and starts to hum.
The answer hides in his slate-gray beard,
like a cat nestled behind an old wood stove,
peering out from its womb of comfort,
evasive, hard to reach, harder to move.
The professor slowly rises from his seat,
and piles his papers in a leather bag.
He dons his coat and quietly leaves,
giving his feline a contented pat.

Mercy in Utuado

Summer Smith

In the past there is no mercy.
The dead are not stripped of their faults
White-washed and made kind in reflection.
It is false that the quarreling parents
With voices like grasping fingers will
Stammer in their children's dotage;
That memory is like the houses
In the rain forest where she grew up,
Sticks perched on hills, treacherous
In sudden rain, prone to disorder.

My great-grandmother speaks of her husband.
He brought her his book of poems like
A schoolboy who has found a garter snake
Or a toad, all guilty smiles. His elegy
For their daughter, typhoid victim
Faces an ode to his secretary, mistress.
She is still opening the book
Recalling the stilted rhyme
When he read to her in the rain forest
Of El Yunque, the States promised like
love words. He went alone.
He is fifty years dead and still not forgiven.

White Coffee

Samuel Shawnson

Plaid pedestrian pants
green and striped purple
lead me to the screened porch
He sits there, his scalp bleeding
from a tree branch
too low to avoid, I guess

His pipe is full in the ashtray
and his thoughts linger
from World War II and go astray
until his twenties
and the ships he built are back

Then, during his favorite Garbo film,
his wife drops off

a pot of coffee on the white iron table
Unable to lift himself up, he asks for milk
And she hesitates, shaking, by the doorway

By eleven he says the limbs in his yard
need to be piled and burned
In his shed, he says, is gasoline
He offers me a five dollar bill
and tries to smile, but chokes

When I leave, he thanks me for the coffee
and looks for his roadmap stashed
under back issues of *Reader's Digest*
He tells me to have a good trip
He forgets I live in the little white house

next door

Bahamas

Kathy Dority

Jeremy and I went to the Bahamas
      over spring break
Went canoeing, swimming, horseback riding
Couldn't leave the hotel after dark
Dangerous that Freeport, Bahamas
People didn't like him holding my hand
Oh, he's white
Didn't go to Williamstown because tourists
      go there and never return
Get robbed of their money and thrown into
      the ocean
It's scary there in the Bahamas
No, we didn't like Freeport, Bahamas

Ring for Ring

Tamara Mills

Few steps separate the streetlamp's ring
of brilliance from the dusk,
and the subtle change of gray
to black promises, in the whispered
movement of dead leaves,
to renew images of the past.

But, so many small things are now past
recollection, like flower chains, rings
of grass, and the leaves
from the trees under which we whispered
to each other in the dusk.
They're edges of memory, gray

dusty things, like photo albums in gray
jackets, and pictures that are fading past
perception. Turning pages have whispered
of still moments in time: ring after racing ring
expands from pebbles tossed in dusk
dark liquid, mountains of leaves

in which we burrowed until leaves
were in our clothes, everywhere. Gray
turns black, and the sound of dusk
change into the silence of night, hours past
the curfew of childhood. The ring
of phones searching for us whispered,

telling us, that soft whispered
excuses, as quiet as the wind through leaves,
would not stop the ring
of parental voices in our ears. Gray
company we were then, as we walked past
house after hours, our spirits in a dusk

deeper than the electrically lit dusk
of the streets. We whispered
then, in a time now past,
and pulled handfuls of leaves
from each other's hair. We traded one ring
for another and walked head high from the gray

street's dusk. No more am I a child covered with leaves,
I have whispered over and over. My hair is gray
like memories lost to the past, but I remember our trade, ring for ring. [2]

You and I—Our Different Worlds

Van Mong Trinh

You call it designer clothes—colors for the seasons
I call it shelter—a cloth to cover my skin

You call it water—turn a knob on a faucet
I call it treasure—digging from a deep well

You call it entertainment—color TV and radio cassette
I call it heaven—watching a black and white screen

You call it a pain—waking up early to class
I call it a privilege—not having to work in the jungle

You call it dictatorship—people telling you what to do
I call it parents—my second gods, people who gave me birth

You call it crazy—my thought, my way of thinking
I call it awareness—reality of forgotten facts.

Questions

1. For each poem, which attributes of poetic technique do you most notice?

2. Do any of these poems extend, contradict, or illuminate the discussion and definitions I've provided?

3. What, if any, are the commonalities among these student writers?

4. What are these writers best at?

5. Which of these poems do you prefer? Why?

6. Which of these poems need the most revision? Why? In what way?

Writing Fiction

A loose definition: *Fiction* is a piece of prose that portrays imaginary characters and events: as a story, a series of connected events, told to entertain or inform; as a novel, connected events that usually form a complex plot. Traditionally, in prose fiction, experience and invention are shaped to explore an event that has a crisis and depends on conflict, and is often told from a particular point of view, developing characters and their dialog in a way that makes the reader want to know what happened and why.

Writers' Definitions

My novel is a thirteen-year conversation, but in the end it represents a whole thought. . . . The process is very complex; it's not just what I sit down and write. It's what I think and what I teach and what I do and who I see and what I feel and who I become. In every sense it's my whole life.

—Paula Gunn Allen (qtd. in Coltelli 34)

It is no less difficult to write sentences in a recipe than sentences in *Moby Dick*. So you might as well write *Moby Dick*.

—Annie Dillard (71)

If a book could be made in two hours, like a watercolor picture, lots of people would write books; but the plain duration of writing a novel discourages most people.

—Wallace Stegner (qtd. in Bunge 12)

Plot might seem to be a matter of choice. It is not. The particular plot for this particular novel is something the novelist is driven to. . . . It is what is left after the whittling-away of alternatives.

—Elizabeth Bowen (qtd. in Murray 149)

Writers face off against the page, put one letter down after another to make a word, one word after another to make a sentence: the sentence has to have a certain shape, a certain melody. Then you have to make another sentence. Then you have to make sure the two of them harmonize—at every level, from sound to semantics. Story vanishes in this process. Move back far enough and, yes, a "story" emerges at a certain point—in the same way that, if you move back even farther, you can see the story's theme; and, if you can get back even farther still, you can see its genre. But up close, it's just words and sentences and sounds and syntax, one following another in a variety of patterns, while you try to make those words relate to all the others you've put down in a variety of ways—a very few of which *may* relate to "story."

—Samuel Delany (qtd. in McCaffery and Gregory 103)

Basic Terms

Plot, Story, Scene   A plot is a plan for a narrative, and the story puts that plan into action. "What comes next?" is the essence of plot. "Why?" is the essence of story. Since most story action takes place *chronologically* (including the use of flashbacks, reported past actions, and so on), action may be moved forward scene by scene. Scenes may momentarily represent a full and immediate imitation of reality.

Conflict   Conflict is the natural result of the "why?" of fiction although the term *conflict* sounds more forceful than it has to be. Stories may depend on the tension and conflict created by the internal choice a character needs to make (or avoids making) or the external situation she finds herself in; the best writing may develop from a blend of both types of conflict. In prose fiction "something happens." The interested reader has been convinced by the writer to keep reading in order to discover more about unfolding events.

Setting Stories happen somewhere, whether in the imaginary but coherent worlds of science fiction or in the about-to-be ficionalized backyard you can see from your study window. The setting of a story can provide worlds of information about a character and can support the conflict (tonally) or complicate the plot. Settings can be enriched by detailed description, using all the senses; setting can take advantage of (and usually needs to be consistent with) a particular historical time, a season, a cultural geography.

Characters Fiction happens to characters; the author may be telling a character's story. Other characters may help readers understand the main characters or they may simply inhabit the world that is being created, necessary functionaries to a fabricated reality. Characters may have complete histories, parts of which are instrumental to the unfolding story; characters move, talk (share dialog), and think (experience interior dialog). Through these characters, the main work of the story is often completed.

Point of View Point of view is the angle from which the story is told; authors are expected, by convention, to hold to a single point of view, particularly in short fiction. As a rule of thumb, the longer the work, the more time you have to prepare readers for following shifts in point of view. Kelly Cherry says, "Point of view is a very minor problem. . . . All you have to do is remind the student that if one pair of eyes is being used, you can't jump into another pair of eyes unless you've built preparatory platforms for making that leap" (qtd. in Bunge 28). Traditionally, the two most used points of view are first person singular (I) and third person singular (he/she), with a limited ability to see into the motives of others. Other options include the less used, generally experimental, second person singular (you), first person plural (we), and third person singular omniscient, which provides a God-like ability to enter the mind of any and all characters.

Comparisons and Contrasts

How is prose fiction different from everything else?

- It is language that works to get somewhere, relying on chronology and intentional analogy to "real life," inviting the reader to participate or relate.

- Fiction writers depend on characters; they often talk of following a character into a story, living with, being taken over by characters.

- When writing stories, the author shapes time, places characters into scenes, and creates a flow that seems "inevitable," all to avoid a "so what?" response. The author wants the created world to matter.

How much can prose fiction change and still be itself?

- Compelling narrative prose has many attributes of poetry, but language is less important overall than movement; a story has to go toward some end. Narrative approaches drama when it depends less on exposition (telling) and more on dialog.

- Traditional narrative relies on duration of time (compared to the poetic instant), and it depends, heavily, on created *verisimilitude*, a sense that this narrative scene or story is much like real life. Prose fiction is generally longer than poetry and most often takes longer to write. Many fiction writers prefer steady composition, a number of hours each day, to fast and irregular drafting. Fiction attempts a bigger breath than poetry, weaving together many characters' lives and voices. Novels take longer than novellas, which take longer than short stories, which take longer than short short fiction. Conversely, ascending sized fictional canvases allow for more development, more characters, more potential for verisimilitude.

How does prose fiction fit into larger systems?

- Fiction is one of the three main genres favored as "literature" by English departments. It is shaped, "fictional," and gains its writers a great deal of prestige. Due to the state of current publishing markets, the novelist has more potential to become commercially successful than the poet. Fiction encompasses many popular subgenres (mystery novels, romance novels, science fiction stories, and so on) and is considered more accessible and less esoteric than poetry.

- Fiction is the macrocosm of literature, sharing many attributes of nonfiction prose, taking many popular literary forms. It is accessible in ways that poetry, which requires a sophisticated interest in and skill with language, is not, and in ways that drama, which requires performance, cannot be.

Student Fiction: A Sampler

The Cosmic Cat

Matt Shepard

"Can I help you?"

"Huh?" The boy glances up from the *X-Men* comic book he has been intensely studying for the past five minutes.

"You're not supposed to read the comics. This is a bookstore, not a library."

The small boy sheepishly places the comic back on the shelf with the new arrivals, then turns to leave. Wes feels slightly guilty for being so harsh, but only slightly. After all, this isn't the sort of clientele that keeps this place in business.

Wes had begun to recognize the various types of customers who drift through the store. There are, of course the very young kids who come in and read everything in the store, but rarely buy anything. They patronize the store with annoying regularity and must be constantly reminded not to read the books. Wes imagines the mentality of a dog that refuses to be house trained, that continues to smile and piddle on your carpet, no matter how often you swat it on the nose with a newspaper.

The store where Wes works is called the Cosmic Cat, which sits proudly in the East Lake Shopping Plaza, nestled in between Pantry Pride and Payless Shoes. Inside, several tall shelves along one wall are filled with the new month's arrivals, next to a small sign that says "Please do not read." The shelf on the opposite side of the room displays hardcover books for "Dungeons 'n' Dragons" and other role-playing games. The long table that occupies the center of the room holds several boxes of old, back issue comics, all alphabetized and neatly stored in protective plastic bags. The subdued, off-white colored walls are interrupted by splashes of garish color; Posters of Spiderman, Batman, Wolverine, the Punisher, and Teenage Mutant Ninja Turtles hang from walls and ceiling. Behind the cash register, a locked glass case is filled with some of the more valuable items in the store, a "trophy case" of sorts. A mint copy of *"The Dark Knight,"* first printing, sells for thirty-five dollars. *"X-Men"* #94 has a price tag of one hundred twenty-four dollars.

Wes imagines he couldn't have had it any better. When the Cosmic Cat opened a year and a half ago, Wes saw the opportunity of a lifetime. By then, he had been collecting comic books for four years. His parents admired his interest in comics, but grew weary of financing his growing collection, so they encouraged him to get a job. Wes's high school buddies all had aspirations for Publix or McDonalds; Wes had other ideas. Wes hugged the owner of the Cosmic Cat until he gave in and let Wes work part-time hours. Aside from working the cash register, there was not much actual work involved, except on Thursdays when new shipments came in. Plus, he could pick out copies of all his favorite titles and put them in his own personal bin behind the desk. The price was deducted from his paycheck, with a thirty-five percent employee discount. The reality was that most of Wes's paycheck went towards comics.

A tall, lanky man in his mid-thirties puts a stack of comics next to the cash register.

"So, I hear the Hulk is hot this month."

"Yeah, we've had to reorder it three times this month," said Wes. "That'll be eighteen dollars and sixty-four cents."

The man's name is Bill Weatherbee. Bill is a good example of the sort of customer the Cosmic Cat smiles upon. They come in and grab exactly what they want. These are mostly young adults who think of comics not merely as a hobby, but as an investment. To say a comic is "hot" is to say it will appreciate quickly in the months ahead. Bill knows what's hot. Bill is the sort of customer that makes a store like this cost effective.

A third group is the odd breed of customers who live and breathe comic books. Wes remembers one such individual who stopped by just a week ago. He looked to be in his mid-to-late thirties, wore suspenders and glasses, and had a receding hairline. Wes remembers ringing up his stack of comics, and listening to the man talk about how Batman's character has changed over the past fifteen years, and how he once found a bunch of old "*Detective Comics*" in a garage sale, and how last week he drove five hours to a comic book convention in Atlanta, and how he thought that the Cosmic Cat was a much better store than Futureworld Comics, on the other side of town. "They don't know what they're talkin' about over there," he said. This fairly one-sided conversation continued for about forty-five minutes. Wes remembers how he stood uncomfortable and helpless, watching and listening to this man. The way the man talked with a sort of enthusiastic giddiness did not fit Wes's image of how a mature adult should act.

Wes remembers when, once several weeks ago, a group of friends stopped by his house after school. Among the group was one face he didn't expect to see. Lisa Simmons was getting a ride home from a student government meeting with one of Wes's friends. Lisa danced on the drill team, took minutes at student government meetings, and belonged to the clique of popular girls that most guys in school secretly lusted after. Wes was no exception. Once in Wes's English class, he was paired up with Lisa for peer revising and criticism. Lisa had giggled at Wes's essay proposal to replace Shakespeare with Stephen King as the most important figure in Western literature.

Wes fed the group Coke and potato chips. Somebody wondered out loud what the homecoming theme would be this year. Lisa noticed one of Wes's comic books sitting on the coffee table.

"YOU read comic books, Wes?"

"Yeah. Here, let me show you."

Wes perked up whenever somebody mentions comics, and he jumped at the chance to impress Lisa. He led her to his bedroom, where his collection sat proudly on display in a special bookshelf that his dad had made for him. The five hundred-or-so comics were sorted neatly, each in its own protective mylar bag, with a cardboard back to keep it from bending. Lisa skimmed over the titles.

"Iron Man, the Incredible Hulk . . . oh, this is such a gas! Can I read one?" Lisa removed *Spiderman* #128 from the shelf and proceeded to remove it from its bag.

"Carefully . . . " Wes was always nervous watching someone else handle his comics. Each one was delicate and sacred, and every bent corner and wrinkled page decreased its market value. Lisa flipped quickly through the pages. She pauses and giggles at a picture of Spiderman as he nearly falls to his death from a twenty story building. Wes beamed.

"I always thought comic books were for little kids," Lisa said flatly.

Wes was wounded by this statement. It caught him off guard. He quickly spoke up in defense of his hobby.

"Oh, no. Lots of adults buy them as investments."

"Do you?"

Wes glared at Lisa.

"That one you've got there is the first appearance of the Punisher, in 1973. I bought it four years ago for fifteen dollars. Today, I could sell it for a hundred."

"This is worth a hundred bucks?" Lisa held the book like a dead fish, between her thumb and index finger.

"Here, you're not holding it right. Give it to me." Wes took the book from Lisa's hands and carefully began to replace it in its bag.

"God, Wes, you're so touchy." Lisa turned around and returned to the living room. Five minutes ago, Wes was overjoyed to be able to talk to Lisa Simmons, in his own house, no less. Now, he was shocked at how she so carelessly snubbed his hobby, his job, his recreation. . . . At once he realized that he was in the minority of people his age who still read comic books. Suddenly, on a relative, global scale, comics didn't seem that important any more.

The minute hand approached four o'clock. An unusual number of customers filled the Cosmic Cat, waiting in quiet anticipation. Every Thursday afternoon was always the busiest part of the week, the only time it was really necessary to have more than one person working at a time. Today was an unusually large crowd.

At four o'clock sharp, a UPS delivery man dropped off two large cardboard boxes at the backdoor to the Cosmic Cat. Wes and Greg, one of Wes's older coworkers, hauled the two boxes inside and set them on the floor next to the new arrival shelf. The customers quietly looked on, some staring at the boxes, some staring at Wes and Greg. Wes imagined the ritual of feeding time at a zoo; a dozen or so monkeys lining their cages, waiting for the zookeeper to throw a scrap of food.

Greg went over to the front desk to get some inventory lists. Wes began sorting the comics on the shelf, making room for the new ones. Wes turned around to see two guys grabbing handfuls of comic books out of the newly torn open boxes.

"What are you people doing?" Wes shouted. "Can't you people wait five minutes?" The two violators, both much older than Wes, chose to ignore him.

"Stop that! Are you guys that hard up for comic books? Why don't you people get a life?" Wes shouted as he jerked the box away from them. At this moment, Greg stepped in.

"Wes, why don't you go in the back and cool off for a while?"

Wes stomped off to the inventory room. Greg said something to the two guys that Wes couldn't quite hear.

Wes got off work at six. He felt exasperated and uneasy. Never before had he lost his temper like that. Wes remembered the defiant arrogance of the two guys in the store, and he remembered Lisa's cold indifference. Wes thought of monkeys in a zoo fighting over a piece of banana. He pictured a small cocker spaniel joyfully leaping down the aisle of the Cosmic Cat, urinating on the floor. He pictured the man with the glasses and the receding hairline sitting alone in his apartment, eating a T.V. dinner and reading a comic book.

The next day there were several new additions for sale in the "trophy case" behind the cash register. Among them was a copy of *Spiderman* #128, in mint condition.

The Bassoon Blues

Aimee M. DeFoe

Reginald Brodsky was beside himself. No, Reginald Brodsky was not just beside himself, or stressed out, or even at the end of his rope; he was downright hysterical. It seems that on this fine May morning Reginald had noticed the peculiar absence of his bassoon. Reg was standing in the "dining area" of his duplex, hands on his little round head, eyes bulging, mouth hanging open wide enough to allow the entry of a small songbird. A small sound began to form in the proximity of the cavernous opening. Soon the sound became a moan and then a full blown wail as Reginald stamped his feet and turned around in two complete circles.

"Okay," Reg muttered, managing to get a handle on himself, "Alfred will be here soon. He'll know what to do. Just don't panic."

Reginald paced the apartment and began looking. He looked everywhere, turning up couch cushions and opening cabinets as if a four foot wooden musical bazooka was going to be hiding in one of these places.

"Oh, heavens," said Reg. "Oh, oh, heavens."

Reginald thought of the band. The Weekiewachee Two Step Dixie-land Jazz Combo it was called. He remembered two years ago when the boys down at the lodge were just thinking of forming the band. Gracious they were tipsy. They hadn't mentioned needing a bassoonist, but Reg had volunteered anyway. They had needed him.

Reg walked out the front door. Where was Alfred? He walked back in and slammed the door. Reg slammed the door again.

"Reginald?" said a voice from down the hall. "Is that you doing all that slamming and bamming around?"

"Oh heavens," thought Reg. There was Alfred, finally. What was he going to think? There was that time when Hank Fowler had left his trumpet in Denny's before the Weston VFW gig. The boys had never let Hank live that down. Well, anyone could have made that mistake.

Reg did his best to rearrange the couch cushions. Just then the door opened and in strode Alfred Feemster. He took off his gray derby and hung it carefully on the hat rack, which was otherwise empty except for a pair of brown gloves each on a separate prong, which made the coat rack look like it was waving.

"Alfred, thank God you're here. What took you so long, anyway?" Reginald's voice wavered from preadolescent tenor to deep bass.

"Reginald, my boy, just calm down. What seems to be the matter?"

"It's my baby, Alfred. It's gone. Missing. Abducted, pilfered and otherwise absent, never to be seen again!"

"Your bassoon is gone? Now just get a hold of yourself, Reginald. When was the last time you had it?"

Reg had no answer, but remembered the trip to Maryland last fall to get the bassoon. He and Marie had taken a side trip to Washington, D.C., and gone to the Smithsonian. A picture of the massive dinosaur bones flashed across his mind. They were just so magnificently extinct. Marie had stared at the Hope diamond for ages. Reg remembered the only way he could get her to go was by promising her that the "Woodwinds of the Baroque Period" display was just in the next hall. The ancient ancestors of the modern day bassoon had fascinated Marie almost as much as that big blue rock had. "Oh, Reginald," she had said, "do you think you could play one of those old bassoon daddies?"

"What about in the car?" Alfred was asking.

"Oh, the car," said Reg, lost.

"Come on, Reg, let's go look in your car."

Alfred led the way out the door and Reg dragged behind as they began the descent down the stairway.

As they went down the stairs, Reginald waxed nostalgic about the first time he had taken Marie out. On her lapel she had worn the yellow mum he had brought her. Reg remembered the lovely dinner at Bonanza and the way she had nibbled ever so delicately on her hot fudge sundae cake. Afterwards they had gone back to Reg's duplex and he had crooned out Marie's favorites, "Tiny Bubbles" and "The Blue Danube" in long mellow tones on his bassoon. The thought of never playing for Marie again almost brought another wail to his throat.

Just then, Alfred and Reginald burst into the bright light of late morning. They crossed the parking lot to the old blue '79 Coronado and Reg opened the trunk, all the time preparing himself for the inevitable disappointment of not finding his bassoon. There, behind the spare tire and the emergency flares Reg always kept handy was the corner of a brown—could it be—bassoon case! Reginald gave the precious instrument a gentle yank and hugged it close to him. He grinned at Alfred who was busy polishing his glasses, trying not to look amused.

"Thanks, Al," muttered Reg.

He carried the baby upstairs, thinking of Marie. She'd surely be at the Weekiewachee gig tonight, sitting as always to the left of the band at what she called the perfect "bassoon angle." Maybe afterwards she'd be up for a verse or two of "Tiny Bubbles."

The Man in the Woods

Beth Powell

John folded the baby-blue sheet length-wise and then width-wise and laid it across the card-table, which had five holes on its surface and rusted metal legs. One of the legs was slightly bent in the middle, which made the table lean towards that corner. He was humming and whistling his own tune as he removed the two Hostess cupcakes from the clear plastic wrapper and placed them each on an individual napkin.

Every day for the past two months, nine-year-old Katherine had gone to the woods to have her snack with John. John took the Ronald McDonald watch that Katherine gave him for his fifty-third birthday out of a zippered pocket in his baggy green army jacket. Ronald McDonald's red gloves pointed out 3:55 P.M. Katherine always ate her after school snack with John at 3:30 P.M. and this absence made three in a row.

John sat on a black Borden milk crate in front of his tent. With his feet spread shoulder-width apart, he put his elbows on his knees and rested his forehead on the "heel" of his hands. He combed his thick brownish-red hair with his fingers, which made the silver flecks more prominent. Then he rubbed the curve under his bottom lip with the side of his finger, coarse hairs of his red beard against the dry cracked skin on his hand.

He stood up and rubbed the middle of his chest with his fingertips and then entered his tent. He rolled up his royal-blue bed-roll, tied a piece of rope around it and set it in the corner of the tent. He gathered his necessities, such as his toothbrush, pots, eating utensils, matches, dog leash and rifle. He put everything except for his rifle into a knapsack. He carried these belongings outside and placed them under a pine tree.

The other items in the tent were things he had collected over the one year he lived in "Katherine's Woods." He took the rest of the items out of the tent and threw them on the ground. He pulled the pegs of his tent out of the ground and put them in the knapsack. He removed the metal rods and tossed them next to his knapsack. He clenched his fists and jumped on the tent and stomped on it. One of the tent ropes caught his ankle and as he tried to free himself he swung his leg in front of his body. The tension in the rope made him fall to the ground. He landed flat on his back and stared up at the sky. It was cloudless, brilliant blue with golden highlights. He looked at the circular piece of sky that was shaped by the top of the trees and noticed the similarity of this day to the very day he met Katherine.

On that day, John walked through the woods carrying a bucket full of fish that he caught for dinner. He thought, "Now this is the kind of day I live for. A day where the sun warms my face. A day where the fragrance of green life mixed with that of the earthy smell of the moist soil gives me a sense of home. A day where the birds sing their beautiful songs for me to hear. And a day when I catch enough fish to fill my belly."

As John approached the portion of the woods where lightning had struck a few weeks ago, he heard a scratching sound and noticed something moving by some fallen oak trees. He got closer and saw an armadillo stuck upside down between the trunks of two trees. The leaves crunched under John's feet as he walked towards the armadillo and with each step the armadillo would wiggle even more. John set down his bucket and fishing gear and lifted the squirming armadillo out of the "trap." The armadillo jumped out of John's hands and scuttled into the brush. John smiled, picked up his belongings and headed for home. When he reached his tent, he found a little black-haired girl snooping around his belongings.

"What are you doing?" John asked.

"Nothing. I uh, I'm trying to get home," said Katherine as her voice shook.

"Well, try a little harder because you're not going to get home through my tent."

John carried the smelly bucket of fish over to his outdoor stove that consisted of sticks.

"I'm lost. I was hoping that you could help me get home," she said with her head bowed.

"Sorry, don't have time."

She whispered, "Nobody ever has time for me."

He glanced at her humble form and then stared back into the bucket as he asked, "Do you like fish?"

"Yeah . . . sometimes."

"Would you like some now?"

"I guess so."

He turned to the woods and shouted, "Beau! Come here Beau!"

John whistled three short times and clapped his hands.

Five seconds later a little short-haired dog with white paws ran up to John and sat at his feet. John vigorously patted Beau on the head.

"Go keep her company," he commanded Beau as he pointed his finger at Katherine.

Beau walked over to Katherine with his head held high and licked her hand. Katherine sat "Indian style" and Beau lay down beside her and rested his head on her left thigh. Katherine bent down and put her cheek on Beau's cheek and her left hand on his side and she gave him a hug.

"What a day that was," John thought as he got up off the ground and folded his tent neatly. He reached into his right jacket pocket for his red bandana to wipe his face but instead he pulled out a polaroid snapshot of Katherine and him at his "private" birthday party.

For his party, Katherine showed up in a frilly pink dress with a white ribbon in her hair. She brought a paper bag that contained steak and lobster (leftover from dinner at her house the night before), three paper birthday hats, two chocolate cupcakes, a candle and a polaroid camera. John held the camera at arm's length and took a picture of the both of them. Then Katherine put a hat on Beau's head but it only stayed there for about five seconds. Beau jumped every which way to get that hat off and he finally did; he hit it with his paw and broke the thin elastic. Katherine laughed and laughed until tears came to her eyes but John tilted his head to the side and shook it back and forth.

Katherine lit the candle on John's cupcake and sang happy birthday to him. He blew out his candle and made a wish. As Katherine took a second bite of her cupcake, Beau jumped on her and the white cream covered her nose. Before she regained her balance completely, Beau stole her cupcake. John smiled at the white cream on her nose and scolded Beau.

"John. I've never seen you smile before," Katherine said.

"Here's a napkin."

"I might just walk around all day with white cream on my face to keep you smiling."

"No, no, don't do that. Bugs might get stuck on your nose."

"John . . . I love you," she said as she gave him a hug.

He felt as if he had just gone down a big hill on a rollercoaster ride. He put his right hand on her head while she was still hugging him and stroked her hair as he said, "I love you too, Katherine."

They broke away from their embrace and decided to play fetch with Beau as Katherine told John about her day at school.

John rubbed the polaroid snapshot between his fingers as he stared into the woods. He scanned the trees with his eyes and his eyes stopped when he saw the small opening in the woods where Katherine usually appeared. He thought to himself, "Three days and I have not heard from her. She promised that she would always keep me informed on what was going on in her life. I guess time changes but people never will."

The little red Ronald watch told him it was 4:45 P.M. He slowly turned to the card-table and placed both the watch and picture next to Katherine's cupcake. He picked up his own cupcake, lifted it into the air and made a toast.

"Good-bye, Katherine."

He brought the cupcake to his lips and took a bite. He could not swallow it, however, because his stomach heaved and his insides felt all knotted. He spit out the bite in his mouth and gave the rest of his cupcake to Beau.

John took a swig of water from his canteen to rinse his mouth. His eyes searched the opening in the woods once more in hope of seeing Katherine. He thought back to the many snack times that he and Katherine had together. One particular meeting would not leave his thoughts. This meeting took place about a week ago. Katherine seemed more depressed that day than any other day they had talked.

"Katherine, what's wrong?" John asked.

"Nothing," she said softly.

Looking at her watery eyes, he put his hands on his hips and said, "Come on now, you can tell me anything. We're friends. Besides, Beau is the only other one I talk to and he's good at keeping secrets."

"Well . . . I'm going to run away."

"Why?"

"Because my Mom doesn't have time for me any more. We were supposed to go to a mother-daughter dinner last night and she forgot. She said that we would go to dinner together some other night when she wasn't so busy."

"Katherine, running away won't solve anything, especially running away from the people you love. I'm sure your mother loves you very much and she would want to know how you feel."

Beau's barking brought John back to the present and John watched as Beau chased a squirrel up a tree. John put his watch back on and slowly re-pitched his tent in its old position and began to set up his home.

Questions

1. For each story, which attributes of fictional technique do you notice most?

2. Do any of these stories extend, contradict, or illuminate the discussion and definitions I've provided?

3. What point of view does each author choose? What difference does it make to the story?

4. How does each author develop his or her characters?

5. How effective is the dialog in each story? What dialog rules are being followed?

6. What do you think about these authors' plots? Many beginning writers think their own experiences are too mundane to write about; do you think writers have to gain worldly experience before they can tell engaging stories?

7. What, if any, are the commonalities among these student writers?

8. What are these writers best at?

9. Which of these stories do you prefer? Why?

10. Which of these stories needs the most revision? Why? In what way?

Writing Drama

A loose definition: *Drama* is a piece of writing that uses dialog and action to tell the story of a human or humans who are often in conflict. Drama utilizes many of the techniques of both poetry and fiction but has the particular attribute of being written for production, for characters speaking aloud. Drama can be both realistic and unrealistic, and the staging of the piece and actors' interpretations of their parts predict that the work will become more resonant during performance than it appears in the author's text.

Writers' Definitions

> A play's an interpretation. It is not a report.
> —Arthur Miller (qtd. in Wager 20)

> I'm convinced that there are absolutely unbreakable rules in the theater, and that it doesn't matter how good you are, you can't break them. . . . You must state the issue at the beginning of the play. The audience must know what is at stake. . . . The theater is all about wanting things that you can or can't have or you do or do not get. . . . One other thing: You can't stop the action for detours.
> —Marsha Norman (qtd. in Murray 153)

> The process goes like this: I discover that I have gotten an idea somewhere. I never *get* an idea—I discover that I *have* one. Then over the next six months or a year or two years, it gradually, slowly develops—I think about it occasionally. The characters are forming at that time, and eventually after a certain period of time when the idea seems both vague enough and clear enough to start working on, and the characters seem three-dimensional enough to carry the burden of the work by themselves, then I go to the typewriter. So the actual

writing time is very short—anywhere from a month to three months. But the prewriting process—which is a form of writing, I suppose— takes a good deal of time.

> —Edward Albee (qtd. in Wager 38)

The theatre is the place for the anarchist to throw his bomb. . . . Theatre is the art of explosions, the trick is to have them go off at the right time in the right spot.

> —Eric Bentley (303–4)

Quite often I have a compelling sense of how a role should be played. And I'm proved—equally as often—quite wrong.

> —Harold Pinter (qtd. in Wager 182)

I find it very easy to get along with the cast. . . . I don't talk to them. I talk through the director. I get along with the director fairly well. We have most of our arguments before rehearsals start. A few large ones during rehearsal. But not too many.

> —Edward Albee (qtd. in Wager 39)

I said, "I can't believe it, I am fifty-four years old now, and I think the reason it is so incredible to me that I have suddenly reached this age is that each year is not another year to me—it's a play." And sometimes three years are a play and my life seems to be chalked off not in years but in plays and pieces of work.

> —Tennessee Williams (qtd. in Wager 226)

Basic Terms

Live and Continuous Performance   The playwright creates the script for a visual, audible, and continuous narrative. Characters' speeches are used *both* to show and tell and to move the action along, and viewers, unlike readers, cannot go back and review a portion of the action; drama has to work, now.

Dramatic Questions   Drama focuses on a question that can be narrated, encountered, or examined. Steven Minot lists the seven most traditional dramatic questions as: Will he come? Who did it? Will he or she succeed? Will he or she discover what we know? Will a compromise be found? Will this episode end in violence? What's happening? These questions remind us that in drama, something does happen (Minot 263–64).

Scenes and Acts   Since exposition is limited in drama, acts and scenes provide the beats of action: Characters enter, interact, and exit, and the scene changes; acts unfold, providing necessary information for answering the dramatic question. A drama may take place in a single act of several scenes or several acts, also consisting of several scenes. Not all acts or scenes need to be as full or as strong as others, but all need to keep the viewer engaged, through a building rhythm and progression.

Dialog and Character   While fiction can use direct and indirect dialog, drama relies on direct dialog only to develop what we know about characters (details have to be included in speeches that might normally be "told" in fictional exposition by a narrator). Most dramatic dialog is close to actual speech—repetitive, fragmentary, capitalizing on tag questions, and body language. Directions for body language cannot, however, be written in; the author expects actors to interpret and add. Dramatic monologs, one character speaking alone at great length, are often opportunities for saying more than would normally be said in a conversational exchange. Characters' speech patterns help to identify their personalities, through regionalisms, and so on; common accents don't have to be written in, though, since actors expect to provide the desired British or Brooklyn accent.

Staging   The playwright needs to visualize the play and to rehearse it aloud. He or she expects to provide basic notes about costuming, setting, lighting, and production, but also expects to be interpreted by the director and actors and those hired to design and support the stage production. The playwright has the responsibility for providing useful preliminary stage directions, supporting the script with logical, functional exits and entrances, and so on. He or she should expect to give up power beyond the script, but to write the script so that it can be played. Since an audience agrees to sit for the duration of a performance, the playwright relies on dramatic tension and climactic action to keep the audience engaged and involved.

Comparisons and Contrasts

How is drama different from everything else?

- It is language shaped for verbal presentation and performance, telling a story—often about the human condition—and requiring an interactive audience; the dramatic script, like the musical score, is always interpreted.

- Dramatists visualize characters in a particular scene and find themselves both asking questions and allowing the characters, through their monologs and dialogs, to answer the questions. Revision of a play, in some sense, takes place both in the act of writing the script but equally in the production, as actors and directors offer interpretations of the work. Drama can be large or small, highly improvisational or extraordinarily plotted and planned; it is always contingent on the chemistry among the script, the actors, and the audience. For this reason, "a play" can vary widely among companies and among performances.

- When writing drama, the author's auditory imagination is the canvas as much as the print and paper; the dramatist uses both narrative and poetic techniques but always within the framework of speech.

How much can drama change and still be itself?

- Drama becomes narrative in verse or a verse narrative when it is written for reading rather than for performance; it is then a representation of drama rather than *a drama*.

- Dramas are composed individually but realized most fully through a live reading or performance, where all aspects of the form are activated and actualized.

How does drama fit into larger systems?

- Drama is one of the three main genres favored as "literature" by English departments. It is shaped, "fictional," and somewhat limited by its performance aspect; productions may be expensive and complicated to stage. For most readers, therefore, reading a script is a thinner and less satisfying experience than reading poetry or stories.

- Drama is the voice of literature—alive, variable, interactive.

Student Drama: One Scene

Executive Decisions

Stuart Taft

(A white, nondescript waiting room. Far up left is a door, in front of which sits a desk. There is a sofa, one-quarter left, at right center. There is a table in front of the sofa and two chairs either side. One chair is up center, facing full front, and the other is down right in profile. The table is covered with old copies of various religious magazines and several tattered copies of the Bible. Seated at the desk is DORIS, a woman of indeterminable age, dressed in a white robe. She has the bored expression of a civil servant and is usually filing her nails—a stereotypic secretary. Seated on the upstage side of the sofa is JESSIE. He sits hunched over with his elbows on his knees and his head in his hands. He has a very dejected look. He is six feet tall with shoulder length hair and a beard. He is

dressed in a white suit and is wearing gloves. LOUIE enters through a door, right center. He has on an obnoxious Hawaiian shirt and plaid Bermuda shorts with sandals and black socks. He has short black hair and wears black sunglasses.)

LOUIE: Heeyyy, Doris. How ya doin', gorgeous? How 'bout Saturday night? I got one humdinger of an evening planned!

DORIS: Have a seat, Louie. I'm fine. And you know the answer to the other question.

LOUIE: Can't blame a guy for tryin', can ya?

DORIS: After the billionth time, yes, I can. He'll be with you as soon as possible.
(LOUIE crosses to the upstage chair and sits, rifling through the magazines.)

LOUIE: C'mon!! I've been comin' here for, well, forever and you still have the same magazines layin' around. Oh look! "The Black Plague: Effective Business Through Terror." Some nice, light reading. I really liked this article—THE FIRST THOUSAND TIMES I READ IT!! You'd think the big guy could afford some new subscriptions. Geeze! Hey Buddy, what do . . . Jessie!! Well Hell's bells! It's good to see ya! You here to see the Old Man?

JESSIE: Yeah. You?

LOUIE: Yeah.

JESSIE: Must be pretty big.

LOUIE: It is. I'm sure you'll find out. Let's just say that I need to see your father immediately.

JESSIE: So do I. And I'm next.

LOUIE: The hell you are.

JESSIE: I was here first.

LOUIE: You know that doesn't matter. He goes in order of importance.

JESSIE: Right. Like I said, I'm next.

LOUIE: Oh yeah? What's up?

JESSIE: Never mind. It's not important.

LOUIE: Oh, stop being such a martyr.

JESSIE: You don't want to know. Trust me. Besides, it's personal.

LOUIE: Y'know, that's always been your problem. You never confide in anyone. You're always taking on everyone else's problems. That could kill ya.

JESSIE: Tell me about it.

LOUIE: No, why don't you tell me about it?

JESSIE: Oh sure. And listen to your ridicule? No thanks.

LOUIE: AAH!! I'm shocked! What do you take me for?

JESSIE: An insensitive clod who cares for nothing but himself.

LOUIE: At one time, yeah, I was a little devil. But times have changed and so have I. I've—and I hate to use the word—matured.

JESSIE: Sure you have. And Hell's frozen over. I've heard that line before.

LOUIE: I mean it this time.

JESSIE: Ha! You expect me to believe that?

LOUIE: I swear by the River Styx. Look Jessie, I'm not kidding. I HAVE changed. When have you ever heard me swear an oath? Huh? (*Pause.*) But hey, you don't wanna talk about it, fine. I can entertain myself endlessly with the fantastic reading selections.

JESSIE: You're really on the level? No horse crap?

LOUIE: You heard my oath. No horse crap. Now what's the problem?

JESSIE: I hate my job.

LOUIE: Humm. That is a problem. Especially in your position.

JESSIE: Oh, good for you. Now you see why I need to see the Old Man.

LOUIE: Hold on, chap. I said it was a problem but it's not unsolvable. Now why the sudden change of heart?

JESSIE: Have you seen it down there? I just finished my market research for my next tour. People are jaded, crime's rampant, compassion's disappeared. Buck's stronger than he's ever been. *I* saw his influence everywhere. I mean, it's Hell! No offense.

LOUIE: None taken. I understand your problem better than you think. Believe me. But you knew the risks when you first took the job.

JESSIE: Yea, but it was so easy then. The Boss was throwing his weight around. Sure, it had been a while, but the locals were used to miracles. It wasn't hard to fool them. A little deception and they thought you could walk on water. Simple tricks for simple people. If you tried that now, though, they'd laugh you out of town.

LOUIE: Hey, you have to roll with the changes. You can't expect to go down there and fool them with the same old scam. If the audience is more sophisticated, you've got to come up with the angle they can't explain. It's a matter of being one step ahead of your flock.

JESSIE: That's just it. This is my first field operation in eons and I'm lost. The market's totally changed. I've been up here attending souls, power lunching with Saints, arbitrating the Angels' strike—I'm management, not a field operative. I'm afraid I've lost the touch.

LOUIE: That's a bunch of baloney. You're the best field op the Big Man's got right now. Sure, you're a little rusty, but, with a little practice, you'll be back in fighting trim. Hey, I should know. We went our distances together and you always came out on top.

JESSIE: I was lucky.

LOUIE: Luck my ass. You licked me. What you need now is confidence. In fact, I think we all need some more confidence. It's the same for everyone out there. Buck and Mo are hurting just as bad as we are.

JESSIE: No, I've talked to Mo, seen his volume. He's doing big business.

LOUIE: Yeah, but Mo's a fanatical sonuvabitch. He's going to kill himself by killing his flock. Sure, he's doing large volume but at what cost? Hey, at least we're still in the business. Look at guys like Odie and Zoo. Hell, they're not even in the game anymore. And it's not any easier for me, either. It may seem like I'm doin' O.K. but it's startin' to get outta hand. My name doesn't carry the same weight it used to. I used to scare the crap outta people by just sending a plague or two. Now it's all chalked up to science. And yeah, I've got my fanatics, but it's nothing like the Middle Ages. The witches really knew how to throw a sacrifice back then—not this chickens and goats crap. Ya know, I really hate "civilized" civilization.

JESSIE: Yeah, but you don't have the P.R. nightmare that we do.

LOUIE: What're you talking about?

JESSIE: Haven't you heard of the televangelists? They've all been in the news and it's been a publicist's nightmare. Sex scandals, shameless money grubbing, air-conditioned dog houses—and they all say they're doing it for ME! So far it's been confined to the American Market but it could grow.

LOUIE: So?

JESSIE: What do you mean "so"?

LOUIE: Hell's bells, I've had to deal with bad press my entire career! The Old Man loved those smear campaigns. Hell, he's the original politician. I feel a strong sense of déjà vu when I watch political ads these days. But you have to work around it.

JESSIE: That's different. You built your business on bad publicity. What would happen if some of your agents started doing kind and benevolent deeds? Your reputation would be shot.

LOUIE: It'd certainly change.

JESSIE: That's exactly my point. And I don't even want to think about the new moral problems! It used to be "Don't sleep with anyone but your wife. Don't steal or poach. Go to Sabbath." Now there's contraception, abortion, homosexuality, premarital sex—I don't know where to start! I'm supposed to be His top field op and I'm drowning. So you can see why I need to see the Old Man.

LOUIE: No, I can't.

JESSIE: What do you mean no? Are you deaf? You haven't heard a word I've said.

LOUIE: I've heard every word you've said. It's just that the answer's so obvious. Look. Where'd ya start from the last time?

JESSIE: What?

LOUIE: Hell's bells, you are an administrator! What did you do on your first tour? How did you plan your campaign then? Seems to me to be as good a place to start from as any.

JESSIE: That's real easy for you to say. You're sitting outside it all and probably laughing.

LOUIE: Outside it all my ass. I'm right in the thick of it. But hey, if you don't want to listen to me, I understand. You go right ahead and wallow and flounder and complain. It's not my reputation that's at stake. I can just see it. "Hey, whatever happened to that savior guy?" "Ahh, I saw him whimperin' and . . . "

JESSIE: O.K., O.K.! I didn't say it wasn't good advice. I'll think about it. (*Pause.*) Why are you doing this, Louie? I thought you'd be happy to see me fail.

LOUIE: At one time I would've agreed with you but, quite honestly, I miss the competition. It can get kinda boring without any direct opposition. I like head to head competition, the thrill of the hunt. Maybe I win, maybe I don't, but it's the fight that counts. That's what I live for. As for the other reasons . . . well, that's why I have to see the Old Man. I'm sure you'll find out. There's no use spoiling the surprise, is there?

DORIS: Louie, the Boss will see you now.

LOUIE: I told you I was next. (*Rising.*) See ya 'round, kid.

JESSIE: You bet you will. And Louie . . . thanks. You'll live to regret this, y'know.

LOUIE: Let's hope so. (*Exits through up left door. Blackout.*)

Questions

1. What would this playwright have to do to change his basic plot from an imaginary setting to a realistic setting?

2. The playwrite tells us what Louie looks like but not Jessie. How would you cast Jessie and why? What details in the dialog suggest how he should look?

3. This scene reads somewhat slowly in text. What is the dramatic question? Is there enough tension? If yes, what do you find successful in the presentation? If not, how could more be added without drastically changing the author's text?

4. Briefly, explain how you would stage this scene. If you can, read it aloud with a partner and start to sketch in both the characters' stage moments and the delivery of their speeches.

Notes

1. See Britton, Burgess, McLeod, Martin, and Rosen.
2. Poem by Mills is reprinted from Bishop.

Sources and Readings

Anderson, Chris. *Literary Nonfiction: Theory, Criticism, Pedagogy.* Carbondale: Southern Illinois UP, 1989.

Bentley, Eric. *Thinking About the Playwright*. Evanston, IL: Northwestern UP, 1972.

Berg, Stephen, ed. *Singular Voices: American Poetry Today*. New York: Avon, 1985.

Bishop, Wendy. *Released into Language*. Urbana, IL: National Council of Teachers of English, 1990.

Britton, James, Tony Burgess, Alexander McLeod, Nancy Martin, and Harold Rosen. *The Development of Writing Abilities (11–18)*. London: Macmillan Education, 1975.

Bunge, Nancy. *Finding the Words: Conversations with Writers Who Teach*. Athens: Ohio UP, 1985.

Christie, Agatha. *An Autobiography*. London: Collins, 1977.

Dillard, Annie. *The Writing Life*. New York: Harper and Row, 1989.

McCaffery, Larry, and Sinda Gregory. *Alive and Writing: Interviews with American Authors of the 1980s*. Urbana: U of Illinois P, 1987.

Minot, Stephen. *Three Genres: The Writing of Poetry, Fiction, and Drama*. 3d ed. Englewood Cliffs, NJ: Prentice-Hall, 1982.

Murray, Donald. *Shoptalk: Learning to Write with Writers*. Portsmouth, NH: Boynton/Cook Heinemann, 1990.

Ponsot, Marie, and Rosemary Deen. *Beat Not The Poor Desk*. Upper Montclair, NJ: Boynton/Cook, 1982.

Shapiro, Nancy Larsen, and Ron Padgett. *The Point Where Teaching and Writing Intersect*. New York: Teachers & Writers, 1983.

Wager, Walter, ed. *The Playwrights Speak*. New York: Delacorte, 1967.

Winterowd, W. Ross. *The Rhetoric of the "Other" Literature*. Carbondale, IL: Southern Illinois UP, 1990.

Chapter 10

Other Forms

The problem is finding the correct organic shape and the emotional shape for a piece.

—EDWARD ALBEE

Form comes for me in a perfectly natural way. I have never said to myself "now I'll write a sonnet." I write a few lines that interest me and discover they become a sonnet.

—RICHARD WILBUR

To write well in one major genre—poetry, fiction, or drama—is a challenge for any writer. However, the conventional wisdom that you should apprentice yourself to one form and that form only, for life, seems to me less than productive for beginning writers. Playwrights and poets, such as Albee and Wilbur, indicate that form is a matter of being found as well as of finding, and novelist E. M. Forster is famous for the phrase: "How do I know what I think until I see what I say?"

I'd like to steal Forster's phrase and apply it to form: How do you know your best genre until you have explored and "thought" in a variety of forms, and in the forms between forms—scenes and fragments and prose poetry and so on? The following writings will help you explore other forms. You might consider each in the way I considered the major genres, trying to answer the basic questions that all writers have about form. Don't limit yourself to the forms I've included here, however. You may want to discuss detective fiction or songs or soap operas and radio plays.

With any forms you choose to discuss, it can help to define, compare, contrast, and examine the writing of that genre. First, offer a basic definition of the genre. Second, if possible, read what published writers say about that genre's limits or benefits. Third, identify basic techniques of the genre that you already know.

To explore the genre more fully, compare and contrast it with other genres; that is, place it within the universe of genres. For example, how do songs connect to free or formal verse? How does a children's story use techniques similar to those in an adult's story? And also, what limitations exist in writing children's stories that aren't present in writing adult fiction? And so on.

Finally, discuss the techniques used by actual writers in these forms. Choose your favorite published authors as well as some of the following pieces by student writers; examine them carefully and name the techniques and tricks you find in action. Generally, like most of the writing in this book, the student writings that you'll be reading represent works-in-progress.

Sketches and Prose Poems

Trailer 10

Author Unknown

Big hair is what Ethel has, big hair and a body that is held in by a girdle like the stuffings in a sausage. Her fleshy body is covered with scratchy polyester and cheap, animal tested, Avon perfume. Ethel's eyebrows are plucked daily and drawn on with brown pencil.

Trailer #10 with the plastic, pink flamingo in the front yard is hers. With sequined, poodle magnets on her fridge and a lava lamp in the den, Ethel watches her soaps. Barbie and Ken shaped images glide across the screen and say all the right words. Shoveling Fisher's peanuts in her mouth, she is mesmerized by the tube while waiting for her company to arrive.

T.V. trash completed and peanut can emptied, Ethel gets up and unwraps a new, shimmering package of Cashmere soap. In its perfectly smooth, crisp edged form, it is placed in the guests' bathroom, and the former, twice used, bar is chucked. New, lacey, K-mart special towels are placed on the rack just for show, not use. Sizzling sparks of grease come from a pan in the kitchen as Ethel cooks her ground globules of dead cow. Soggy, oil-drenched fries sit in a bowl on the counter, and in the fridge is green jello with marshmallows swimming in it.

Ethel reaches into the shelf above the stove and takes down a bottle of gin. With a few swigs of this, her preparation is complete.

The company has arrived, and a little cherub runs from the car to Ethel.

"Hi, Grandma."

Untitled

Author Unknown

The cancer has spread. It doesn't look good. A week of ups and downs. Mom was still holding her own. In a way she kept me anchored. She kept everything in perspective. She kept waving her wand and making it all better. Money was short. I started working two jobs. I don't know if this helped or harmed. Sure I was bringing in more money but I wasn't around much. I wish I had been. Somehow the bad news had leaked to my friends and I was shelled with questions. Their parents also bombarded my mother with "if there's anything I can do." This started to become annoying. But they were our friends and were only doing what they could. All we could do was wait. Wait for Dad to get better and get home. We sat in the living room. No television, just us. Mom, Misty, and I. We talked and waited for the answers.

Lizards

Luis R. Amadeo

In the bathroom, two iguanas, inside a tub, flick long tails and glide through a mock river, trying to evolve. They have no heat of their own, and it's cold. They seek a warm body, a desert rock. How many times will they shed their skin? They would lose those tails if they got mad at us, and leave them there, wriggling, for us to look at. But today, they will only stick their dewlaps out, and bob chunky, square-like heads up and down.

Yesterday you threw a bottle of wine at me, and it didn't even break. You must not have meant it. Heavy dosages always served us much better, and I've had plenty of you, and you've had plenty of me. Look at those two swim. When they're cheery they turn green, but when they're angry they turn shades of gray. Lizards were never meant to live in aquariums. They're not happy, and they quarrel. But outside, alone, they may not find a warm body to lie on. They shrivel up and die. Don't fight me. Let them chew on lettuce and be happy. We've built a cage for one another. Open more wine, and I'll pick up the glass.

Cygnets

Summer Smith

She stands on a worn spot on the oak floor bruised by years of pirouettes, the revolutions eventually wearing down the polyurethane gloss and sheen. Little cygnets must practice—they are imperfect vessels —the flesh is hard to conquer. Her mentors have to work around the architecture of the female form; her pelvic arch is ideal for childbirth, not turnout. Her sickled feet bear the pain of overcompensation, honorably winged with bunions, her blisters no longer burst watery and bleed against the lambswool she wraps her oily toes within. She goes barefoot where she isn't dancing, but her feet mutilated blur the texture of asphalt grass soil. Finely articulated skeleton, stopped menses, hands transparent at their hinges, she becomes an El Greco figure. Her boyfriend wishes she had breasts.

The rotation begins from the hips and she turns, unwilling, following the directions of her teacher. His imagery disturbs her. She is a balloon in the Macy's Thanksgiving Day Parade, Betty Boop or Bullwinkle, guide wires running from her clavicle to the ceiling, her legs jerking to invisible retainers. "Elevation." A strong man wrenches her legs apart and she must draw them shut. "Equilibrium." A series of straightpins like swords, a foot long and an inch thick, pin her stomach and soft muscles to her spinal column. "Carriage." The pins wed her to an invisible vertical plane, sticking her to it like some entomologist's specimen. She carries the vertical plane with her everywhere, turns with it, sleeps with it, even takes it to high school. The pins are permanent—even when she exits the floor abandons the barre she walks with the swayback outthrust thighs straight spine of the cygnet.

Questions

1. Define these pieces as sketches and/or prose poems. Compare and contrast them, perhaps, with the student stories you have read.

2. Why do writers use and experiment with these forms?

Science Fiction

Message from Ogaron

Katy Bethune

He wasn't sure just when it had begun, he never noticed until it had already occurred, but when he saw it Tom could only stare in wonder. The petals opened outward in a fantastic spiral and the early morning light reflected off of the crystalline surface, spattering the walls of his studio with rainbow colors. The plant was a mutated cactus from an outlying planet on the Ogaron system, brought to Tom for evaluation when found by biologists, who attributed its strange properties to high doses of radiation received from an ancient nuclear fuel dump near which it had grown. Only a few others like it were ever found, and scientists were trying to grow more but were having little success. Growing plants in radioactive waste is not an easy task.

Tom stood in wonder, absorbing the beauty of the crystal bloom perched atop the gnarled, scaled trunk of the cactus, its fishhook thorns reaching out below to tear at the flesh of unwary passersby. He moved closer, reaching out to touch the petals, examining everything about it in minutiae. His fingers trembled in excitement, but stayed clear of the threatening thorns. Incredible, absolutely incredible. Real crystal! I didn't believe it when they told me. My God, the ramifications! I've got to call Bob. It's beautiful. Tom turned and hurried to his desk, rooting under instruments and lists of calculations till he located his comunit, then hurriedly punched up the number for the Botanichem Director. A robotitron secretary answered, flashing a scene of a Terran Japanese garden on the screen while asking the usual "May I help you" in her simulated voice.

"Let me talk to Bob, this is Tom Granay, it's very important."

"Section number and title, please," the robotitron intoned, driving Tom into a frenzy while he typed the requested information into the machine.

"There! Jesus Christ, will you let me through to him now. I haven't got all day." Hardly even that, if what I'm told is true. "Bob, Bob, it's happened, it's true, it's true what they said, it's incredible, and it's real. A plant that can permutate into mineral, its absolutely unbelievable; you've got to get over here right now and see this."

"Wait, wait a second here, Tom, slow down. I haven't the slightest idea what you're talking about. A plant that does what? What's happened?" The Director's pudgy face appeared on the comunit screen, his Klan tattoo showing blue and purple above his right eyebrow, which was drawn down into a frown. Tom explained what had happened and the Director's eyes grew large as he listened.

"I'm coming down immediately, don't do anything to it, I'll bring a team with me. Get ready." Bob ended and abruptly cut off the communication. The Japanese garden reappeared. Tom clicked off the comunit and began collecting his calculations, stuffing them in drawers out of sight. His work, though of dubious ethical quality, involved complex research into the interaction of radioactivity with certain plants and life forms which could be of monetary value to his company. He didn't want any stray eyes to *accidentally* see his work, even though he said he felt no qualms about his research. Then Tom sat down in front of the plant, reaching out to caress the crystal petals. He was a tall, thin man with lank dark hair that never stayed in place and whose total wardrobe consisted of a couple of jumpsuits of a monotonous gray-green, which he wore under an ever-present blue lab jacket. Tom was one of those men whose entire life consisted of his work, to whom recreation was "just a few more calculations before bed, dear."

Bob soon arrived with his team of scientists and photographers. He stood in front of the plant, gazing at it in wonder. Reaching out, he tapped a petal with one finger. "My God! It is real crystal. How did this happen?"

Then quickly, "I want a full analysis of this plant right now. I want it photographed and documented and the file sent me immediately. Tom! What do you know about this plant? How does it do this? And how can we get more of these?" Yes, how? You know how much money I can make if we can get plants to permutate? And even if we can't, these things'll sell on the market for a billion credits. God, I'd be rich. The Director's face lit up with thoughts of a swelling credit count. He grabbed Tom by the arm and pulled him off into a corner. "Tell me about this plant," he said.

It was late in the evening before Tom finally had his studio to himself again. The plant sat in its corner next to the window, the bloom glowing faintly in the lights from the city outside. Scientists had run tests on it all day, trying to crack its secret, to find out how it transformed plant matter into a crystal flower, how it permutated into mineral. Nothing had been revealed by all their efforts. Tom stood in front of the plant once again, gazing into its center, questioning, wondering. Complicated calculations and formulas ran through his head. He formed, tested and reformed hypotheses. None seemed to come near to any answer. Suddenly Tom was drawn out of his musings by a realization that the flower was beginning to glow, its center pulsing violet and green, at first slow, then faster. He stared into its depths, caught by the glow. It seemed to have some sort of pattern—Tom's mind worked to understand, to learn. He could almost . . . understand. He leaned closer, he was directly over the flower now. The crystal petals drew up toward his face. He stood there for a long time, though it only seemed minutes to him, held by the pulsing lights. He struggled, fought with his slow brain to understand the pattern, to learn the language. He felt as if he were swimming in mud, in a river of mud flowing in the opposite direction he wanted to go. He couldn't understand, he was a babe, his mind was retarded. Then there came a light, and he began to learn, to grasp the pattern, but it was too late, for the pulsing light had begun to fade, was dying away. Tom cried out, and pitched forward onto the floor just as the magnificent crystal petals folded in upon themselves, sealing into a small pod. The crystal pulsed violet once more, then was dark.

Tom slowly regained consciousness and sat up on the floor. There was a smell like burned ozone in the air. What happened? I almost learned . . . can't remember. . . . What did it say . . . ? It was important, so important. Oh God. . . . He hugged himself and rocked on the floor. What . . . ? It slowly faded from his consciousness. Shaking his head Tom got up and turned up the lights in the studio. On top of the cactus there was a fist-sized oval pod, hanging downward from a slender stem. He touched it, and the dry leaves crumbled into dust. A small black rock fell into his palm. He looked at it, wondering. Granite? What? A stupid rock? Tom turned to toss the rock into a waste disposal, but instead his hand slipped it into his pocket. Knowledge is not easily thrown away.

Questions

1. What techniques did this writer use to make a futuristic world comparable yet distinct from your present world?

2. What characteristics of science fiction writing distinguish it from literary writing?

3. Is this world engaging enough for you to be willing to read Tom's further adventures? Why or why not?

Children's Fiction

Percy the Puny Poinsettia

David Rowe

Outside Mr. Bimble's store snow floated softly down from the cloudy midday sky. It was the day before Christmas and all day people had been running into the store hoping to find a last minute present or decoration. Percy watched each person from his shelf near the back of the store. Every time the little bell that hung on the front door rang and a new person entered, Percy would whisper to himself "I hope they pick me. Please pick me! Oh, please pick me!" But no one had.

Two hours before Mr. Bimble closed the store, a large woman in a flowery dress came bursting through the front door. "I need a Christmas plant!" she yelled at Mr. Bimble.

Mr. Bimble took her over to the shelf with Percy on it and smiled weakly. "I'm afraid this is the last one we have," he said, pointing to Percy. "It seems like everyone wanted a Christmas poinsettia this year."

"Well, he looks sickly," the woman said. "A poinsettia should have big red leaves and a healthy green stem to hold it up tall. This one is drooping and pale. And he's much too small for a proper plant."

Percy felt a sad tinge run from his roots to the tip of his leaves. It was the same unloved feeling he had felt every time someone had come to his shelf and chosen another plant to take home. He remembered how most of the people had looked at each of the other poinsettias when trying to decide which one to buy, but they never looked long at him. The few people who had seen him said he was too small or not bright enough.

On the very first day the poinsettias arrived at the store a man had picked up Percy and said aloud, "This plant is puny!" After that, all the other plants teased him and called him "Percy the Puny Poinsettia." Not being chosen was bad, but having his fellow plants turn on him hurt just as much. Percy knew that with a little love and care he could be a wonderful plant.

At 8 o'clock Mr. Bimble locked the front door and began to clean up his shop. Percy watched as he straightened up the shelves and picked pieces of paper up from the floor. When Mr. Bimble got to Percy's shelf he stopped and stood looking at Percy. "Well, little fellow. It doesn't look like anybody's going to buy you," said Mr. Bimble.

Percy wanted to answer but he was too sad and could not think of anything to say.

"No need to keep you around. You look so pitiful," he continued.

As he left to go home, Mr. Bimble threw Percy on the foot of a huge pile of trash that was stacked at the corner. Percy felt as low as a plant can feel. The snow gathering on his leaves made him shiver, but it could not make him feel any worse. He could feel himself wilting inside. All hope of a happy Christmas was gone. He felt empty.

Percy sat in the cold Christmas Eve silence for almost an hour until a car stopped by the curb. A little girl bundled tightly in a warm blue coat jumped out the back door and ran to Percy. She grabbed him and skipped back to the car joyfully.

"Thank you so much for stopping," she said to her father. "I just knew the second that I saw that plant that he needed me. I could almost hear him calling."

New life rushed into Percy. He no longer felt unwanted or unloved. Finally, someone had noticed him and someone wanted him. He felt a tingle all over, but it was not like the sad tingle that he was used to; it was a warm red and green tingle that made him feel good. He was as happy as a plant can be.

When the girl arrived home she took Percy into the friendly house and set him beside the tall brilliant Christmas tree. "You'll be OK here," she said. "I'll take good care of you."

The next morning Percy awoke to find a large family gathered around the tree. They were singing carols and talking and laughing, and everybody was smiling. It was better than he had dreamed Christmas could be, and it made him feel special and full of life.

As he was beginning to wonder if he was in heaven, an elderly woman bent over him and said, "Oh my! He is such a wonderful looking poinsettia. He's so green and tall and his leaves are so very red!"

Percy glowed outside and inside.

Writing Percy

David Rowe

This story was written for children in the five- to nine-year-old range and would likely be published in a magazine such as *Highlights*, *Jack and Jill*, or *Humpty Dumpty*. The vocabulary is purposely chosen for a child. In some places a more sophisticated word would be more effective, but only for a more sophisticated reader. Another tactic that is necessary is repeating character names often, rather than resorting to pronouns. This is to make the story easy to follow for a child. The last point I feel a need to defend is the simplistic plot. Remember, you are reading this as a six-year-old, so even the oldest most worn plots are still relatively fresh and new.

Follow-up: I figured that simply finding a five- to nine-year-old test subject would be the hardest part of my follow-up. Back home in Boca, I would have no problem rounding up an entire circle of attentive youngsters to read to, but here in Tally I just don't have the connections. The one eight-year-old I do vaguely know was my only chance.

Chris is an eight-year-old Deon Sanders. He looks small, but he talks big and plays a mean game of catch. My only previous contact with him had been to toss a football or baseball around the yard of the apartment complex both he and my best friend live in. I knew he would be a tough audience for a cute kid's story but I had to give it a shot.

I sat him down on the stairs outside his apartment. It was obvious to me that he wanted to run around and play football but I knew that my story was short and I hoped it could hold his attention for a few minutes.

He sat politely and listened to the story. I could tell he easily understood the action and could follow the plot. However, it was difficult to determine just how much (if at all) he enjoyed it. After I finished he said, "Hey! It's good! Now let's go play some catch!" I had hoped for a slightly more enthusiastic response to the story, but still I considered it a minor success. It was about the reaction I had expected from Chris.

I learned at least one thing by reading the story to Chris. Kids are smarter than adults often give them credit for. I think perhaps the age range I had originally assigned for this story might be off by at least a year. I believe that a five- to seven-year-old range would be better suited to enjoy this story. Somehow, the ideas, plot, and language seemed too simple for Chris.

Writing for children is a challenge that I love. I hope to produce many more stories and perhaps even publish. I think the secret to writing for children is to respect your audience. It is important never to "talk down" to a child when writing. Yet, it is also important to consider the age of the child and make appropriate considerations. The writer must write clearly and be able to think with an uncluttered, wondering mind.

Questions

1. Do you agree with David that kids are often smarter than adult writers give them credit for being? Do you remember ever reading a book that seemed to "talk down" to you as a child-audience?

2. Do you agree that when writing for children the story plot elements (even sentences) need to repeat and vocabulary has to be kept simple?

3. What techniques in general did you notice David using?

4. Compare David's story to some of your favorite children's fiction.

5. What would illustrations add to this story?

Nonfiction: Journalists' Columns and Family Stories

[*Note:* Sarah's process cover sheet, describing how she came to write these columns, appears in Chapter 8.]

Attack of the Foibles

Sarah Proud

Column 1

Monday is always one of those days when you know it's gonna be one of those days. Two mornings of sleeping late are not enough. Monday brings the return of the alarm clock, a sound from hell that jolts your eyes open and electrocutes your brain. Remember, in old movies, the shock treatment given to Frankenstein? A mother's kiss compared to the voltage of the Monday morning alarm.

I do not awaken gracefully, but then that's why God invented coffee. It's too early to wonder why He put it in the same geographical area in which the plant for cocaine grows, but there's probably a connection there somewhere. I'll ponder upon that later; I have other problems now.

I've found my way into the kitchen to meet with catastrophe; I'd forgotten to load and set the automatic coffeemaker last night. With the intelligence of a store mannequin, I open a cupboard, into which I stare for an immeasurable length of time. I never keep the coffee in the cupboard. It's in its usual place, on the counter in a cannister which now appears to be laughing at me.

Cannister in hand, I turn back towards the coffee maker only to whack my head on the cupboard door I'd left open. The resulting head injury does not help my thinking ability, and I lose count of how many scoops of coffee I've put into the filter.

In the bathroom, I await the brewing process. Hearing water running in the kitchen, I assume I've forgotten to turn off the tap after filling the pot. But I've got more immediate concerns right now; there's no bathroom tissue in sight.

Eventually returning to the kitchen, I find that the source of running water is the coffee maker. Coffee is exiting from the filter onto the hotplate where I'd forgotten to place the carafe. That same carafe that seems to be snickering at me as it sits on the counter next to the equally jovial coffee cannister.

I think that perhaps the world will be a better place today if I return immediately to bed . . . even though it's only been fifteen minutes since the sound of the alarm.

Column 2

This morning, sitting on the patio with my coffee, I noticed a tiny silver object on the table. I picked it up and stared at it in much the same manner as an entomologist studies a species of insect. What was it? Where had it come from?

I suspect that we have a troll that probably lives in the unused closet of the guest room and comes out at night to scatter these mysterious parts of something around the house. The problem is—parts of what?

A screw gleams up at me from the coffee table, nowhere near anything requiring one. How did it get there? Is it the crucial piece that makes some unit whole? Is something in my house about to fall apart because it's not there?

And what about this stray coil? I'm not mechanically minded, but surely there's some function it performs within something. It must have fallen out of something. I'll find a tiny battery, a nail, a nut without a bolt, and, once, a key with no known lock. Each time, I look around and find nothing in the immediate radius to which the object might belong.

I've established, by talking to family and friends, that this phenomenon is not limited to my house and yard. Everyone polled had his or her own particular troll; no one had ever solved the mystery of any of the parts' origins.

Sitting on the patio, with the latest mystery part, I began to imagine wider-ranging implications for what seemed, at first, a mechanical game of trivial pursuit. What if the U.S. Defense System is victim to a relative of my troll? Regular viewing of the news seems to indicate a real possibility. There's often a story about some new multi-million dollar piece of defense equipment that doesn't work. The new Stealth Bomber leaps immediately to mind, and just this Sunday, "Sixty Minutes" did a segment on a transducer, a thumb-sized part in missiles carried by Air Force jets. I can't prove it, and Mike Wallace didn't ask, but could it be possible that the military is hounded by the same mystery-part syndrome that plagues my home?

Whether it's true or not, the thought of an ICBM missile with a screw loose is not a comforting thought. Especially when I consider how much the Pentagon paid for each screw . . . compared to the cost of the one laying on my patio table.

Column 3

The new puppy is adorable, a furry black bear cub full of kisses and love. His breed: a Chow, reputed to be fierce, loyal, and protective. His impeccable lineage hangs, framed, on the wall. In anticipation of his heroic deeds, I named him Marquis de Lafayette.

From my earliest memories, I've always had a dog. Each one has had its own peculiar personality, each its share of traits both endearing and annoying. Lafayette has grown to be no exception.

He's as faithful as the sunrise. He plays vigorously, but gently, with my son and his friends. And, he lovingly follows my husband around like the black shadow he is.

He's my running buddy, even though he'll crash through me like a running back with the ball to get away from a rustling noise in the woods. But then, it might be a squirrel—or worse.

He's sharp as a tack. I'll hold a dog treat in front of his eyes. I move the treat to the right, his head turns with it. I move the treat to the left, his face, still turned right, assumes a puzzled expression. I return the treat to the right, his face lights up. He's found it! He did this once for fifteen minutes.

He'll lay for hours staring into a blank, white surface, i.e., clothes dryer, wall, bathtub, inches from his nose. He's not chanting mantras, but he must be deep in contemplation of something.

And what a sense of humor he has. He'll bark when a doorbell rings on TV, but never at our own. And he purposefully naps in the darkest corners of our house, waiting for us to come walking down the hall burdened with a basket of laundry, a pile of papers, or a cup of coffee, and have our foot encounter this unmovable black concrete block, who doesn't even bat an eye.

But that's just when he naps. When he sleeps, the entire Red Army could invade our home and not wake him. And he snores as though we have a Brontosaurus curled up at the end of the hall. Which, now that I think of it, may be his most endearing quality. If you were a prowler, would *you* go down a dark hallway with that kind of noise emanating from the other end?

Column 4

Communication is important in maintaining, among other things, a good marriage. I learned this the other morning when the World War III of marital spats started over the definition of the word "shortly." *Webster's New World Dictionary*—"new world" meaning that it weighs just over a ton—defines "shortly" as "in a short time, soon." I needed a 2,240 pound book to tell me that.

The scene opens on a weekday when we both have to shower and dress for our respective occupations. I was in the middle of my morning workout; he, having just awoken, passed me on the way to the coffee and asked, "When are you going to need the shower?" Sincerely enough, I answered, "Shortly."

It was only a half hour by the time I'd finished my workout and cooled down enough to hit the shower. I found him pouting in the bedroom. Now, I admit that there are times of the month when I'm less reasonable than others; I don't know, maybe it's the moon. This happened to be one of those times.

My sarcasm had the potency of boric acid when I asked him what his problem was. Thus commenced a dramatical, not grammatical, "discussion" about the meaning of the word "shortly."

"I thought you said you'd be done 'shortly,'" he groused.

I retorted, "I was—a half an hour. That's 'shortly.'"

"'Shortly' is just a few minutes," he shot back.

"Ohhh," I rejoined, "you mean like when you're out of town and will call me 'around' six and the phone rings at nine?"

From there it went from bad to worse, comedic theatre in its lowest form.

Sure, we can laugh at it now. But what if we'd been two rival countries with billions of dollars worth of planes, ships, and bombs pointed at each other? Or even two smaller nations with less military hardware? Regardless of the size of the conflict, perhaps it is equally petty squabbles over the meaning of some word like "shortly" that allegedly justifies the planes, ships, and bombs.

But that leads me to something I don't understand. The highest art form of communication is, I thought, diplomacy. And when I watch the latest skirmish on the news, I wonder where that vital means of communication is.

Not Just Another Weekend in the Big City

Greg Kilgore

Ya know, "Life is funny." (Funny strange? Or, funny ha ha?) To be, or not to be? Life's a beach, and then you die. (And, I think there's another cliché that sounds a lot like that one." Live and let live. Do or die. Don't worry, be happy. Have a nice day. Just do it (copyright, Nike). Just say "No."

So many philosophies, so little life to live. It strikes me that we spend a lot of time trying to sell ourselves a better way to live. Or worse, someone else spends a lot of time (and money) to sell us a product while trying to sell us a better way to live.

I was attempting to come up with a more efficient way to manage my time the other day when I paused to answer the phone while sorting some mail. Following that phone call, I took a short trip to Dothan, Alabama, with a friend. Her name is Kendra, for future reference. She needed to get fitted for a bridesmaid's dress and said she'd appreciate some company. While in Dothan, we visited with her maternal grandparents, her father's mother and her uncle's family, each in their own home. In an afternoon and an evening, I had the rare opportunity to scratch the surface of the lives of total strangers and, furthermore, encounter several generations of a family.

With Kendra's mother's parents, we watched a little bit of the Alabama vs. Vanderbilt game and discussed how gramps and grandma were getting along in their new suburban home. They discussed who was still alive and who wasn't, who wasn't getting out much and who was, and that grandpa's new cough is probably caused by working out in the shed too much after the doctor told him what too much sawdust was going to do to him. (I won't even mention the Southern drawl that a South Floridian like me, with no accent whatsoever, can notice immediately upon entering Dothan.)

Next, we arrived at Uncle Tim's, where the smell of Beanie Weenies wafted through high-vaulted rooms which were supported by rustic wooden beams that Uncle Tim had designed and constructed. Family and friends were throwing a birthday party for the twins, Caly and Clinton, who claim emphatically, "We are now five years old." While Kendra and the folks talked as if they were writing a *Who's Who in Dothan*, I played with the children who had come for the free cake and ice cream. We built a house out of Lego's wherein, if you peeked through one of the windows, you could see a miniature Christmas tree one of the little boys had insisted needed to accessorize the interior of the imaginary home.

We also watched the ending to E.T. One of my new playmates claimed, "I've seen E.T. at least a hundred times." I responded, "Oh, yeah?" in disbelief. She retorted, "Yeah, I have the tape at home." No doubt jaded by her incessant exposure to the film, she shrugged off my teary-eyed response to the ending of the movie which I have seen at least twice. Oh, and by the way, this little girl, in particular, produced a charming and gentle giggle when I tickled her.

After the party, it was off to see Grandma Parish. From the outside, her light blue paneled home appeared weathered and unkempt. Once inside, the house appeared the same. In the living room, I eyed numerous Kodachrome family portraits on a mantle above a cement-filled fireplace which had two electric heaters placed in front of it, as if they were placed there to simulate the heat that may have once emanated from the now mock fireplace.

I also surveyed countless black and white family portraits on the walls. Meanwhile, Kendra and Grandma Parish spoke of the norm for the day: friends, family and daily follies. Sometimes, they spoke of nothing at all and would just sit there for minutes in silence, rocking in recliners covered in a pattern of fading pastel colors. I would adjust myself on the rough textured couch, left and right and left again, staring around, glancing at my watch, or peering over my shoulder at a small dirty window to the rear of the room.

As we drove back to Tallahassee that evening, it rained. Kendra and I listened to the SuperGold Network on Sunny 98 FM, singing-along to an hour of Fab Four Faves.

As I arrived home remembering it was time to sit down and write this article, I realized I had less to say about how we should live our lives, and more than nothing to say about just living them for the sake of all that we might notice.

Fragments of Paul

Nancy Shook

When Mom thought we were both still young enough, Paul and I would bathe together. I gave my blinking baby dolls a bath while Paul played scuba with his mask and snorkel. Paul was the first to point out the differences in our soapy bodies we'd both noticed. I went crying to Mom that Paul had told me I'd been naughty and mine had fallen off.

Crouching in the dense brush until our thighs and knees ached, Paul and I watched the latest drive-in movies for free. While Paul tried to explain the bedroom scenes (both on screen and off), I nursed my barbed-wire scratches and mosquito bites. Just after the movie started, we'd move close enough to the cars to hear the dialogue. Paul always brought his Boy Scout sleeping bag but seldom shared the luxury. Every now and then we'd find some friends who would let us sit in their family car, but their parents cramped our style, eventually called Mom and Dad.

Leaping from Paul's last footprint to his next, I managed to dodge most of the sandspurs in our path. Beyond the winding sand driveway to Uncle Fred's house, we would come to the hot, black, asphalt road that curved to follow Lake Minnehaha. Our scorched, bare feet could soon cool as they dangled along with our cane poles from Lee's dock into the murky-brown lake water. Trying to teach me to dive, Paul held me upside-down by my ankles over the edge of the dock while I squirmed and screamed all the way down. As soon as I surfaced, Paul had a gun and was shouting for me not to move. Afloat in water several feet over my head, I watched Paul kill his first water moccasin. Later, after skinning it with his Swiss Army pocket knife, Paul stretched the moccasin's skin out to dry on Lee's dock. Glued to a piece of leather, the trophy was hung in his bedroom.

Playing Junior High football was proof of Paul's strength. His football friends came over to run through the orange grove's sugar-sand as training. They claimed to be strengthening their legs for the up and coming football season. While they were drinking Gatorade and resting after their run one night, I was playing Barbie dolls on the living room floor. Maybe to impress his friend, Jerry, or just to rub salt in an ever-open sore, I teased Paul that he was a wimp. Catching my head between his calves, he squeezed like a hydraulic vice-grip. "Momma!" was all I could get out between my involuntarily clinched teeth. "Paul, leave her alone," came the usual monotone response.

At thirteen Paul was an unwilling babysitter. He tried to ignore me but I was too persistent. I followed Paul and his friends until he'd hit me. Crying more from embarrassment than anger, I would run upstairs. In my room, I would take the case off of my pillow, pack some favorite clothes, and head back downstairs—grabbing a knife and salt shaker on my way out the back door. Heading for the grove, it was my plan to live on oranges and grapefruit until Paul apologized, or more likely, Hell froze over. Before I reached the grove's edge, Paul would have me thrown over his shoulder potato-sack-style. As he carried me back to the house, I'd pummel his back and kick as hard as I could. He'd only laugh.

"Momma, Momma," I'd yell, but as Paul reminded me, "Momma ain't home."

Egg Hunting Season

Sylvia Jimmie

My family and I love to go egg hunting during the season which starts at the end of May and runs to the middle part of June. We who call ourselves Yupik in my native language—meaning genuine person in English—live in Kwigillingok in the southeast part of Alaska by the mouth of the Kuskokwim River.

As I was growing during my childhood, every summer we went out to the tundra to try to find eggs. To me, during those times, I didn't like going hunting for eggs. It seemed that all we did was walk for a long time just for nothing, because I wasn't finding eggs except with my parents. But sometimes, which I got to know later, one of my parents would pretend to have me find some eggs even if they had found them first. This would really make me happy when I saw that I had found big, huge eggs such as cranes' eggs. But then as I grew older and wiser, I began to enjoy going egg hunting. Now I have to go egg hunting during the season because I love traveling, trying to find eggs even if I have to walk a long ways.

Before we go egg hunting, my mother and I pack a grub box with plenty of food for a day or two, depending on how long we will be gone. Also, one important thing we don't forget are hipboots; they are very useful in crossing the creeks or lakes. We usually go egg hunting up river through the river of Kwigillingok. The places we look for eggs are in swampy areas around the lakes and rivers, or on the small islands in a lake that is deep and hard to cross. So, because of this, we usually take a speed boat that will be easy to haul over the land to a lake.

The kinds of eggs we usually hunt for are crane, seagull, arctic-tern, ptarmigan, swan, and several kinds of ducks. However, most of the children like to hunt for small bird eggs that are easy to find and can be found not far from each other.

We know when the time comes when we should stop hunting for eggs. That is if we find some eggs and boil them when we get home. If the eggs are floating on top of the water, it tells us that the bird has developed inside. But mostly our elders like to eat the eggs having a little bird forming inside them. They say they're very tasty.

It's fun hunting for eggs. We go home with lots of different kinds of bird eggs each having its own flavor. We eat those delicious eggs as soon as we boil and cool them. We continue to go egg hunting until we get enough eggs or until the egg hunting season is over.

Questions

1. What techniques did the journalists use to identify their writing as "realistic"?

2. Do you believe these narratives represent reality, or do you guess these journalists shaped events for effectiveness?

3. What is the effect of the collage and discontinuity in Nancy Shook's "Fragments of Paul"?

4. Do you think you would have equally enjoyed reading a ten-page essay by Nancy on growing up with her brother? Why or why not? How might such an essay differ from her fragments?

5. Sylvia Jimmie's story narrates events in essay form. What do you learn about her Yupik culture? What else would you like to learn?

6. How does Sylvia's writing vary from the "traditional" essay form and with what effects?

Sources and Readings

Anderson, Chris. *Literary Nonfiction: Theory, Criticism, Pedagogy.* Carbondale: Southern Illinois UP, 1989.

Murray, Donald. *Shoptalk: Learning to Write with Writers.* Portsmouth, NH: Boynton/Cook Heinemann, 1990.

Winterowd, W. Ross. *The Rhetoric of the "Other" Literature.* Carbondale: Southern Illinois UP, 1990.

Appendix A

Resources for Writers

Writing Directories, Organizations, Newsletters

Standards

AWP Chronicle and *AWP Catalogue of Writing Programs*
Associated Writing Programs
Old Dominion University
Norfolk, VA 23508
AWP publishes articles for writers. The association was formed to serve academic creative writing programs across the United States.

Poets & Writers and *A Directory of American Poets and Fiction Writers*
Poets & Writers, Inc.
72 Spring Street
New York, NY 10012
A membership with Poets and Writers assures you of craft and market information in regular newsletters.

Fulton, Len, ed. *The International Directory of Little Magazines and Small Presses.*
Dustbooks, Box 100, Paradise, CA 95969.
An annual listing of all the small presses you'll ever want to contact; excludes commercial presses and magazines.

Literary Magazine Review
Department of English
Kansas State University
Manhattan, Kansas 66506
Publishes reviews of most new launchings of literary magazines.

Writer's Market
Cincinnati: Writer's Digest Books.
(Published yearly).
A listing of *every* type of commercial market in any (and every) genre.

Worth Reading or Knowing About

The Academy of American Poets
177 E. 87 St.
New York, NY 10128

Coordinating Council of Literary Magazines (CCLM)
666 Broadway, 11th Floor
New York, NY 10012

Grants and Awards Available to American Writers. 15th ed. 1988/89.
PEN American Center
Division of International PEN
568 Broadway
New York, NY 10012

Mystery Writers of America, Inc.
236 W. 27 St.
New York, NY 10001

Romance Writers of America
5206FM 190 West, Suite 208
Houston, TX 77069

Science Fiction Writers of America, Inc. (SFWA)
Box H
Wharton, NJ 07885

Western Writers of America, Inc.
1753 Victoria
Sheridan, WY 82807

Writers' Retreats and Fellowships

All retreats have different deadlines, facilities, and financial support. Write
for information.

Cummington Community of the Arts
Cummington, MA 01026

Fine Arts Work Center in Provincetown
24 Pearl Street
Box 565
Provincetown, MA 02657

The MacDowell Colony
100 High Street
Peterborough, NH 03458

The Millay Colony for the Arts
Steepletop
Austerlitz, NY 12017

Montalvo Artists in Residence
Montalvo Center for the Arts
P.O. Box 158
Saratoga, CA 95071

Ragdale
1260 North Green Bay Road
Lake Forest, IL 60045

The Ucross Foundation
Ucross Route Box 19
Clearmont, WY 82835

Virginia Center for the Creative Arts
Sweet Briar, VA 24595

Yaddo
Box 395
Saratoga Springs
New York, NY 12866

Appendix B

Response Questions for Writing

Poetry

To provide an early response to a poem, respond to any of the following questions:

1. What are the strongest images in the poem? Write them below.

2. What does this poem make you think of? How does it make you feel?

3. Is there a surprise in this poem? Where? What's the surprise?

4. Where could the poem expand? Give two or three places if possible.

5. Are there rhymes in this poem? Where do they work well? Are there places the rhymes draw attention to themselves—distract the reader? Write down some samples, lines, and words.

6. If there are clichés in this poem, list them below. Also write some examples of the writer's use of fresh and interesting language.

To provide a late response to a poem, respond to any of the following questions:

1. What are the strongest images in the poem? Write them below.

2. Is there a main emotion in this poem? If so, what? Are there other emotions that also work in this poem?

3. Is there tension, surprise, or conflict in this poem? Where? Does it work for you? If so, how?

4. Does the poem have a sense of closure? How does the writer achieve that effect? Or do you still expect more from the poem? If you expect more, what do you expect?

5. Where do the poem's rhythms work best? Where do they work the least? Is there rhyme, alliteration, assonance? Do they contribute to the effectiveness of the poem?

6. What are some of the words this poem doesn't need? Write down the word and what line it appears in.

7. Mark the clichés in the poem with an asterisk. List examples of fresh and interesting language here.

Short Fiction

To provide an early response to a story, respond to any of the following questions:

1. What is the best part of this story? Why?

2. Does the story have an understandable structure? How would you describe it?

3. Are the characters developed well enough? Which characters are most believable? Which could be improved?

4. Do you have a sense of the story's setting? What is it? How might it be improved?

5. Does the story have a clear point of view? What (whose) is it?

6. Are there problems with verb tense shifts? Sentence structure? Syntax? Grammar? If so, please note here and mark them on the draft.

7. Has the writer avoided clichés? Where could the writer be more careful about word choice?

8. Try to sum up what happens in this story in one sentence.

To provide a late response to a story, respond to any of the following questions:

1. a. Do the characters' actions and the progress of the story (the plot) make sense to you? Why or why not?
   b. Is the tension sustained? How?

2. Is *everything* in the story *essential* to the story's success? What could be deleted?

3. Are the characters developed (that is, do they seem like real people to you)? How are the main characters different from each other? Consider dialog, physical gestures, description.

4. Where is the language most vivid, or à la Pound, "charged with meaning"? Where does it go flat?

5. What is the story's point of view? Is it consistent? How is it *appropriate* for the story's purposes? Could a different point of view improve the story? How?

6. If you described the story's *texture* (that is, the way it feels), what would it be? Why? Does the story seem three-dimensional? Where could that quality be improved?

7. Could the sentence variations be improved (that is, do the rhythms vary sufficiently)? Where?

8. Does the story's pace fit its content? How?

9. Is the story's ending satisfying? Why or why not?

10. Why does the story fit its title?

11. What did you like most about the story?

Nonfiction

To provide an early response to nonfiction, respond to any of the following questions:

1. What part of the essay do you remember best?

2. Be nosey. What do you want to know more about? Think of three questions to ask the writer about his or her piece.

3. Was there anything that you didn't understand? If so, what part?

4. Which sensory details were most effective?

5. What do you wish the writer would leave out in the next draft?

6. Suggest some aspects for the writer to experiment with. (Examples: past to present tense, changing point of view, serious to sarcastic tone, first to third person, moving ending scene to the beginning, emphasizing a different theme.)

7. If you could have lunch with one of the characters in the essay, which one would it be? What would you talk about?

8. What do you think about the beginning? What made you keep reading? What did you think of the end? Did you wish it had continued? Ended sooner? Or was it just right?

9. If this were your paper, what would you do next?

10. Tell the writer what he or she does best and encourage her to do it some more.

To provide a late response to nonfiction, respond to any of the following questions:

1. Why do you think the writer wrote this piece?

2. Why could or couldn't/should or shouldn't this piece be a short story?

3. What do you like best about this piece?

4. What other titles might be good, or is this title the best one you can think of (and why?)?

5. Which sentences or paragraphs did you have to reread in order to understand?

6. Which sentences sound especially good out loud?

7. Which sentences sound awkward, too slow, too long, too heavy, or out of tune?

8. Which words or sentences need more spice!?

9. Where could dialogue be added, or is there enough?

10. On the writer's paper, mark all the mechanical errors (syntax, grammar, spelling, punctuation, typing format) that bugged you or distracted you, or that you'd just like to point out to the writer. Use editing/proofreading marks if you wish.

11. Is there anything else you'd like to tell the writer?

Any Genre

To provide an early response to a piece in any genre, respond to any of the following questions:

1. Find several words, lines, or passages that stand out in this piece of writing. Underline/highlight them on the paper. Is each one effective? Distracting? Out of place? Unusual? Interesting? Explain for each example that you choose.

2. After reading this piece, what did you still want to find out? Why?

3. For you as reader, were there any words, lines, or passages that left you unsure or confused? If so, find several and explain what you felt unsure about.

4. How do you feel about the writer's use of language in this piece? Give some examples, using page numbers and sentences or by quoting lines:
    a. Examples of fresh, interesting, and/or appropriate language—language that you especially liked
    b. Examples of clichéd, too familiar, and/or out-of-place language—language that you think could be rewritten more effectively

5. Suggest the most important change(s) you feel the writer could make to improve this piece while redrafting.

To provide a late response to a piece in any genre, respond to any of the following questions:

Higher-Order Concerns

1. Describe how you felt after you finished reading this piece. What impressions did you leave with?

2. List three places where the author could streamline this piece by trimming certain words, lines, or passages.

3. List three places where the author could improve the piece by adding more information.

4. Do you feel this piece is complete? If yes, why? If not, what is missing?

Lower-Order Concerns

1. Did the author use punctuation in any way that concerns you? If so, where and why?

2. Were there any places in the piece where you were dissatisfied with the author's choice of words? Where and why?

3. What do you think of the title? Does it suit the piece? Why or why not?

Response questions are taken from Bishop, Wendy. *Released into Language: Options for Teaching Creative Writing.* Copyright 1990 by the National Council of Teachers of English. Reprinted with permission.

Index